THE TYRANNY OF CONCEPTS:
A CRITIQUE OF MARXISM

The Tyranny of Concepts:
a Critique of Marxism

GORDON LEFF

For words are wise men's counters, they
do but reckon by them; but they are the
money of fools, that value them by the
authority of an Aristotle, or a Thomas
or any other doctor whatsoever, if but a
man.

Thomas Hobbes: *Leviathan*

UNIVERSITY OF ALABAMA PRESS
University, Alabama

CONTENTS

To the memory
of my sister Angela

PREFACE TO THE SECOND EDITION

Apart from the new Introduction and corrections, the main changes in this second edition occur in Chapters I and II. They arise principally from what is I hope a less naïve view of knowledge. This has led me to rewrite the last part of Chapter I and recast a number of arguments in sections one and six of Chapter II. I have also sought to make more explicit the continuity of the Hegelian elements in Marx's thought, above all the notion of alienation, which now receives fuller treatment. It was tempting to pursue this theme, but to have done so would have meant embarking upon another book. This one is not primarily an exegesis of Marx; adequate books on his thought exist in growing numbers. My purpose, as I stated in the first edition, was to consider Marxism as it has become, and to treat Marx's meaning in the context of the meaning it has taken on in the evolution of Marxism. The dialectic between them forms the subject of this book. I am grateful to the publishers for enabling me to revise it, including references to subsequent literature and new editions.

York GORDON LEFF
November 1968

INTRODUCTION TO THE SECOND EDITION

The theme of this book is contained in its title: Marxism has become one more closed system, imprisoning its adherents in its categories. For Marxism in its official form this is, if anything, more obvious now than when I first wrote nine years ago. As recent events in Czechoslovakia and France have shown, it is not from communist orthodoxy, even in its present fragmented state, that the ideological or intellectual challenge of Marxism any longer comes. But, as sympathetic critics of the first edition of this book stressed, orthodox communist Marxism is not the only, or indeed the authentic, Marxism. This, too, is more true now than nine years ago. The study and evaluation of Marx's writings, especially his earlier ones,[1] have further disclosed the radical divergence in

1. Among the works on Marx that have appeared since the first edition of this book, mention may be made of three that have a special bearing on its theme: R. C. Tucker, *Philosophy and Myth in Karl Marx* (Cambridge, 1961); E. Kamenka, *The Ethical Foundations of Marxism* (London, 1962); and S. Avineri, *The Social and Political Thought of Karl Marx* (Cambridge, 1968). Together they have firmly established the continuity of Marx's thought and its Hegelian inspiration especially over the concept of alienation. They differ, however, in their interpretation of Marx. In particular Tucker mars a good book by committing the genetic fallacy of arguing that Marx's own outlook was a projection of the 'urge to be Godlike' which he found in Hegel. To attempt to assess the validity of an outlook by its genesis is to fall victim to one of the shortcomings of Marxism. Whether or not Marx was psychologically alientated is no more a test of the significance of his ideas than Columbus's search for the Indies is a test of the significance of his accidental discovery of America.

Avineri's book is among the most perceptive studies of Marx that I have read. Although disagreeing with much of his interpretation for giving a consistency and explicitness to Marx's thought which I do not believe it possesses, he succeeds in displaying its underlying coherence. Much of this Introduction has been framed as a response to Avineri's book as the footnotes will show.

Kamenka's book provides an important pendant to Avineri in stressing the unreconciled tension in Marx's thought between its ethical presuppositions and its relativist treatment of other outlooks.

the philosophical foundations of his own outlook and those of official Marxism. The gap begins in Marx's own lifetime between his approach and that of Engels. Their differences cannot be regarded as merely individual variations upon a common theme; they spring from different conceptions of materialism and dialectics. Much at the theoretical level that has passed into the official Marxist canon is from Engels rather than Marx. As further developed by Lenin it has helped to distort the whole shape of Marx's thought. The desire to restore it has given a new impetus to Marxist thinking.

The growing impoverishment of Marxist orthodoxy has thus been accompanied by a new diversity, indeed hetero- doxy. The breakdown of monolithic communism has also freed Marx from the syncretism of Marxism–Leninism. His ideas are now the focus of rethinking and their interpretation is once more open; for the first time since Lenin one can meaningfully be a Marxist without being a communist. In these circumstances it may well be asked what is to be served by continuing to flog the dead horse of orthodoxy. Why not bury the corpse and return to the living source in Marx's writings?

There is much in this contention. As I hope this book makes plain, there are vast areas of Marxist thought that are not the work of Marx: in the present context, chapters one, three, and a considerable part of chapter four. In nearly every case they are the outcome of misconstruing Marx or importing elements alien to his thinking, invariably for the worse. But the restoration of his or any outlook, however skilful, is more than a matter of exegesis. If it is to be other than a scholastic exercise, it demands acceptance of its categories and the belief that they can serve as a *Weltan- schauung*. It is precisely here that the difficulty arises; for such an attitude rests upon the very grounds that in my view invalidate orthodox Marxism.

The first is the general one—that to treat Marx's or any other system as an independent body of truths whose efficacy depends only upon correct interpretation and application is to close it. A system is defined by its structure. We can either keep within it and observe its tenets or we pass beyond it to something else. An outlook can only be open if it can be transcended and this implies treating it as provisional. Otherwise it becomes received truth, which, for all that is not given in immediate experience or known demonstratively, means holding it on faith. However much it may draw upon knowledge or modify its positions in the light of experience, its basic concepts can neither be superseded in the way that a scientific hypothesis can, nor be regarded as factitious and arbitrary. It is in this sense that Marxism has become a faith while claiming to be a science. The return to the true Marx will bring only a change of focus, not of attitude, so long as it rests upon acceptance of an ultimate authority enshrined in the written word. The texts will continue to be the medium of all understanding and its attainment conceived as a perpetual commentary upon them. Submission to the word made Marxism a secular religion; it will continue to do so even if there is no longer a church to impose conformity.

To treat any system that claims to be founded on natural reason as the repository of truth is therefore self-defeating. It can only mean displacing reason by authority. Regardless of content the obligation to accept it takes precedence over the reasons for doing so. The demands appropriate to faith are transferred to the secular world. This is what has already happened once to Marxism; the remedy is hardly to begin the process all over again.

This leads to the second consideration, of the status of Marxism as a body of knowledge. It is here above all that relationship between Marx's ideas and Marxism–Leninism is to be seen. For all their divergences it is important to remember that they arose from within a common set of assumptions. The contemporary stress upon their disparateness is in danger of falling into the same mechanistic mistake of which it accuses Engels and Lenin: it opposes one to the other without recognising that they belong together. However irreconcilable they may have become, one engendered the other. In that sense theirs is a diversity within a unity. If it was not necessary nor was it random. Leninism

3

was at once a debasement and a development of Marxism as for that matter much in Engels was; neither was inherent in what Marx held but each nevertheless sprang from it. Or put another way, Engels and Lenin as we know them are inconceivable without Marx and often irreconcilable with him. Their relationship is dialectical; and it is as misconceived to believe that orthodox Marxism can be explained independently of Marx merely through vulgarisation as to insist that his teachings could have had no other outcome. There is a causal nexus between them, but as in all human activity it is contingent upon the individuals involved and not ineluctable.

How it evolved in this case is the subject of this book. It rests upon the contention that there is a continuity not only within Marx's thought but between it and subsequent Marxism. It is not, however, a direct or simple continuity but came through the very discontinuities engendered by Engels and Lenin, so that the Marxist orthodoxy that has resulted is an amalgam of reason and myth, empiricism and teleology to which the thinking of Marx himself can justly be opposed, but from which it cannot be dissociated.

Central to this continuity was Marx's conception of man, above all in his present state. Marx reached it through his criticism of Hegel that began with his *Critique of Hegel's Philosophy of Right* in 1843.[2] His mode of thought remained throughout Hegelian. This more than anything else accounts for the form it took and with it that of Marxism as a whole. There can accordingly be no adequate understanding of the way in which Marx's thought developed that does not recognise its Hegelian character. It owes its central premise to Hegel, namely the dichotomy between appearance and reality, conceived as alienation, and its progressive resolution dialectically. So much has rightly been made of the role of alienation in Marx's thinking that there has been a danger of overstressing it; and it was a fault of the original edition of this book to react against this tendency by not emphasising

2. For a good discussion see Avineri, *op. cit.*, p. 13 ff.

it enough. Far from its marking a phase in Marx's own development, the concept of alienation underlies his entire outlook. For him, unlike Hegel, it signifies man's lack of control over his own life, both the products that he creates and his relationships with other men. He becomes subjected to alien economic and social forms—property, the state, institutions, law, religion, and so on—so that instead of being part of society he feels separated from it; it stands outside him as something alien. Only by abolishing the material conditions that engender this divorce can man become reintegrated with society and so truly human. Transposed thus to the real world alienation becomes a radical critique of all class society, particularly capitalist society. Marx arrived at it by following Feuerbach in inverting Hegel. He took alienation to refer to man's actual experience of the real world in which he lived and not as spirit's awareness of what was outside it and ipso facto alien. From being a state of consciousness which it was for Hegel, alienation expressed for Marx man's actual state of existence; its resolution lay not in the emancipation of the spirit from its material confines but in man's revolutionising of his material conditions. Self-consciousness as the transcendence of the material world was displaced by man's self-activity in changing his world. It was here, in giving primacy to human praxis over consciousness taken for itself, that Marx's system has its point of departure. It substituted man for spirit.

This was not the overthrow of Hegel but his transformation. In Marx's words Hegel was 'turned right side up again'. The main facets of Marx's thought stand as an inverted image of Hegel's.

To begin with they began from the same epistemological assumption of an independent, self-subsisting reality that could be directly apprehended. But whereas Hegel recognised its conceptual nature, Marx apparently believed that he was seizing reality directly as it existed outside consciousness in the real world. As he later wrote in the Introduction to the second edition, volume one of *Capital*, for Hegel 'the real world is only the external, phenomenal form of the "idea". With me, on the contary, the ideal is nothing less than the material world, and translated into forms of thought'. But it is this very notion of translation, however dialectically conceived, that impoverished Hegel's epistemology; for it transferred the dichotomy between the ideal and the material exclusively to man's activity in the external world. To subsume consciousness under praxis is not to resolve their contradiction; it is to subordinate one to the other causally. Marx in seeking to overcome Hegel's idealism was not thereby dispensing with the ideal element inherent in all cognitive activity; he was substituting one conceptual system for another. To describe even the most simple physical occurrence entails placing it in a category, whether a colour or species, by abstraction and conceptualisation. The more generalised and complex our categories, including all those that bear on social phenomena—for example class or the state—the more abstract and conceptional they become and the further removed from any direct correspondence to actual objects. To put *homo faber* instead of the cunning of reason as the motor of history and to conceive its development dialectically is to employ one set of abstractions for another; their justification lies not in any direct correspondence to things as self-subsisting entities, which they manifestly do not have, but in making intelligible the phenomena to which they refer.

Consciousness, like being itself, is an abstraction; and in omitting to treat it as such Marx was taking his own definition of each for an independent reality. He thereby left a yawning epistemological void, which was filled by Engels and Lenin and indeed drew in Marx himself. In the first place it has made Marxist materialism scarcely less one-sided and mechanistic than that which it superseded. So long as being is conceived in terms of objects, and consciousness as translating experience of it into thought, consciousness remains causally dependent upon being. The dependence is not overcome by positing consciousness as itself creative activity, in the way that Marx did. To make every change by man of his environment *ipso facto* a change in the man who effects it implies one of two consequences: either it can be taken to mean their inseparability to the point where they are indistinguishable, which is tantamount to denying any independent role to consciousness, or it posits all consciousness as manipulative and/or creative, which does not bear examination. We are as much recipients as agents, and our awareness is not solely active but also reflective and contemplative. Man is not solely a producer, whether of goods or ideas; indeed, apart from a possible first man, man is a consumer before he is a producer, while much of human activity is neither productive nor conscious. Marx's materialism overlooks the distinguishing feature of all human activity: that it takes place within a system of values, which far from being necessarily consciously directed owes as much to the past as to the present and to habit, tradition, and preconception as to actual perception or conscious direction. Accordingly there is at once a time-lag and discrepancy between how men conceive reality and how it really is. This rather than any ontological antinomy between being and consciousness is the *Leitmotiv* of human development. It is therefore as diverse as the ways in which men can act and be conscious; for it owes as much to men's conceptions of themselves and the world as it does to what exists outside them. If each changes in relation to the other it does so not according to any regular sequence in the manner posited by Marx. Otherwise we should be unable to explain how men in the same condition can envisage their circumstances differently, or why some accept what they find as given while others achieve something new, or even why there could be different ways of expressing the same experience. Yet the difference between a Kant and a Hegel, a Blücher and a Napoleon form the irreducible data of human history; and with it the autonomy of intention, imagination, and intuition. It may be granted that men respond to their circumstances, but they do so in their own way. The ability to create a conceptual or imaginative world that does not correspond to the external world and only exists conceptually or imaginatively is central to human consciousness. Whatever it may owe to men's experience of the world no theory of translation in the way enunciated by Marx can account for its mental products. As a recent Marxist writer has truly said, 'Round the margins of his workaday existence there has been a wilderness given over to fancy, suggestibility, dreams, and inspiration. We must look here, as well as in the narrow sphere of practical activity, for the origins of art and magic. . . .'[3] Men live on different levels: the abstractions that we call art and religion are not a unitary mode of inverting real experiences; they are themselves diverse modes of experience as real for those to whom they belong as they are unreal for those who cannot share them.

The attempt to relate consciousness to men's productive activities leads to one of two alternatives. Either it is limited to the way in which men produce or it reduces all forms of consciousness to the mode of production. The difference between these courses is also the difference between Marx on the one hand and Engels and subsequent orthodoxy on the other.

Marx, who conceived nature itself as the product of human agency, made no distinction between consciousness of nature and social consciousness. His concern was with men's relationship to nature and it was in their interaction that the dialectic between consciousness and activity lay. To that degree Marx recognised no independent order of nature outside human agency and hence he made no provision for the different forms that other modes of consciousness could take. But consciousness is not unitary, just because it varies according to what is to be known. There is all the difference between knowing the structure of rock crystal and that of the state: one refers to a set of physical laws, the other to modes of human behaviour.[4] To seek to apply

3. V. G. Kiernan, 'Notes on Marxism in 1968' in *The Socialist Register, 1968* (London, 1968), p. 205. This is a challenging series of reflections, but it does not, I believe, go far enough in its analysis.

4. I have considered it in my *History and Social Theory* (London 1969), chaps. 1 to 6.

the same criteria to both can only lead to epistemological nonsense. This occurred when Engels attempted the dialectical treatment of nature. The result has been the pseudo-categories known as dialectical materialism. As further extended both by Engels and Lenin to our perceptions it firmly reinstated the mechanistic mode of thinking that Marx had expressly sought to overcome by confining consciousness to men's own activities.

In the second place, however, even Marx's dialectical thinking did not save him from the element of determinism that could so easily become reductionism. For it revolved around the very need to reconcile the two central premises of his outlook: that the mode of production is the ultimate determinant in man's life and outlook, and that men are their own agents in changing their history and themselves. His system thereby stands or falls by whether this reconciliation can be achieved. It is my contention that it cannot, and that neither Marx himself nor his successors have been able to do so. Just as it is logically impossible to posit an order of priorities based upon an ultimate cause without making the consequent dependent on the antecedent, so it is empirically. However dialectically their relationship is envisaged, one must precede the other. Marx's system rests upon a clear order of priorities. 'Social being determines social consciousness'; and whether or not being is itself shaped by human consciousness, consciousness remains bounded by the social reality from which it springs and to which it is directed. As expressed in Marx's image of society divided into a material base and an institutional and ideological superstructure, the determinist element was accentuated; the superstructure stood for the preservation and rationalisation of the prevailing productive relationships. As such it took on a much more derivative role, justifying and legitimising the social reality that already existed. The dangers of economic determinism to which this led stirred Engels in later life, after Marx's death, to try to correct the balance by stressing the word 'ultimate'. But, as I have considered in chapter two, section five, this becomes a mere play upon words

9

that is an invitation to sophistry. A cause is a cause or it is not. To make it ultimate is to return to a scholastic hierarchy of causes. The detailed arguments belong to the text of the book. Here I wish to point to what I regard as the three major misconceptions that the notion of basis and superstructure has engendered.

The first is the epistemological one: that Marx took it as expressing social and historical reality. It shared none of the methodological status of Max Weber's ideal types. Recently an attempt has been made to refute Weber's contention that this was the fundamental difference between him and Marx.[5] It rests upon the contention that Marx also distinguished between capitalism as an abstraction and its imperfectly developed forms in which it was to be found in Western Europe. That is true enough. But this is not the same as treating capitalism as a category of historical explanation, in the way that Weber did, rather than as an historical reality: only that Capitalism had not emerged fully fledged. It was indeed the enormous achievement of Marx to treat social evolution historically. He did so, however, not by denying the reality of his categories but rather by hypostasising them as historical realities. There is nothing to suggest that he ever regarded them as devices.[6] Here above all Marx remained true to Hegel. He invested human history with the dialectical qualities that Hegel had applied to the unfolding of the absolute idea, so that Marx, no less than Hegel, saw in their operation the laws of historical development. The *dramatis personae* changed but their reality remained. No one reading Marx from his early *Critique of Hegel's Philosophy of Right* to the final pages of *Capital* can doubt that his world of abstractions, 'proletariat', 'capital', 'class struggle', 'mode of production', stood

5. Avineri, *op. cit.*, p. 158.

6. Nor for the same reason will the contention of I. M. Zeitlin, *Marxism, A Re-Examination* (Princeton, 1967), chap. 1, hold that Marx's approach was purely inductive. It is surely time that the myth of a purely inductive attitude devoid of presuppositions, as the paradigm of a scientific attitude, was buried once and for all.

directly for historical realities. They constituted models only in the sense that they enabled us the better to reach the independent order of phenomena that underlay them and to which they corresponded. They were translations of reality, not, as for Weber consciously selected segments that could therefore (*a*) have been different and so were arbitrary and (*b*) carry their own evaluations. For Marx, on the contrary, there was a clearcut epistemological division between objective and subjective that excluded any such mingling of our own preconceptions with what was to be understood. When he spoke of social reality he meant what existed independently of however we might envisage it. In his own words, 'a non-objective being is a *non-being*'.[7] That Marx considered he was enunciating the laws of society in the manner of a natural scientist explaining nature is the surest indication of his belief in the reality of his categories. As he put it in his letter of Weydemeyer in 1852: 'And now as to myself, no credit is due to me for *discovering the existence of classes*. . . . What I did new was to *prove* (1) that the *existence of classes* is only bound up with particular, historic phases in the development of production; (2) that the class struggle *necessarily* leads to the dictatorship of the proletariat; (3) that this dictatorship itself only constitutes the *transition* to the abolition of all classes and to a classless society.'[8] Setting aside the content of this passage, which is discussed in chapter four, the words I have italicised illustrate, as clearly as could be, Marx's assumption, first, that history is the repository of objective reality, which is there to be discovered as it exists; second, that this enables us to seize the elements that constitute its laws of development; and, third, these operate according to a necessary order that enables us to predict or at least to prognosticate its future course. Together what do they signify if not that the data of history are independent objective truths that owe nothing

7. Karl Marx, *Early Writings*, translated by T. B. Bottomore (London, 1963), p. 207.

8. Letter No. 18 to Weydermeyer, in K. Marx and F. Engels *Selected Correspondence* (London, 1943), p. 57.

to our particular angle of interpretation and everything to grasping them as they truly are? Where praxis is the criterion, as it was for Marx, there is room only for *the* truth. The dialectic between consciousness and activity is also that between present and future; what exists is there to be changed. It must therefore first be understood. This gave Marx's thought an entirely different epistemological orientation from Weber: its goal was 'not criticism but revolution'. Hence partial understanding was not enough.

This gave rise to the second misconception: namely that it excluded the possibility of an alternative interpretation. Society has its own laws that govern its evolution and in terms of which alone we can understand it. Here, too, Marx owes his conception to Hegel. Transposed to society the Hegelian dialectic produced a conflict model of society; but again, unlike Max Weber's ideal types, its manifestation in class struggle was seen as the real motor of history so far. This led Marx to explain its evolution as the successive overcoming of one mode of production by another in an ever-rising series until with the proletariat all classes would be at once abolished and transcended. This notion of change as coming through the resolution of contradictions at a higher level has made of history at once a metaphysics and a teleology. It is the medium in which men evolve and through which they will become emancipated. For Marx history was as necessary to explain man's state of alienation and how it would be overcome as it was for Hegel.

The consequence has been to instate dialectical change as the universal law of development. If Marx was not responsible for the subsequent Marxist epistemological assumption that there must be central contradiction in everything from barley to mathematics by which it can alone be explained, he provided Marxism with its conflict model of society. Although he did not conceive it in such terms, for the reasons already given, his almost exclusive preoccupation with struggle and revolutionary change led him to make them the motor of history. In that sense Engels was only doing for nature what Marx did for society. But in neither case does it make sense when exalted to a first principle. A society is a structure; and like any other the condition of its survival is a minimum degree of equilibrium. Social relations are thus dialectical not only in engendering contradictions but also interdependence. Social conflicts arise from within a relationship, which, however unequal, is reciprocal. Only exceptionally do interests become so contradictory as to be irreconcilable because that means jettisoning the accepted framework in which men live and have their expectations. Struggle itself for the most part takes place within a socially sanctioned framework, whether legally recognised or not. If it is endemic in class societies, it acts as much as a safety-valve as an explosive force.[9]

This is an historical fact that Marx and Engels in reading all history in class terms overlooked. The overwhelmingly greater part of history has been devoid of revolutionary change. For all the conflict between 'freeman and slave, patrician and plebeian, lord and serf, guildmaster and journeyman, in a word oppressor and oppressed', endemic resistance to change of any sort, let alone of society, is an almost universal law of mankind. It is as much a datum of human behaviour as man's ability to change. Yet Marx made social revolution the driving force of history and invested the proletariat with the mission to bring about the final revolutionary transformation. In spite of a hundred years of proof to the contrary, new revolutionary groups are now arising upon the same assumption that revolution is inherent in proletarian being, and needs only stirring into consciousness to become actual. Thus does the dialectic become mechanistic: and as the direct legacy of Marx.

As I have sought to show in chapter two the gearing of social change to revolutionary transformation has paradoxically made Marxism incapable of accounting for revolutionary change itself, since most of the far-reaching developments in history have taken place within an existing social order and not through its supersession. The periodic

9. For a development of this theme, see my *History and Social Theory*, chap. 9.

explosions in consciousness that have occurred throughout history, e.g. in Greece in the fourth century B.C., in Western Europe in the twelfth, fifteenth, seventeenth and twentieth centuries, provide no correlation with productive activities. They cannot be explained therefore as expressions of the latter; they have their own dynamic, which is to be found in the experience of those who engendered them. Indeed, contradictions of any kind, within a body of knowledge or a society, only become such when men consider them such.[10] A revolutionary situation arises when individuals refuse to accept the present. What makes them do so belongs to the contingency, not the laws, of history. When Marx said that 'mankind sets itself only such tasks as it can solve', he was substituting teleology for freedom;[11] for he was discounting the discontinuities that spring from the actions of individuals and that can as well be unintended, like the discoveries of Columbus or Copernicus, or forced upon men, like Napoleon's conquests or the law of gravity, as be in harmony with the prevailing outlook. Indeed the entire notion of society acting as a whole is a figment. Human development is not governed by the inexorable movement of social wholes but by individuals and groups acting in diverse ways. For all his stress upon change Marx could only conceive it in inverted Hegelian terms as part of a necessary and autonomous revolutionary sequence. As such it can have no meaningful application to most of history, the development of which is neither necessary nor revolutionary.[12]

Finally Marx's conception generated its own central contradiction. It has no place for its own evaluations. Like each of the other consequences that I have mentioned this is once again the outcome of his epistemology. To hold that what is true exists objectively, independently of our knowing

10. Kiernan makes a similar point, *art. cit.*, p. 187.

11. Avineri, *op. cit.*, p. 80, argues that this itself reflects Marx's vision of the future: that a human need is itself a product of a concrete historical situation and cannot be determined a priori. This however still does not allow for the autonomy of consciousness.

12. For a fuller treatment of this theme see my *History and Social Theory*, Part One.

it, entails also accepting it independently of our evaluations. But since men so far have not been able to see themselves objectively, because they are alienated from society, on what grounds are we able to posit objective truth? To do so, we must assume that we can stand outside the historical process and are able to see what is not yet socially true since it does not exist.[13] Alternatively, we must accept that our own conception of what man should and could be is an ideal and derives from our evaluation of him as a species. In the first case we have to exempt ourselves from the limitations of knowledge so conceived and thus recognise that consciousness can operate beyond the confines of objective being. In the second case, we have to make our conception of history part of our conception of man evaluatively. Both consequences seem to me inescapable in any viable epistemology; but there is no provision for them in Marxist terms. Instead justification is sought in an appeal to history.

By turning to history for evidence of what man is and has been Marxism claims to show what man can be. History for Marx subsumes man as a species and so what he ought to be under what he is. The force of Marxism lies principally in this dynamic conception of history; but it does so just because Marx, not history, is the arbiter of what man should be. As his early writings show he began from a moral vision of man as the subject of his own world and not its object. His notion of man's present alienated state derives from his notion of what it is to be truly human. In that sense Marxism as conceived by Marx is a humanism. It is also a morality. It appeals to the realisation of man's full nature. There is nothing reprehensible in such an outlook except to pretend that it is something else. To act in the name of history can only subvert the very vision that is the warrant for changing history. It can too easily lead to substituting a belief in necessity for human agency and destiny for humanity. It then becomes not only amoral but irrational as Stalinism so clearly showed. Only if men act for moral reasons can they

13. Avineri, *op. cit.*, pp. 84–5.

hope to act with reason. They are not however the same: and Marx in turning away from his early notion of man divided from himself, as a species, to man divided into classes blurred the central dynamic between man as he is and as he could be; he did so not only because he directed his attention almost wholly to economics and politics, but also because he never reconciled his own moral vision with his epistemology. Where subject remains ontologically distinct from object, the dualism between *is* and *ought* remains unbridgeable. If the return to early Marx succeeds in reinstating man, not history, as subject it will be an immeasurable gain for Marxism; but it will only be preserved if it is recognised that the shift from one to the other in the first place was immanent in Marx's own outlook; for no matter how dynamically men's condition is conceived, if it is made to occur according to a regular historical sequence, man is made a hostage to history. The charge against Marxism is not determinism but reductionism, which can too easily be turned into necessitarianism. Marx largely avoided both by holding to a morality that remained outside his system. But to those who lacked either his humanism or the ability to discern it, increasingly overlaid, in his later writings, the dialectic between its pull and the demands of his system was displaced for the merely mechanistic interpretation of the latter.

The lesson of the failure of Marxism is that of any orthodoxy. The personal insights of the founder become lost and only its formal expression remains. Taken for reality it encloses its adherents within it. If Marxism is to be revitalised, the condition is to dispense with the system and rethink its assumptions. Marxism could then, in ceasing to *be* the truth, once again join the search for truth, which has no exclusive repository.

I

DIALECTICAL MATERIALISM

◆

Marxism, as a doctrine, is a series of paradoxes. It claims to be a science yet regards its truths as transcendental; it upholds the inexorability of change while remaining frozen in its century-old categories; it asserts the conditional nature of all outlooks and claims exemption for its own; it condemns pragmatism but makes success its criterion; it denounces metaphysics while labouring under its own metaphysical presuppositions.

Nowhere are these inconsistencies more prominent than in its philosophy. Despite all the protestations to the conrary, dialectical materialism is indelibly imprinted with the image of nineteenth-century science. In the hundred years or so of its existence, it has undergone virtually no development: its emphases are still those of its epoch; its categories remain Hegelian; the range of its problems has scarcely been extended or deepened to meet the vast changes in knowledge that have since come about. Today, as in the time of Engels, its main tenets still comprise a few bald generalisations which, to all practical purposes, can be accepted, rejected, or disregarded with no real consequence; for in truth Marxism has never been a philosophy in the strict sense. Its concern has always been with the social and political; its starting-point has been society rather than nature; its arena, history not the cosmos; its search, not for abstract truths abstractly arrived at, but social change. Hence knowledge for its own sake and truth as an independent pursuit have no place. Practice is the supreme arbiter to which all theorising must bow. In the words of Marx's Second *Thesis on Feuerbach*: 'The question whether objective truth is an attribute of human thought is not a theoretical but a practical question. Man must prove the truth.'[1]

This onus upon proof is the core of Marxism and the source of its dynamism. Its appeal has always been to man's power to act. It has conquered not by the perennial truths of its philosophy or by the scientific enlightenment of its theories, many of which are mythical, but by infusing men with a faith in their own historical destiny. In effect Marxism has supplanted the old gods by a new deity, that of history; but whereas men mainly worshipped the former in passive obeisance, they have served the latter by fighting for its commandments. Resignation has been superseded by revolution.

Nothing therefore can be more misleading than to interpret Marxism in abstract terms. From the first its founders set themselves strictly practical objectives, the attainment of which has been the end of all its theory. Marx set the tone in his famous Eleventh *Thesis on Feuerbach* when he declared: 'Hitherto the philosophers have only interpreted the world; the point, however, is to change it.'

Consequently when we come to examine dialectical materialism as the officially appointed philosophy of Marxism, we are not in fact dealing with a philosophy in the strict sense; we are confronted with an artifact, a series of rather vague principles grafted onto what is essentially a sociology. Both logically and temporally it is not untrue to say that dialectical materialism is extraneous to Marxism. Its tenets had no formative part in the evolution of Marx's central positions, and the latter stand in their own right independent of any so-called philosophical foundations. Indeed dialectical materialism, as officially formulated in the handbooks of Marxism, is a later and disastrous importation of Engels; even if its main features, as enunciated in *Anti-Dühring*, received Marx's tacit assent, it is hard to see

1. Published in Karl Marx and Frederick Engels, *Selected Works*, Vol. II (London, 1950), pp. 365-7, and K. Marx and F. Engels, *The German Ideology* (London, 1965), pp. 651-3.

their place in his own work. So far as Marx was concerned, his outlook was formed from his critique of Hegel and Hegelian philosophy during 1843 and 1844. It was crystallised in the *Communist Manifesto*. 1848 was the watershed in Marx's development. Henceforth he devoted himself principally to the study of capitalism together with day-to-day political activities. The principles that he had enunciated in the *Economic and Philosophic Manuscripts of 1844* and *The German Ideology*, during 1845 and 1846, were now given application in both political economy and politics. Engels, on the contrary, roamed farther and farther afield taking in developments in the natural and social sciences, and interpreting them in the light of Marxist materialism; in that way there gradually emerged a series of *dicta* that have come to constitute dialectical materialism.

Now nothing is more enviable than the breadth of Engel's interests; the range of his knowledge and his power of assimilation were outstanding, measured by any standards. But this is not to say that he was a creative thinker or a genius; and the more one compares his contribution with that of Marx, the greater the disparity between them appears. After the first phase of their collaboration and the appearance of the *Communist Manifesto* the basis of Marxism had been laid: that is to say, the theory of society and human development. It was Marx who pursued the path to its final culmination in *Capital*, transforming Marxism into the massive outlook it has become, while Engels harried their opponents and instructed their disciples; effective polemicist as he was, most of his writings have been ephemeral. They depended too much upon transitory knowledge and too little upon the insight that comes only from a thorough study of any one field. Knowledge of dialectics was not the same as knowledge of economics; and whereas Marx's conclusions were distilled from his own personal investigations and insight, Engels refined upon the findings of others. Marx produced a series of general propositions that, even if they cannot be accepted, have transformed the study of society and have made Marxism the main intellectual challenge of this century. Engels on the other hand succeeded in reducing the complexities of nature to a series of sterile generalisations that provide no further point of departure for scientists or philosophers. They have become a padlock on Marxist thought, which from the time of Lenin has acted as a barrier against new knowledge. It is for that reason that they are important.

The fallacy of dialectical materialism lies in attempting to apply the same criteria to nature as to society. The materialism about which Marx wrote in his early philosophical writings, notably *The Economic and Philosophic Manuscripts of 1844*, *The Holy Family*, *The German Ideology*, *The Poverty of Philosophy*, and the *Theses on Feuerbach*, was essentially concerned with human beings, and more specifically with the nature of men's ideas about themselves; he sought to confute the prevailing Hegelian belief in the autonomy—or tyranny, as it was called in *The German Ideology*—of concepts and to show that they could not be taken as sovereign in themselves. 'Hitherto', wrote Marx in the preface to the last-named work, 'men have constantly made up for themselves false conceptions about themselves, about what they are and what they ought to be.' The way to liberation from these false conceptions was not merely to combat them on the intellectual plane by criticism and ideas; it was to 'quit the realms of philosophy' and 'the independent existence of ideas' for 'their real premises'. These were 'the real individuals, their activities and the material conditions under which they live, both those which they find already existing and those produced by their activity'.[2] In thus turning to men's material conditions, Marx and Engels cut themselves off root and branch from idealism. They renounced not simply Hegel's Absolute Spirit but also 'the rule of religion, of concepts, of an abstract general principle in the existing world'.[3] It also took them beyond Ludwig Feuerbach's concept of a human essence with which he had countered the bloodless abstractions of the Hegelians. In Marx's

2. *The German Ideology*, Preface, p. 23.
3. *Ibid.*, p. 30.

eleven *Theses on Feuerbach*, the quintessence[4] of Marx's early thinking, can be seen the emergence of what Marx called the 'new materialism': its standpoint was 'human society or social humanity' (Tenth *Thesis*), in contradistinction to the passivity of the older materialism, on the one hand, which understood reality 'only in the form of the object of contemplation', and idealism, on the other which had developed 'the active side' but confined it to the abstract and non-sensuous (First *Thesis*). In fact, 'our sensuous nature [is to be understood] as *practical*, human-sensuous activity' (Fifth *Thesis*). Man, that is to say, is not a 'sensuous object' but 'sensuous activity'.[5]

The effect of this reorientation was to foreswear philosophical enquiry for social analysis; or more exactly to refuse any longer to regard the products of consciousness—religion, philosophy, ethics—in their own terms, but as expressing a definite social situation. As Marx put it, 'Life is not determined by consciousness, but consciousness by life'.[6] Consequently 'men are the producers of their conceptions, ideas, etc.—real active men, as they are conditioned by a definite development of their productive forces and of the intercourse corresponding to these, up to its furthest forms. Consciousness can never be anything else than conscious existence, and the existence of men is their actual life process'.[7]

We shall reserve for a later chapter consideration of the relationship between ideology and social life: here it suffices to show the light in which Marx regarded all thought. Ideas have no independent existence; indeed they are the substitute for real knowledge, and 'when reality is depicted, philosophy as an independent branch of activity loses its medium of existence. At the best its place can only be taken by a summing-up of the most general results, abstractions which arise from the historical development of men. Viewed

4. N. Rotenstreich, *Basic Problems of Marx's Philosophy* (Indianapolis, 1965) provides a detailed commentary on them.

5. The *German Ideology*, p. 58.

6. *Ibid.*, p. 38.   7. *Ibid.*, p. 37.

apart from real history, these abstractions have in themselves no value whatsoever'.[8]

It follows therefore that the way to truth lies in going beyond ideas for the reality that underlies them. But what is this reality? Here we come to the other feature of Marx's critique of philosophy. Not only is the idea not the repository of truth, but the reality that it expresses is not nature in the raw as such but as man has made it: that is to say, all consciousness is not only socially conditioned; it is from the outset 'a social product' changing as men's 'life activity changes'.[9] At first it is consciousness of a nature that appears to men 'as a completely alien, all-powerful and unassailable force with which men's relations are purely animal and by which they are overawed like beasts'.[10] Later it 'receives its further development and extension through increased productivity', until such time as 'through the division between mental and physical labour', consciousness breaks away onto its own course. It is then in a position 'to emancipate itself from the world and to proceed to the formation of pure theory, ethics, etc.'.[11] Once consciousness reaches this position it is no longer prepared to acknowledge its dependence upon existing practice but takes on an autonomy in virtue of which it gives a distorted picture of reality.

Reality is seen in terms of immutable essences, such as Nature and Man, whereas in fact these are the result of an historical process. Man is not 'man' but 'real historical men'; the sensuous world is 'not a thing given direct from all eternity, ever the same, but the product of industry and of the state of society'.[12] Even the simplest natural object, such as the cherry tree was 'only a few centuries ago transplanted by commerce . . . and therefore only by this action of a definite society in a definite age . . .'.[13] The external world, therefore, and consciousness of it are governed by a given state of society. 'The nature that preceded human

8. *Ibid.*, p. 38. 9. *Ibid.*, p. 40.
10. *Ibid.* 11. *Ibid.*
12. *Ibid.*, pp. 56–7. 13. *Ibid.*, p. 57.

history is not by any means the nature in which Feuerbach lives';[14] and the ruling ideas at any one time are 'nothing more than the ideal expression of the dominant material relationships, grasped as ideas; hence of the relationships which make one class the ruling one; therefore the ideas of its dominance'.[15] Ideology, then, cannot be taken in its own right, as true or false as such; it is engendered by a particular set of social circumstances, of which it is the expression. Once this is realised, it will be seen that 'all forms and products of consciousness cannot be dissolved by mental criticism . . . but only by the practical overthrow of the actual social relations which gave rise to this idealistic humbug'.[16]

Such was the reply of Marx's materialism. Its importance need hardly be stressed. In the first place it meant the rejection of philosophy and criticism as the way to understanding: truth lay not in consciousness but in men's productive activity; history, as the study of men's changing social relations, supplanted abstract thought. Society became the only legitimate reference. The standpoint as Marx said was now social humanity. This led, in the second place, to an entirely new outlook; Marx's materialism was more than the reassertion of the primacy of being, or nature, as Engels defined it;[17] it marked the redefinition of being itself. Here if anywhere its distinctiveness lay. Society as 'the product of men's reciprocal activities' now constituted the framework in which all human activity was to be judged. The traditional categories were displaced, or rather they were subsumed under it. This can be seen with especial clearness in Marx's *Theses on Feuerbach*, in which what were hitherto regarded as abstractions become facets of social practice. Reality is no longer an object of contemplation, or abstract thought, but 'revolutionary', 'practical-critical' activity (First *Thesis*); truth, likewise, 'is not a theoretical but a practical' question (Second *Thesis*) and 'the reality or non-reality of thinking . . . isolated from practice is a purely scholastic question'

14. *Ibid.*, p. 58. 15. *Ibid.*, p. 60.
16. *Ibid.*, p. 50. 17. See below, p. 63.

(Second *Thesis*); 'the essence of man is no abstraction inherent in each individual but the ensemble of social relations' (Sixth *Thesis*). In every case knowledge is to be found in the actual conditions in which men live and act. 'All the mysteries which urge theory into mysticism find their rational solution in human practice and in the comprehension of this practice' (Eighth *Thesis*).

Marx's materialism, then, was essentially a doctrine of society: its beginning and end were directed to men's way of life and the attitudes to which it gave rise. It is important to stress this essentially social-practical emphasis, for it governed Marx's entire outlook; philosophy in the strict sense, nature as an independent entity, human experience other than in socially objective terms had no place. If it is to be called a philosophy at all, it was a philosophy of society, and all its concepts were determined accordingly.

It is in this context that we must view his use of the Hegelian dialectic, the most abstract element in Marx's thinking. Only by considering it as an aspect of his view of society does it make sense in a way in which it does not when applied by Engels and orthodox Marxism to the universe at large. As with his materialism, Marx's treatment of dialectics is inseparably bound up with society; or, put another way, it is in the study of society that Marx conceives its laws of development in dialectical terms. It receives no independent treatment except for the discussion in the *Economic and Philosophic Manuscripts of 1844*, and the few ironical pages in the *Poverty of Philosophy*.[18] More to the point, however, is his preface to the second edition of *Capital* many years later, where he summarised the role of dialectic in his outlook thus: 'My dialectic method is not only different from the Hegelian, but its direct opposite. To Hegel, the life process of the human brain, i.e., the process of thinking, which, under the name of "the Idea", he even transforms into an independent subject, is the demiurgos of the real world, and

18. Chap. 2, 'The Metaphysics of Political Economy', Observations 1-4 (London, n.d.), pp. 89 ff.

the real world is only the external phenomenal form of the "Idea". With me, on the contrary, the ideal is nothing else than the material world reflected by the human mind, and transformed into forms of thought. . . . In its mystified form dialectic became the fashion in Germany because it seemed to transfigure and to glorify the existing state of things. In its rational form it is a scandal and an abomination to bourgeoisdom and its doctrinaire professors, because it includes in its comprehension and affirmative recognition of the existing state of things, at the same time, also, the recognition of the negation of that state, of its inevitable breaking up; because it regards every historically developed social form as in fluid movement, and therefore takes into account its transient nature not less than its momentary existence; because it lets nothing impose upon it, and is in its essence critical and revolutionary.'[19] This was the sense in which Marx conceived the dialectic, as describing the mode of social development. It was a process of change that took place through what, a quarter of a century earlier, he described as 'the coexistence of two contradictory sides, their conflict and their fusion into a new category'.[20] It was the motive force in all societies and the outlooks that accompanied them; for all were subject to the contradictions that led to their ultimate supersession by a new and higher order. Accordingly, the dialectic was, as it were, embodied in society, and was not an abstraction to be regarded in itself.

We are not at present concerned with Marx's doctrine of historical development; what I wish here to establish is the essentially social nature of his dialectical materialism (to use an expression that he never employed). His dialectics, as his materialism, were not conceived in any but social terms designed for the purpose of comprehending men as they are, as they had been and would become. Being was social being; consciousness was social consciousness; move-

19. Karl Marx, *Capital*, edited and translated by Dona Torr (London, 1946), pp. xxx–xxxi.
20. Karl Marx, *Poverty of Philosophy*, p. 95.

ment was social movement through the struggle of classes; change was from one social system to a higher one. Within this context, the Hegelian dialectic provided a dynamism that has helped to make Marxism the force that it is. In Marx's hands it became the most potent social and political doctrine to be formulated.

It is when we turn from its application to society by Marx to its gradual crystallisation into a self-contained, all-embracing system that dialectical materialism changes character. Where previously it had been located within the configuration of society it now became increasingly defined and formulated in its own terms; it was a gradual, almost surreptitious, change and, as so often, took place through the very process of more precise definition. Inevitably, the effect was to create a new metaphysic, to worship the abstraction for the reality, to turn guiding principles into precepts and prohibitions, to transform a method into an absolute. The very consequence that Marx and Engels had sought to avoid—the tyranny of concepts—came about.

The reason for this lay primarily in the failure of Engels in particular and Marxists in general to adhere to their own canons. Marxism is no more immune than any other outlook from the effects of time. As with any other outlook it took its rise from a particular set of circumstances; in this case the dominance of Hegelianism, the backward political state of Germany, the horrors of early industrialism, and the ineffectiveness of contemporary socialism. Marx's thinking was a revulsion against all these and in this sense was shaped by them. The core of his materialism lay in the primacy it allotted to men's economic activities in society. It was from the outset, as we have remarked, a social doctrine, translating all truth and reality into terms of social existence. It had no time for the abstract or the contemplative.

Clearly such an outlook was unconcerned with and unadapted to either the individual or the universal: man and nature, other than as categories, were outside its purview; the dialectic of being and change were, as Marx said, treated not abstractly but as facets of social development, and so was thought. Indeed the strength of Marx's materialism was its comprehension of man as a social being. With Engels and subsequent Marxist orthodoxy, however, Marxism was made to overstep these limits and exalted into a universal philosophy of nature and being. As such it has become a metaphysic, the repository of those principles— and by implication truths—that govern all existence. In doing so it has doubly infringed its own canons, firstly in ignoring the circumstances and assumptions in the light of which Marx formulated his outlook, and secondly, in taking as eternally valid the categories of Hegelian idealism and the science of Engels's day. If, according to Marxism, all thinking reflects the underlying social reality, where is the justification for exempting Hegel's dialectic? The reply that this comes of his very recognition of movement and change is hardly to the point when the process is explained entirely in terms of Hegel's idealist categories—as the clash and interpenetration of opposites. Even more to the point, however, is the failure of dialectical materialism, as an instrument of a universal knowledge, to progress beyond the boundaries set by Engels and, by implication, Marx. This atrophy has come about not only because of its very nature it is unfitted to cope with non-social matters, but Engel's attempt to make it do so has inevitably meant distorting its entire pattern, as we shall shortly observe. The result of its grandiose claim to have the key to all knowledge has been one more nineteenth-century attempt at synthesis, albeit a mere skeleton of propositions. Like all its kind it suffers from the burden of being comprehensive and yet true, immortal and yet contemporary, and like them it faces the choice of adaptation of fossilisation. Unfortunately Marxists in refusing the first course, have suffered the fate of the second

The process begins with Engels; as we have said, after his early collaboration with Marx over the early writings that culminated in the *Communist Manifesto* he increasingly turned his attention to the more general implications of their materialism while Marx pursued his study of capitalist society. But where Marx had the necessary instruments for this task in his conception of history, Engels had not; he was unequipped to make the transition from society to nature, and he never succeeded in doing so. It is no denigration of Engels to regard him as a talented expositor rather than as an original genius. His range and versatility were outstanding, and probably no man had a wider knowledge of the natural and social sciences of his day. But this is not the same as being able to disclose new truths, and both he and Marxism have suffered from not observing the distinction. Instead his every jotting and scribble have been solemnly incorporated into the canon; his pronouncements on science, philosophy, and anthropology have been treated by official Marxism with the same finality as Marx's words. Yet as we have said there is a crucial difference between speaking from a profound personal understanding, as Marx did, and generalising at second-hand from the knowledge of others. In Engels's own words, 'What I contributed—at any rate with the exception of my work in a few special fields—Marx could very well have done without me. What Marx accomplished I would not have achieved. Marx stood higher, saw farther, and took a wider and quicker view than all the rest of us. Marx was a genius; we others were at best talented.'[21] We do Engels fullest credit by accepting this characteristically generous testimony.

We can perhaps best discern the source of the trouble in a passage from *Ludwig Feuerbach*, written towards the end of Engels's life, where he traced the emergence of Marxism: 'The separation from Hegelian philosophy was here also the result of a return to the materialist standpoint. That means it was resolved to comprehend the real world—nature and history—just as it presents itself to everyone who approaches it free from preconceived idealist fancies. It was decided relentlessly to sacrifice every idealist fancy which could not be brought into harmony with the facts conceived in their own and not in a fantastic connection. And materialism means

21. F. Engels *Ludwig Feuerbach*, Marx and Engels, *Selected Works*, Vol. II, p. 349, note 1.

nothing more than this. But here the materialist world outlook was taken really seriously for the first time and was carried through consistently—at least in its basic features—in all domains of knowledge concerned.'[22]

Now two comments can be made here. The first is the assumption—perhaps due to deliberate over-simplification on Engels's part—that there is no difference between comprehending nature and history, and that all knowing consists in approaching reality 'just as it presents itself to everyone who approaches it free from pre-conceived idealist fancies'. There could hardly be a more reckless assumption: it entirely begs the question of what it is we are knowing and the ways in which we know it. How do we compare for instance knowledge of a mathematical formula with knowledge of a stick? Or the way in which a scientist knows the sun and a layman knows it? We shall return to these questions later. For the present it is enough to point to what has become one of the occupational diseases of Marxism: its inability, or refusal, to recognise different kinds and different levels of knowledge, or an intitial set of assumptions without which nothing is known. For this Engels must bear the primary responsibility. With it has gone the reduction of the process of knowing to a simple and direct act of reflexion on the part of the knower. Or as Engels puts it a little later in the same work: 'We comprehended the concepts in our heads once more materialistically—as images of real things instead of regarding the real things as images of this or that stage of development of the absolute concept [of Hegel]'.[23] The word 'image' has done more than any other to bedevil Marxist epistemology. It denotes an essentially passive role, disregarding the active 'this-sidedness' of which Marx speaks in his First *Thesis on Feuerbach*. It takes no account of the individual role of the knower, or how one man may know more or differently than another, or of habit in enabling us to know at all. The second comment is that Engels conceives the source of such true knowledge as dialectics; for strictly speaking Marxist philosophy, as envisaged by

22. *Ibid.*, pp. 349–50. 23. *Ibid.*

its founders, is not a dualism, or syncretism, of materialism and dialectics but, as both Marx and Engels averred, a materialist dialectics. That is, the portrayal of reality as it really exists—dialectically. In Engels's words, 'Thus dialectics reduced itself to the science of the general laws of motion—both of the external world and of human thought— two sets of laws which are identical in substance but differ in their expression in so far as the human mind can apply them consciously, while in nature, and also up to now for the most part in human history, these laws assert themselves unconsciously in the form of external necessity in the midst of an endless series of seeming accidents. Thereby the dialectic of the concept became merely the conscious reflex of the dialectical motion of the real world . . .'[24] For Engels and Marx, then, dialectics thus conceived were materialism, or rather to think in truly materialistic terms was to be dialectical; it was not until Lenin, when materialism came to receive separate consideration, that the full implications of Engels's doctrine of reflexion, alluded to above, were made apparent. Accordingly, I propose first to examine dialectics in order to ascertain whether it can be truly regarded as 'the science of the general laws of motion—both of the external world and of human thought'; and then to pursue the arguments of my first observation in the light of this enquiry, so that it may be possible to discern how far dialectics are really materialist, and conversely, how dialectical Marxist materialism is. In each case we shall begin with the basic propositions of Engels and trace their development through to Lenin and subsequent Marxist orthodoxy.

I. DIALECTICS

As we have mentioned, in the absence of any treatment by Marx, Engels is the main authority for what has come to be called dialectical materialism. Most of his emphasis was directed to dialectics, in terms of which he attempted to

24. *Ibid.*

explain all reality, but especially nature. The primary sources are *Anti-Dühring*, *Ludwig Feuerbach* and *The Dialectics of Nature*, where his wealth of knowledge, ingenuity, and often gaiety, were brought to bear in a manner that compels admiration if not conviction. In *Anti-Dühring*, the most comprehensive and systematic exposition of dialectical and historical materialism, Engels defined dialectics as 'nothing more than the science of the general laws of motion and development of Nature, human society and thought'.[25] These he described in general terms as follows: 'When we reflect on Nature, or the history of mankind, or our own intellectual activity, the first picture presented to us is of an endless maze of relations and interactions, in which nothing remains what, where and as it was, but everything moves, changes, comes into being and passes out of existence'.[26] Although, Engels continued, it was not enough to leave this 'primitive, naïve . . . conception of the world' as it stood, it was intrinsically correct; and it is through the indispensable process of refining upon it, in examining the details individually and separately, that this overall dynamic picture is lost. 'The analysis of Nature into its individual parts, the grouping of the different natural processes and natural objects in definite classes, the study of the internal anatomy of organic bodies in their manifold forms—these were the fundamental conditions of the gigantic strides in our knowledge of Nature which have been made during the last four hundred years. But this method of investigation has also left us as a legacy the habit of observing natural objects and natural processes in their isolation, detached from the whole vast interconnection of things; and therefore not in their motion but in their repose; not as essentially changing but as fixed constants; not in their life but in their death'.[27] This second mode—christened by Hegel metaphysical—of viewing things has always been regarded as the antithesis of dialectics; indeed since the time of Engels it has become

25. Marxist Leninist Library, Vol. I (London, 1943), p. 158.
26. *Ibid.*, Introduction, pp. 26–7.
27. *Ibid.*

common Marxist usage to expound dialectics by means of contrasting them to metaphysics, a point to which we shall return later.

The assumptions underlying the Marxist view of dialectics were twofold. First they were the means of overcoming the rigidity into which abstract thought had been frozen through its very need to extrapolate as mentioned by Engels above. Dialectics meant a return to viewing things in their interconnection, and so of overcoming 'the insoluble contradictions' that 'absolutely discontinuous antitheses' engender. Instead of the 'Yea, yea, Nay, nay' of the meta-physician, for whom 'a thing either exists or it does not exist', dialectics recognised their interdependence: 'positive and negative are just as inseparable from each other as they are opposed'.[28] Accordingly the entire realm of meta-physical method, of conceiving nature and our ideas as static, separate and self-contained, was rejected. Secondly, dialectics were not simply an alternate mode of thinking. Contrary to Hegel—and ironically enough to Stalin, who described dialectics as 'the method of studying and appre-hending the phenomena of nature'[29]—their *raison d'être* lay in reality itself. Dialectics provided 'an exact representation of the universe, of its evolution and that of mankind, as well as of the reflexion of this evolution in the human mind'.[30] Hence dialectics were materialist in that they were the recognition of material reality as it existed, 'not as a com-plex of ready-made *things* but as a complex of *processes*, in which the things apparently stable no less than their mind-images in our heads, the concepts, go through an uninter-rupted change of coming into being and passing away . . .'.[31] The 'general actions of becoming and ceasing to be, of pro-gressive and retrogressive changes' constituted the actual state of all that was, whether nature, history, or human thought. 'Thereby, the dialectic of concepts itself became merely the

28. *Ibid.*, pp. 28–9.
29. J. V. Stalin, *Problems of Leninism* (Moscow, 1945), p. 569.
30. *Anti-Dühring*, p. 29.
31. *Ludwig Feuerbach, Selected Works*, Vol. II, p. 351.

conscious reflex of the dialectical motion of the real world'.[32]

We are thus confronted with two basic propositions in dialectical materialism. The first, that reality lies in the external world, and the second that it is the function of our thinking to mirror this reality as it actually exists, that is, dialectically, in a constant state of movement and flux. Let it be said at once that there was a boldness and freshness in this programme to which we can only pay tribute. Engels—I refer to him solely here, as Marx took no overt part in these developments—was one of the few thinkers who was truly prepared to submit all our concepts to the test of reality, in this case the science of his day. He constantly emphasised not simply the provisional nature of our findings but the displacement of philosophy as an independent pursuit by the sciences themselves: '. . . modern materialism embraces the more recent advances of natural science, according to which Nature also has its history in time . . . modern materialism is essentially dialectical and no longer needs any philosophy standing above the other sciences. As soon as each separate science is required to get clarity as to its position in the great totality of things and of our knowledge of things, a special science dealing with this totality is superfluous. What still independently survives is the science of thought and its laws—formal logic and dialectics. Everything else is merged in the positive science of Nature and history'.[33] Abnegation in the interests of truth could not go further. Yet this very desire to make reality, interpreted dialectically, the sole consideration had a fatal flaw. Everything depended upon the validity of the interpretation; and when we come to examine the workings of dialectics in detail we are presented with a series of propositions that are no less arbitrary and subjective than the metaphysical and idealist concepts they were designed to replace.

The reason is that dialectics are themselves metaphysics. They claim nothing less than to be above all positive knowledge. In Engels's own words, 'What still independently survives of all former philosophy is the science of thought and

32. *Ibid.*, p. 350.   33. *Anti-Dühring*, p. 31.

its laws, formal logic and dialectics. Everything else is merged in the positive science of Nature and history.'[34] Their role is therefore as the supreme arbiter of reality, the means by which it is rendered intelligible.

In itself this is not reprehensible. On the contrary dialectics must like any other conception of reality stand beyond mere experience. There can be no intelligibility without some framework of interpretation. What is indispensable to the attainment of truth is to recognise the factitious and in a sense arbitrary nature of the standpoint adopted. To that extent all human knowledge is unavoidably subjective. It either conforms to a formal order, or it is a refinement on experience. In each case it must have its own emphases and priorities, including and excluding according to some determined order. This is precisely what Marxism has never admitted; and its failure to do so is due less to any dishonesty than a genuine confusion of terms—a classic example of Marx's warning not to take a man at his own estimation. Dialectics, it is averred, are the laws of movement: since they recognise the unceasing flux in everything there is no question of going beyond reality or of aspiring to final truths. In the oft-repeated phrase of Engels: 'If, however, investigation always proceeds from this standpoint, the demand for final solutions and eternal truths ceases once for all'.[35] But to be aware of the provisional nature of one's findings is not the same as accepting the provisional nature of one's instruments of investigation; and it is in ignoring the difference that Marxists from Engels onwards have sought exemption from their own judgment. The point hardly needs labouring: had dialectics asserted merely the universality of movement it would hardly rank as more than a platitude. In fact, however, it goes much further, and purports to define the laws of movement. These, as we shall now see, are as much the product of a set way of regarding reality as any other.

In the first place, it is worth reiterating that in origin the dialectic is not scientific but Hegelian. As Engels pointed

34. *Ibid.*   35. *Ludwig Feuerbach*, p. 351.

out at length in *Ludwig Feuerbach,* 'According to Hegel, dialectics is the self-development of the concept . . . According to Hegel, therefore, the dialectical development apparent in nature and history, that is, the causal interconnection of the progressive movement from the lower to the higher, which asserts itself through all zig-zag movements and temporary retrogressions, is only a miserable copy of the self-movement of the concept going on from eternity. . . .'[36] The need was therefore to strip away its idealist content and thereby place it 'upon its feet'. Marx, too, speaks to the same effect in the introductory passage to *Capital* quoted earlier. Neither evinced any doubt that a method that had been engendered by the entirely different purposes of Hegel was appropriate to a materialist standpoint, and that the same arbitrary preconceptions that informed his metaphysics might not also be present in the dialectic. In this they omitted to apply the standards that they employed for all other ideologies, where they posited a definite correlation between form and content.

The reason is that Marx's thought grew out of Hegel's, as we shall discuss in the next chapter. His own materialism consisted in inverting Hegel's concepts, not dispensing with them. He first enunciated his outlook in his *Critique of Hegel's Philosophy of Right* written in 1843, under the influence of Ludwig Feuerbach. In that work he adopted Feuerbach's transformative method[37] of reversing the order between subject and predicate. Henceforth instead of treating religion, art, philosophy, law, the state and so on, as Hegel had, as manifestations of the absolute spirit standing outside man, they were to be seen as the expressions of man's own essence or nature. In making man the subject and these ideal forms the predicates, the latter now belonged to man as their subject and not man to them as their property. This entailed turning to man as he actually existed in the natural world. 'Only perception of objects and experiences in their objective actuality can free man from all prejudices', wrote

36. *Ibid.,* p. 350.
37. For this see Tucker, *op. cit.,* p. 85 ff. and Avineri, *op. cit.,* p. 11 ff.

Feuerbach. 'The transition from the ideal to the real takes place only in the philosophy of *praxis*.'[38]

It was therefore Feuerbach who turned Hegel right side up, and Marx was Feuerbach's pupil in following him. But, as we have remarked, Marx went beyond Feuerbach in refusing to stop at substituting a human essence for a divine essence; man was himself to be conceived dialectically as changing according to his mode of life and consciousness. These were the grounds on which Marx criticised Feuerbach in his eleven *Theses*.

If Marx owed his humanism to Feuerbach his mode of thought remained Hegelian. He sought the dynamic of human development historically in the dialectical inter-action of man upon the world and men upon men. He also adopted from Hegel the notion of progress through the overcoming of the contradictions, inherent in all develop-ment, in a higher resolution (*Aufhebung*). This at once destroyed and preserved what had been transcended, so that the new both contained and abolished the old. It was this conception which at the hands of Engels passed beyond the framework of society in which Marx had exclusively treated it, to being in general. It thereby took on the character of a metaphysics that has become known as dialectical materialism. The central tenet of the dialectic is not movement as such, but movement by means of inner struggle. As Marx put it in *The Poverty of Philosophy*: 'What constitutes dialectical movement is the coexistence of two contradictory sides, their conflict and their fusion into a new category.'[39] Or in Hegelian terminology, affirmation, negation, and negation of the negation. That is to say, it is assumed that within everything there exist contradictory tendencies, or opposites, that conflict; and this results in their fusion into a new equilibrium, in turn giving rise to further antagonisms and new combinations, and so on. It is in this process that dialectical movement lies. It is neither a simple progression from stage to stage nor a series of random leaps; but rather a spiral, in which each new level is en-

38. Quoted in Avineri, *ibid.*, p. 12.   39. *Ibid.*, p. 95.

gendered by the struggle that took place previously: thus in negating a previous affirmation a new affirmation is produced that negates the previous negation. Engels described the entire process in *Anti-Dühring*, the following example of which will suffice: 'But what then is this fearful negation of the negation, which makes life so bitter for Herr Dühring and fulfils the same role with him of the unpardonable crime as the sin against the Holy Ghost does in Christianity? A very simple process which is taking place everywhere and every day, which any child can understand, as soon as it is stripped of the veil of mystery in which it was wrapped by the old idealist philosophy and in which it is to the advantage of helpless metaphysicians of Herr Dühring's calibre to keep it enveloped. Let us take a grain of barley. Millions of such grains are milled, boiled and brewed and then consumed. But if such a grain of barley meets with conditions which for it are normal, if it falls on suitable soil, then under the influence of heat and moisture a specific change takes place, it germinates; the grain as such ceases to exist, it is negated, and in its place appears the plant which has arisen from it, the negation of the grain. But what is the normal life-process of the plant? It grows, flowers, is fertilised and finally once more produces grains of barley, and as soon as these have been ripened the stalk dies, is in its turn negated. As a result of this negation of the negation we have once again the original grain of barley, but not as a single unit, but as ten, twenty or thirty fold.'[40]

Again: 'if we take an ornamental plant which can be modified in cultivation, for example a dahlia or an orchid: if we treat the seed and the plant which grows from it as a gardener does, we get as the result of this negation of the negation not only more seeds, but also qualitatively better seeds, which produce more beautiful flowers, and each fresh repetition of this process, each repeated negation of the negation increases this improvement'.[41]

Now there are four main elements in this dialectical conception. Firstly there is the omnipresence of opposites,

40. *Anti-Dühring*, pp. 151–2.   41. *Ibid.*, p. 152.

contradictions, or antagonisms (the terms as we shall notice are interchangeable) which comprise everything and by which and from which all movement and development derive. Secondly all being is regarded as in a constant process of change and all change is regarded as struggle. In consequence, for Marxism struggle has been elevated into the *Leitmotiv* of development whether in history or in nature. This leads, thirdly, to the view of change as something sudden and discontinuous, a leap from one level to another. At a certain point in the conflict between the old and the new, the old is finally negated and the new will emerge. This takes place not as the result of mere quantitative progress, passing smoothly from phase to phase, but through the transformation of quantity into quality. This was defined by Hegel as the 'nodal line of measure relations, in which at certain definite nodal points, the purely quantitative increase or decrease gives rise to a *qualitative leap*; for example in the case of water which is heated or cooled, where boiling-point and freezing-point are the nodes at which—under normal pressure—the transition to a new form of aggregate takes place, and where consequently quantity becomes transformed into quality'.[42] This has led Marxists to view everything in terms of revolutionary change, especially so far as society is concerned. The assumption is that, if not violent, it must be abrupt. Finally there is the implicit belief in progress: 'in spite of all seeming accidentality and of all temporary retrogression a progressive development asserts itself in the end'.[43] Change is not merely a circular process but essentially a progression from 'the lower to the higher which asserts itself through all zig-zag movements and temporary regressions'. It is enshrined in the negation of the negation in which there is an ever-recurring spiral; the old is both 'overcome and preserved'.[44] The effect of this has been to focus attention almost entirely upon that which is to come in the belief that of its nature it will be an advance upon the present. Indeed

42. *Ibid.*, p. 54. 43. *Ludwig Feuerbach*, p. 351.
44. *Anti-Dühring*, p. 155.

so strongly has this become an accepted attitude that Stalin cites as one of the features of dialectics that it 'regards as important primarily not that which at the given moment seems to be durable and yet is already beginning to die away, but that which is arising and developing, even though at a given moment it may appear to be not durable, for the dialectical method considers invincible only that which is arising and developing'.[45]

Opposites and their struggle

Now it would be, I think, more than a little difficult to maintain that these assumptions are to be derived purely from 'comprehending the real world—nature and history—just as it presents itself to everyone who approaches it free from preconceived idealist fancies'. One need only examine them more closely to be made aware of their impalpability. First, let us take opposites, the heart of dialectics: Engels in *The Dialectics of Nature*[46] describes the three main laws of dialectics as those of the transformation of quantity into quality, the interpenetration of opposites, and the negation of the negation. Yet neither there, nor previously in *Anti-Dühring* (where he had separate chapters on both quantity and quality, and the negation of the negation), did he ever treat the middle law. Whether this was entirely fortuitous it is hard to say: what is significant however is that it is the only one of the three that he does not uphold with copious examples from the natural sciences. This is hardly surprising, for the entire conception of opposites is one that is at variance with what Engels elsewhere described as 'the great basic thought that the world is not a complex of ready-made things, but a complex of processes'. The attempt to reconcile the universality of opposites with the view of the whole natural, historical and spiritual world '. . . as in constant motion, change transformation and development'[47] is

45. 'Dialectical and Historical Materialism', *Problems of Leninism*, p. 571.
46. F. Engels, *The Dialectics of Nature* (London, 1946), p. 26.
47. *Anti-Dühring*, p. 30.

indeed, to use a Marxist phrase, one of the contradictions in Marxism. For, to have opposites on the one hand, and their 'mutual interpretation', on the other, is to be vulnerable on two counts. Firstly, even accepting that it applies to nature as opposed to logic, it still posits something that can be called an opposite and is defined as such in virtue of certain distinguishing traits that it actually possesses. But is this tenable? The much-vaunted triumph that Marxists—and Marx and Engels in particular—claimed over Hegel was that while his dialectic was concerned only with the absolute idea, they turned to reality as it actually existed in nature and history. To quote Engels, 'an exact representation of the universe, of its evolution and that of mankind, as well as of the reflection of this evolution in the human mind can only be built up in a dialectical way'.[48] But where are we to find opposites and how do we define them? Is black the opposite of white, or hot the opposite of cold, soft the opposite of hard, in other than human terms? Is there, that is to say, any objective means of measuring and establishing these qualities such that they may be treated as opposites? It would appear not; the very qualities that are denoted when we talk of hot and cold have no such correspondence in physics. We call 150° fahrenheit hot and 35° cold, but so far as their thermometer measurements are concerned there is nothing that characterises the hotness of one or the coldness of the other as contrary qualities; the same applies to black and white, hardness and softness: none of these are self-subsisting qualities susceptible of physical description either in these human terms or as opposites to one another. The case is no better founded with other measurable qualities, such as wetness and dryness, lightness and heaviness. None of these can be called opposites except as the result of an act of mental abstraction. In all these cases, certainly at the macrocosmic level, we find that opposites are abstract concepts of our own devising. They are the work of conceptualisation, and as conceived by Marxism they are also metaphysical in the sense that they cannot be en-

48. *Anti-Dühring*, p. 29.

countered in actuality. Here, Marxism has fallen into the old confusion of treating concepts as entities. It has hypostatised what are in fact categories drawn not from nature but from our own subjective experience. In doing so it has become the slave of its own abstractions. This is on a par with the very idealism that Marxism is designed to avoid; far from being more up to date than the most modern philosophy, it betrays the same traits of rigidity, preconception, and abstraction for which it brands metaphysics.

Quite apart from these considerations of material unreality, however, the actual working of the principle of opposites is no more satisfactory: it becomes either mere triviality or is so arbitrary that it is of no value. An example of both these defects can be seen in Lenin's instances of the unity of opposites, in support of his contention that 'the division of the one and the cognition of its contradictory parts . . . is the essence . . . of dialectics:

In mathematics: $+$ and $-$, differential and integral
In mechanics: action and reaction
In physics: positive and negative electricity
In chemistry: the combination and dissociation of atoms
In social science: the class struggle.'[49]

We must assume that Lenin took these definitions seriously. For the undialectical however they are of interest as specimens of the great Marxian fallacy that anything can be defined in terms of a central contradiction and that this is the key to its understanding. A moment's consideration will show how misguided this belief is. To begin with, all definition is a formal and to some degree arbitrary exercise. To choose to describe mathematics as governed by the contradiction between $+$ and $-$ is only one among a number of possible ways of describing it. But even assuming that it were the best, this would not explain what mathematics is about or what its function is or how it is practised, any more than to classify flora and fauna is to disclose the nature of

49. *On Dialectics*, V. I. Lenin, *Selected Works*, Vol. XI (London, 1943), p. 81.

individual flowers or animals. At most it puts them in a class that enables us to place them and impose an order upon them. But it is we who are doing so; and however closely our categories correspond to what they contain, they remain descriptive not cognitive in Lenin's sense. To take our terms for the reality as Lenin does is to invest them with an independent standing—nearer to idealism than materialism. At the least it constitutes a failure to recognise the conceptual nature of our knowledge; but at worst it can mean distorting the reality it seeks to explain. This is the second charge that can be levelled against Marxian dialectics. To attempt to subsume mathematics under the contradiction between $+$ and $-$ only renders it unintelligible, because it bears no relation to the empirical reality of what mathematics is. Mathematics as the abstract language of quantity embraces a complex of activities that cannot possibly be made intelligible in terms of the contradiction between plus and minus, differential and integral. Many of its branches such as geometry and trigonometry and mathematical logic do not invoke them at all. Even if they did, what relevance does such a contradiction have to the complexities of quantum mechanics or theories of numbers, either as a formal description or in the activities of those who employ them? If it is not central to all that concerns mathematics, then it cannot be taken as *the* characteristic. Since it is the dialecticians who have so far had to contend with the contradiction between $+$ and $-$, the reason may be that they are dialectians rather than mathematicians.

Lenin's other definitions lack even the precision of $+$ and $-$; that of mechanics has all the breathtaking simplicity of sheer nonsense, while in social sciences one would have thought that Lenin's own knowledge would have made him ask himself what exactly his opposites were designed to show. If the class struggle is the basic contradiction of the social sciences, what happens to the study of pre-history, or socialism? What then becomes of much of anthropology, archaeology, ethnology and so on? How are many activities

—such as developments in knowledge or language—meaningfully to be understood by reference to the class struggle? What, for example, is the relevance of the invention of the printing press to the class struggle; or in Leninist terminology how does this express the inter-penetration of opposites?

The pointlessness of these questions is the measure of the futility of the entire exercise. This lies in the apparent inability to realise that the only thing that these different pairs of opposites have in common is that they are conceptual abstractions. They are all artifacts of the mind. Beyond this their similarity ends, though Lenin appeared oblivious to the fact. Whereas + and − are basic symbols bearing a definite connotation, expressions like 'action' and 'reaction' have no correspondence to anything: they describe groupings of events, in this case reciprocal relationships in the most general terms, which possess no specific features which enable us to say *that* is action in the way in which we can write a plus sign. For action, or reaction, we have to translate a series of happenings that can be anything from a man crossing the road in front of a car (action) and the car pulling up sharply (reaction) to the description of complex scientific phenomena. To regard them as opposites is not only purely arbitrary; it begs the question, what is an opposite? This is a question that has never been satisfactorily answered or to my knowledge even considered by dialecticians. Electricity, positive and negative, is a third kind of expression, for here certain kinds of energy are being described that answer to the terms positive and negative. They therefore differ from both a conventional symbol and from groupings of words, in having a specific correspondence in nature. With Lenin's fourth pair, that of chemistry, we are back again at describing not specific events, like positive and negative electricity, but actions that they may undergo, as with the second group. As in the latter definition, to describe the basic contradiction of chemistry as the combination and dissociation of atoms is equivalent to describing the basic contradiction of life as the combination and dissociation of being. It is so general as to be meaningless. Finally, with the class struggle we are confronted with another kind of concept. A class, whether a social grouping or a number, is the result of an act of abstraction, in which all phenomena of a similar nature are brought together. Such a classification is therefore a category, which, while it is founded upon a quality common to a number of different individuals, does not subsist independently of them. In this sense it differs either from a mathematical symbol or from a verbal description of a specific action or from a definable series of events such as positive electricity. Hence none of these can be indifferently thrown together as real living, material opposites, all of which can be encountered as independent entities in nature and society and which exist regardless quite of our knowledge of them. But this is what Lenin has done; he has confused artificial symbols, verbal expressions, and logical categories with real things and sought to explain reality in terms of them. It may be argued that each of the instances he gives can, in fact, be verified in practice, but that is not to the point. For what Lenin has professed to show by them is that they themselves, in their own right, constitute reality as the very essence of the different aspects of nature and history to which they belong. Accordingly it is to these pairs of opposites that we are bidden to turn if we are to understand reality. In fact we are presented with a jumble of classifications that share only their verbal form as abstract nouns in common. Lenin has taken mental categories for reality and thereby has misconceived the one and distorted the other.

Not that Lenin is alone in doing so; it is among the oldest and most misleading of all confusions, which goes back to the Middle Ages at least, to suppose that to every name there corresponds a thing. William Ockham in the fourteenth century and Bertrand Russell in this have attempted to deliver men from this particular bondage. But from the time of Lenin onwards Marxism has been firmly frozen in the same mould; for it was Lenin who, more than anyone else, enshrined the harmful tendencies that we have already remarked in Engels. Marxism has subsequently remained oblivious to the vastly increased sensitivity in the use of language and precision of meaning; it has never even considered, as Stalin's work *Concerning Marxism in Linguistics* abundantly proves, that the structure of language can vary. As the late Benjamin Whorf showed in his revolutionary essays on American Indian languages, our way of thinking is largely determined by our mode of expression. Where through the refinements of analysis we speak and think in terms of subjects, objects and verbs, the less sophisticated languages of the Hopi, Nitinant, and Nootka, for example, have no such clear distinction. Of Nitinant, Whorf says, 'Actually, the terms verb and noun in such a language are meaningless';[50] while in Nootka, 'all words seem to be verbs . . . we have as it were a monistic view of nature that gives us only one class of words for all kinds of events. "A house occurs", or "it houses" is the way of saying house'.[51] Here, as Whorf says, is a mode of expression far better fitted to express the conceptions of modern physics than the subject-predicate structure of our language, that goes against the whole trend of modern physics; indeed it is because of the macrocosmic nature of our terminology, evolved to convey life-sized experience, that we are ever more dependent upon the ultimate refinements of mathematics to compass what lies beyond the immediate realm of perception. This is not, contrary to Lukács's rather facile verdict, because of our growing withdrawal from reality and the substitution of quantitative measurements for real phenomena;[52] it is the result of confronting reality on a new and more microscopic level, where the ordinary delineations and measurements have dissolved into a flux beyond man's capacity to recognise them.

50. *Language, Thought and Reality* (M.I.T., 1956), p. 99.
51. *Ibid.*, pp. 215–6.
52. *Geschichte und Klassenbewusstsein* (Berlin, 1923), p. 125. There is now a French translation, by K. Axelos and J. Bois (Paris, 1960).

As a consequence Marxist terminology is impregnated with the false verbal juggleries and sophisms of the heyday of Hegel; and much of Marxist philosophy consists in resolving verbal problems by verbal solutions. Let us take Lenin again on dialectics as the examplar. His style of argument is characterised by an almost total lack of rigour; his main concern, by its own lights highly effective, is to brand a particular argument as reactionary through showing its affinity with some (by Marxist standards) reactionary standpoint, such as Berkeley or Hume, and concentrating upon its heretical implications. This, as we shall have cause to mention later, is epitomised in *Materialism and Empirio-Criticism*. *On Dialectics*, on the other hand, consists of extracts taken from Lenin's Philosophical Notebooks and therefore we cannot expect to find a closely argued case; what we do see however is the kind of verbal pyrotechnics that in themselves carry no weight but which generate a fog around the entire argument. Thus Lenin:

'To begin with the simplest, most ordinary, commonest etc. *proposition, any* proposition one pleases: the leaves of a tree are green; John is a man; Fido is a dog etc. Here already we have *dialectics* (as Hegel's genius recognised): the *singular* is the *general* . . . Consequently, opposites (the singular as opposed to the general) are identical [!]: the singular exists only in the connexion that leads to the general. The general exists only in the singular and through the singular. Every singular is (in one way or another) a general. Every general is (a fragment, or a side, or the essence of) a singular. Every general only approximately comprises all the singular objects. Every singular enters into the general incompletely etc. etc. Every singular is connected by thousands of transitions with other *kinds* of singulars (things, phenomena, processes) etc. *Here already* we have the elements, the germs, the concepts of *necessity*, of objective connexion in nature etc. Here already we have the contingent and the necessary, the appearance and the essence; for when we say: John is a man, Fido is a dog, *this* is a leaf of a tree etc., we *disregard* a number of characteristics as contingent; we separate the essence from the appearance, and put one in opposition to the other'.[53]

Now the interest of this passage is that it epitomises the fallacy for which we have been criticising Marxist dialectics. It takes logical categories to be those of the real world. Logically we can contrapose singular to universal and, if we so desire, regard them as opposites that are at the same time united; for it is a function of logic to classify, grouping like with like, and distinguishing unlike from unlike. By this means we are able to arrive at concepts of universals and singulars, to recognise that man as a species is made up of individual men, and thereby to say that one is subsumed under the other. Yet this is an exclusively logical process, the result of the ordering of our concepts, that are at best abstractions from the real world. It does not allow us to infer that because we recognise the interconnection between an individual and the class to which it belongs we thereby actually encounter the class each time we meet a member of it. To do so would be to revert to the position of the realists of the Middle Ages, who regarded the universal—man, tree, goodness—as a self-subsisting entity of which the individual was but a particular manifestation. Accordingly, like Plato, they regarded reality as composed of universal essences by means of which individuals came into being.

Now this is substantially the position adopted by Lenin. He has also invested the individual with a universal property by juxtaposing the two as equally real. Accordingly he regards 'Every general as the . . . essence of the singular', and implies that the singular is the 'contingent' or the 'appearance' of the underlying 'necessary' 'essence', by which, it would seem, he means the universal. We have only to compare this with the position attributed to the twelfth-century realist, William of Champeaux, to see how close the affinity between them is: 'One and the same universal comprises diverse individuals none of which is different in essence but only by a number of accidents', so that, 'for example, individual men are of the same substance, man,

53. *Selected Works*, Vol. XI, p. 83.

and the individuals Plato and Socrates differ only in their accidents'.[54] Such a conclusion is inescapable if the categories of logic are to be translated into real terms; to insist upon the reality of the individual's universality, or the universal's singularity (Lenin is remarkably imprecise in his use of the terms) is to posit something like William of Champeaux's self-subsisting essence and to be back at a version of Platonism. At the very least it is metaphysics and for many it is nearer to gibberish.

This shows the perils of treating words as though they were things; such hypostatization is the essence of in dialectics. Far from constituting a new outlook, it represents a return to the realism of the twelfth century, with the same distinctions between accidents and essence, appearance and reality. But whereas the twelfth century had its Abelard to burst its metaphysical bubble and to point to the essentially verbal, conceptual nature of the problem—as one of logical categories—Lenin was not only left to his musings, but they have become enshrined in the Marxist canon. Thus Stalin in the exposition of dialectics in his *Problems of Leninism* talks of 'The struggle between these opposites, the struggle between the old and the new, between that which is dying away and that which is being born, between that which is disappearing and that which is developing, constitutes the internal content of the process of development'.[55] In support he quotes Lenin that 'In its proper meaning dialectics is the study of contradictions *within the very essence of things*', and 'development is the struggle of opposites'.[56]

The same perpetuation of these abstractions can be found in most Marxist manuals; two of the most soundly orthodox, Maurice Cornforth's *Dialectical Materialism* (vol. one, London 1954) and the late George Politzer's *Principes Elémentaires de Philosophie*, both use much the same terminology. Cornforth on page 76 takes Lenin's examples of opposites in mathematics, chemistry, and physics, not

54. In B. Geyer, *Die Patristische und Scholastische Philosophie* (Basel/Stuttgart, 1956), p. 210.
55. *Problems of Leninism*, pp. 572–3.   56. *Ibid.*, p. 573.

surprisingly omitting those of mechanics. He also stresses that 'We find ourselves considering not just a number of *different* things, *different* properties, *different* relations, *different* processes but pairs of *opposites*, fundamental oppositions. As Hegel puts it: "In opposition the difference is not confronted by any other but by *its* other" '. Politzer likewise speaks of things as 'l'unité des contraires'.[57]

Yet in all justice to Lenin, it was he more than any other of the Marxist Authorities who made a really sustained attempt to establish the existence of opposites in things; indeed he alone speaks consistently of opposites where Marx and Engels talk of contradictions or antagonisms. Lenin, it would appear, was prepared to treat them as entities where Marx and Engels thought more in terms of oppositions or interactions. The result has been an unbecoming vagueness in terminology with opposite, opposition, contradiction, and antagonism all treated as interchangeable. T. A. Jackson, in his often scintillating apologetic, *Dialectics*, explicitly treats them as interchangeable when he says: 'without opposition, contradiction and struggle, *resulting* in movement (change, development etc.) would be impossible'.[58] Elsewhere, glossing a passage from Lenin on the unity of opposites, he explains it in terms of opposition, thereby making the concept plausible even if he does not succeed in getting beyond the tortuous Hegelianism which it serves. 'There are', he says, '. . . two radically different kinds of "opposition" contemplated by Dialectics. One is the opposition of things in *objective* nature, which do, in actual fact, *act upon and react against each other*. Two billiard balls in collision upon a billiard table are visibly and obviously at the moment both *opposed and in union*. Their subsequent opposite movement is... the *consequence* of their having been *in union*. Quite another kind of 'opposition' is that of the categories in logic, in which unity is premised as that into which opposites can be reconciled....'[59]

57. George Politzer, *Principes Elementaires de Philosophie* (Paris, 1946), p. 191.

58. T. A. Jackson, *Dialectics* (Benares, 1945), p. 761.

59. *Ibid.*, p. 752.

This passage is interesting in more than one respect. It shows that even when there is a realisation—albeit implied —that opposites are such because they are in a relation of opposition rather than because they possess inherently opposite qualities, dialectics do not become any more meaningful. The metaphysical framework still remains: two billiard balls in collision still 'unite in their opposition', and their 'union in opposition' is the source of their subsequent development. We have only to consider this statement to find how worthless it is. It is simply stretching the meaning of words to call a fleeting external contact between two billiard balls a union; and even if one does so, what has been gained? Are the balls in any way transformed? Do they give rise to a new synthesis that is the result of their meeting? On the contrary, it is only by remaining structurally or qualitatively unaffected by their contact that they are able to carom and maintain the billiard game in being. It is as meaningful to describe any contact between two objects, even without opposition, as a union. When I sit on a chair, I am, according to this line of reasoning, united with it, or when I walk and my foot makes contact with the ground there is a union in opposition. But does that in any way explain the law of my movement from A to B? This mode of thinking exemplifies the real case against dialectics, which is less that it is wrong—for anyone is entitled to invent a language of his own and to call objects opposites, their contacts unions, and their subsequent development the result of the interpenetration of opposites—but that it is at best meaningless and at worst simply misleading. It offends both against clear thinking and reason.

Such a development was no doubt inevitable once the shores of social analysis were left behind. For Marx the antagonisms, or contradictions, in society were its driving force, and the whole strength of his analysis of capitalism derived from it. Yet there is all the difference between its concrete application to a tangible set of phenomena, and the universal attempt at superimposition that Engels set in train. Even so, Engels's firm grasp of science led him to keep the dialectic within bounds; and it is not without significance that neither he nor Marx ever talked in terms of opposites in the manner of Lenin and subsequent orthodoxy; even less did he attempt the kind of dialectical surveys that we have been considering.

This leads us to the second aspect of opposites. For Hegel they were essentially conceptual, conceived as the working out of the idea. As such they belonged to a conception of reality where it was possible to reconcile the one with the many and the many with the one by means of words. But what was fitting for Hegel is totally unfitting for the claims of materialist dialectics: there is, or ought to be, no common ground between envisaging reality as the Absolute Idea and as 'nature as it presents itself to us'; nor can their terms have the same meaning. An opposite for Hegel is a logical concept that owes no allegiance to anything but the mind; it can therefore be contraposed to another concept without doing violence to it. Logically as we have said, individual is the opposite of universal, one is the opposite of many. Combine them and they can be united to give being and number; and, conversely, being and number can be broken down into logical contraries. The same applies to the individual in species and genus: two cats are not the same but together they can be united in the species cat, and, in turn, cats and dogs can be subsumed under the genus animal. There is fertile ground here for any number of permutations and combinations.

Once turn to reality—be it nature or history—and the scene changes. An entirely different set of criteria is required for which these concepts are totally unsuited. It is in their misapplication that, as we have said, the flaw in Marxist dialectics lies; for, it has tried to do for nature what Hegel did for the spirit, with the bizarre results we have observed. The attempt rests upon a hopeless confusion of terms and cannot but fail. It can be seen very clearly in Engels's effort to superimpose a dialectical explanation upon scientific explanation; it means stretching our macro-cosmic object and subject mode of thought to purposes for which it was not designed. That $-a \times -a = a^2$ is proof not of dialectics[60] in nature but of mathematical laws; it harms not mathematics but our own power of reasoning to conclude that, therefore, something is a contradiction, both itself and not itself; for as Professor Popper has pointed out, 'If we were to accept contradictions no kind of scientific activity would be possible; for if two contradictory sentences were admitted any sentence would have to be admitted. . . . Contradictions are only productive because we try to avoid them'.[61] This needs put Marxism in a dilemma. On the one hand, there is the recognition that for us a man is fat, or thin, or bald; on the other, that absolutely speaking there is no exact point at which we can say when a man is fat, or thin, or bald.[62] Hence the attempt to have the best of two contradictory worlds: we are told that nothing in nature can be regarded as clearly demarcated from that to which it is indissolubly connected; and at the same time we are compelled, as we have abundantly seen, to undergo the most tortuous contortions of terminology in order to concede the presence of affirmation, negation, and further negation in everything from billiard balls to electricity. Clearly there is an antinomy here, and one that even a dialectical sleight of hand will not resolve. It arises from the very failing with which Marxism brands 'metaphysics':

60. Cf. Engels, *Anti-Dühring*, p. 153: 'Let us take . . . for example a. If this is negated we get $-a$ (minus a). If we negate that negation, by multiplying $-a$ by $-a$ we get $+a^2$ i.e. the original positive magnitude, but at a higher degree raised to its second power.' M. M. Bober has pointed out that if on the other hand we negate $-a$ by $-a$ by subtracting $-a$ from $-a$ we get not a 'higher degree' but o. *Karl Marx's Interpretation of History* (Cambridge, Mass., 1948), p. 384.

61. K. R. Popper, 'What is Dialectic?', *Mind*, Vol. 49 (1940), pp. 407–8.

62. See for example M. Cornforth, *Dialectical Materialism:* When is a man bald? Common sense recognises that, though we can distinguish bald men from non-bald men, nevertheless baldness develops through a process of losing one's hair, and therefore men in the midst of this process enter into a phase in which we cannot absolutely say either that they are bald or that are not: they are in process of becoming bald. The metaphysical either or breaks down.' Vol. I, p. 75.

namely the conceptualising of natural processes. Engels came near to describing it when he said: 'But although a concept has the essential nature of a concept and cannot therefore *prima facie* directly coincide with reality, from which it must first be abstracted, it is still something more than a fiction, unless you are going to declare all the results of thought fictions because reality has to go a long way round before it corresponds to them, and even then only corresponds with asymptotic approximation'.[63] It is precisely this conceptualisation that dialectics cannot avoid; hence its inability to explain movement except in terms of contradictions, which become entities, in gross violation of the dialectical principles from which they have sprung. Here if ever is a case of the negation of the negation. For it is in the very nature of thought and language—dialectical or otherwise—to engender the definition that dialectics attempts, and claims, to avoid. Baldness, as Cornforth recognises, is a commonsense concept, that bears no correspondence to a quantitatively measurable physical state: it is we who contrast it to non-baldness; and, by the same token, Hegel and the Marxists who then go on to describe them as opposites (with presumably a wig as their reconciliation).

Thus the entire conception of dialectical change, far from having been born of nature, derives from Hegel; it owes everything to the same process of abstraction and classification as the absolutes which it seeks to transcend. Science and scientists have managed, and continue to manage, to survive without its guidance, for they are prepared to recognise what dialectics fails to see: that a different language from that of our everyday usage—quantitative and mathematical—is required for the study of nature at the chemical, mathematical, and atomic levels. Even though Marx was not the last of the schoolmen, dialectics is one more brand of scholasticism.

This confusion in trying to combine the two levels has led

63. Engels: Letter to Schmidt, March 12th, 1895, Marx and Engels, *Selected Correspondence* (London, 1943), pp. 527–8.

not only to the parody of science in the name of dialectics but equally to the violation of logic. Here, too, the source was Engels, though once again at an incomparably higher level of erudition and subtlety than anything that Lenin and his followers subsequently achieved. For where, so far as nature was concerned, the effect of dialectics was to rigidify, categorise, and conceptualise processes that can only be properly described in scientific and commonsense terms, the opposite was the case with logic. Here the essential prerequisites of clear thinking—as embodied in such laws as that of identity (A is A), contradiction (A is not —A), and the exluded middle (A cannot both be B and not B)— were denigrated, as the epitome of so-called metaphysical thinking. Engels expressed this attitude which came about, he said, 'because in considering individual things it loses sight of their connexions; in contemplating their existence it forgets their coming into being and passing away; in looking at them at rest it leaves their motion out of account; because it cannot see the wood for the trees. For every day purposes we know, for example, and can say with certainty whether an animal is alive or not; but when we look more closely we find that this is often an extremely complicated question, as jurists know very well. They have cudgelled their brains in vain to discover some rational limit beyond which the killing of a child in its mother's womb is murder; and it is equally impossible to determine the moment of death, as physiology has established that death is not a sudden, instantaneous event, but a very protracted process. In the same way every organic being is at each moment the same and not the same; at each moment it is assimilating matter drawn from without, and excreting other matter; at each moment the cells of its body are dying and new ones are being formed; in fact, within a longer or shorter period the matter of its body is completely renewed and is replaced by other atoms of matter, so that every organic being is at all times itself and yet something other than itself.[64']

If it served no other purpose this passage would be of

64. *Anti-Dühring*, p. 28.

value as a warning against the intoxicant of dialectic. Quite apart from anything else it implicitly contradicts the entire conception of the 'law of quantity into quality' as we shall discover; for if there is no ascertainable point at which life becomes death we are not in a position to say that there is a sudden discontinuity from one to the other. It is indicative of the virtual impossibility of doing credit to dialectics without doing injury to nature, or history; if everything is forever itself and not itself how is it possible to say what it is or when it becomes such? Nor is this a mere aberration on Engels's part; it has become firmly established in Marxist orthodoxy. Thus Georges Politzer[65] follows Engels almost word for word, and adds his own illustration that 'the beard of a dead man continues to grow; so do his nails and hair'.[66] We have already referred to Cornforth's allusion to the indeterminate state preceding baldness, as well as to Lenin's reflections on 'John is a man. Fido is a dog etc.' To the almost certain rejoinder that this only shows a failure to think dialectically one must reply that at some stage even the headiest dialectician must pause; interpenetration of opposites and quantity into quality are his laws, not ours; and if he wishes to put one or other into temporary abeyance it is for him to do so, but it is idle to pretend that both can coexist when one has palpably cut the ground away from under the other. The same applies to the change in the cellular composition of the body; if quantity changes to quality, then surely there should be as many different individuals as there are cycles of replacement. Yet for all practical purposes Smith remains Smith throughout Smith's life, and Jones remains Jones.

Of greater relevance to the present discussion is the Marxists' inability once again to distinguish between levels of truth. It is one of the most inexplicable failures of Marxism never to have recognised that different criteria are needed to serve different states and conditions and purposes. If one is a physiologist then assuredly the precise point between life and death may well be too nice to decide; and

65. *Op. cit.*, pp. 180–1.   66. *Op. cit.*, p. 183.

within his terms of reference one would not presume otherwise. But the case is not at all the same at the level of what may be called human personality. A dead man's beard and nails and hair may continue to grow, but once his heart has stopped beating and his metabolism no longer behaves as a living creature's, we have no difficulty in concluding he is dead; for we are now judging him as a human being, as one who has the needs, functions, and aura of a person. When these have ceased, so has he. (The case of the child in the womb is not one of fact, either micro-cosmic or macrocosmic, but of interpretation of a fact and therefore has no bearing upon the reality or non-reality of the child's death, but solely upon its cause.) If we were seriously to follow Engels in upholding the simultaneous existence and non-existence of something we would make nonsense of any attempt at definition, abstraction, or investigation. Our knowledge of Smith and Jones is only possible on the assumption that each is who he is. Our own very existence depends upon such hard, discrete facts as that a car which is travelling in our direction will knock us down if we get in its way: the metal of the car may be undergoing constant atomic change, its speed may be the result of a series of contradictions, in which it is here and not here, there and not there, but it nevertheless proceeds in a set direction at a measurable speed. Similarly I may be myself and not myself, all my cells may be in a state of flux, but if I am struck fairly and squarely the odds are that I shall be killed: and even if physiologically the exact moment of my death cannot be precisely ascertained, I shall never again be the recognisable entity that I and not–I represented.

That these implications of Engels have been neglected by his disciples says as little for the value of dialectics as for their judgement. But the truth remains that despite oc-casional disclaimers to the contrary, there is an assumption that dialectics has, to say the least, superseded formal logic.[67]

67. Though recently there has been a rehabilitation in the Soviet Union: see G. A. Wetter, *Der Dialektische Materialismus und Sowjet Philosophie* (Stuttgart, 1952), p. 479. There is an English translation.

We are not here concerned with the shortcomings of the syllogism, nor with the developments that have been made by logicians in the past sixty years; but with the incontrovertible truth that only by the processes of logic are we able to exist, to think, and to communicate with one another. It is by virtue of 'Yea yea and Nay nay for whatsoever is more than these cometh of evil' that these functions are made possible. Thus when Plekhanov, in many ways the most philosophically creative of all Marxist theoreticians, tries to set aside these traditional boundaries he is in fact disregarding the functions that logic alone can and must fulfil, and seeks to impose upon it those that by definition are outside its province. He does so by arguing from the example of movement. 'But what' he asks, 'is movement? It is an obvious contradiction. Should anyone ask you whether a body in motion is at a particular spot at a particular time you will be unable with the best will in the world, to answer . . . in accordance with the formula, "Yes is yes and no is no". A body in motion is at a given point, and at the same time it is not there. We can only consider it in accordance with the formula "Yes is no, and no is yes". This moving body thus presents itself as an irrefutable argument in favour of the "logic of contradiction"; and one who is unwilling to accept this logic will be forced to proclaim, with Zeno, that motion is merely an illusion of the senses. . . . We seem to be between the horns of a dilemma. Either we must accept the fundamental laws of formal logic and deny motion; or else we must admit motion and deny these laws.'[68]

The ground for this rejection of traditional logic lies in a twofold misconception. Firstly, that movement is divided up into a series of heres and theres, but, as Gustav Wetter has pointed out,[69] this is an arbitrary conception; indeed it is positively subjective. Movement is a continuum and we have no objective grounds for splitting it up into such stages;

68. G. V. Plekhanov, *Fundamental Problems of Marxism*: Dialectic and Logic (London, 1946), pp. 112–13.
69. Wetter: *op. cit.*, p. 544 ff.

to do so is to interpose ourselves and to regard it in relation to us, but then we are no longer treating it as a physical, least of all as a scientific, occurrence. Even if this were not so, it is hardly worthy of 'dialectical logic' to base it upon ignorance; for that is what Plekhanov's argument amounts to. In effect he is saying that when we do not know something we cannot judge it logically; but what is this if not a vindication of logic? Logic is possible only on the basis of definition and classification; argument can only advance from what is known to what is unknown; when there is no premise there can be no conclusion. If Plekhanov is prepared to allow the uncertainty that comes of inadequate knowledge to be taken as dialectical, he thereby only impugns the reliability of dialectics. No one in possession of his senses regards 'Yes and No' as anything but a confession of uncertainty, to be overcome at the first opportunity. The onus is not upon the validity of logic, but upon its misapplication. Plekhanov himself appears to acknowledge this distinction when he says: 'To every definite question as to whether an object has this characteristic or that, we must respond with a yes or no. As to that there can be no doubt whatever. But how are we to answer when an object is undergoing a change, when it is in the act of losing a given characteristic or is only in the course of acquiring it?' Yet when he goes on to reply that 'A definite answer should be the rule in these cases likewise. But the answer will not be a definite one unless it is couched in accordance with the formula "Yes is no and no is yes" '[70] we recognise the irresistible spell of the dialectic once again; for what is this if not a state of uncertainty? And what better way of designating it than by the words 'perhaps', 'maybe', or even 'probably'? If Plekhanov cares to substitute the ponderous formula of 'Yes is no and no is yes' he is not exposing the limitations of logic nor giving us a new dialectical logic; he is merely using seven words where one would suffice and in doing so making the truth seven times more confounded. Finally, it may be noted that Plekhanov's approach is

70. Plekhanov, *op. cit.*, p. 114.

hardly a good advertisement for the new dialectical logic. At the outset we are presented with the stark alternatives: 'Either we must accept the fundamental laws of formal logic; or we must admit motion and deny these laws'.[71] As we have seen, the contradiction is of Plekhanov's own making and hence the solution or (to keep to the the dialectical rules) resolution, is not a little specious: it falls to the ground if we do not accept—as there is no reason to—his original dilemma.

Plekhanov's attitude is symptomatic of that of Marxism generally; even T. A. Jackson, one of the few Marxists to give anything like a balanced appreciation of formal logic and its indispensability,[72] shows the same confusion over 'Dialectic logic'. 'It takes over', he avers, 'where formal logic has to stop'. It does so 'by taking as its starting-point the very fact that formal logic is forced to exclude—that nothing can be understood by means of itself alone: everything must be understood as (a) coming *from* something else, (b) moving *to* something else, (c) moving under the impulsion of an active interaction between itself and its circumstances. Therefore Dialectics treats each and every thing as the embodied *movement* resulting from the interaction between other things. . . . Given movement and its transformation as the subject of study and Dialectics is indispensable.'[73]

The Negation of the Negation

The best reply to these, and other like claims, is to be found in the workings of the supereme epitome of dialectical logic, the negation of the negation. As we have seen it denotes the struggle of opposites; we have also seen that the latter, as with the categories of formal logic, are essentially the outcome of a process of mental abstraction and in fact

71. *Ibid.*, p. 113.
72. E.g. '*Both* formal logic *and* the Dialectic are necessary procedures in scientific investigation' (*op. cit.*, p. 760). 'The Dialectic is no more a substitute for plain everyday *formal* logic than algebra or the calculus is a substitute for simple arithmetic' (*ibid*).
73. *Op. cit.*, p. 761.

display the same sin condemned by Engels of 'standing in rigid antithesis to one another' as formal logic: the difference is that whereas logic does not presume to make them interpenetrate dialectics does. But to what effect? Let us revert to Engels's examples of the grain of barley: '. . . it germinates; the grain as such ceases to exist, it is negated, and in its place appears the plant which has arisen from it, the negation of the grain. But what is the normal life process of this plant? It grows, flowers, and is fertilised and finally once more produces grains of barley, and as soon as these have ripened the stalk dies, is in its turn negated. As a result of this negation of the negation we have once again the original grain of barley . . .'[74]

Now we are here presented with what amounts to a series of arbitrary classifications; arbitrary in that they impose a pattern and terminology that are merely factitious. There is nothing in the transformation of grain into barley that need be understood as negation; it could as well be called the affirmation of the true nature of the grain, and how could this be denied? If, however, we did so, the dialectical rhythm would be lost: for it would then be otiose to think in terms of development through struggle. Similarly when the barley, having germinated, loses its stalk we could say that this was its final consummation in the pure emergence of the grains themselves: for what is to prevent us from adding our own dialectical niceties and invoking the further distinction between essence and accident and regarding the stalk as nothing but the external, so that in its withering, the barley, far from being negated, has at last emerged in its true nature? If we did so, we would then have substituted a Life Force for dialectical struggle; we should be viewing the whole of existence as a striving after, and consummation in, a final purpose. We should be called metaphysical certainly, and even mystical, by the Marxists at least. But is their position so very different? They see development in terms of the struggle of opposites, where it could be equally through the assertion of likeness. There is

74. *Anti-Dühring*, p. 152.

nothing, either *a priori* or *a posteriori*, that compels us to view the relation of the grain to the barley in one way rather than another. In either case, the designation is the result of choosing certain criteria by which to judge, select, classify, and draw conclusions: in a word to abstract what is regarded as significant. Without this power of abstraction, men—Marxists as well as non-Marxists—could not begin to describe reality. Were we really to conceive things as we apprehended them, and nothing more, we should be confined to an endless juxtaposition of objects without order or relation. It is only because we learn from experience and from society to associate things, to perceive connections, and to classify, that we are able to think at all. In this sense all thought is subjective. For only by selecting, excluding this, including that, are we able to bring order to what we know. Failure to do so would plunge us into an incomprehensible welter of impressions.

Marxists from Engels onwards have failed to observe the elementary distinction, made for centuries, between sensible and abstract knowledge, between what we immediately experience and the ordering of our experience. In effect their dialectical claims amount to the rejection of the second, indispensable phase—the foundation of all knowledge. 'Look,' they proudly exclaim, 'we have returned to nature as it really is: no more frozen categories for us, but things in the raw.'

> Ships, towers, domes, theatres and temples lie
> Open unto the fields and to the sky.

But it is a testimony to the resilience of the human mind, rather than to the power of dialectics, that despite this Marxists should continue to follow the path of abstraction and categorisation that alone makes meaning possible. The very concept of movement, mentioned by Jackson, is an abstraction. What, in effect, Marxists have done is to theorise about what they cannot, in the nature of language, actually depict. They have sought to describe, or rather to enunciate, the laws that govern the development and interrelation of things. In so doing, they have been reduced to their own conceptual framework, with its own abstractions. But the irony is that, in refusing to acknowledge their dependence upon these mental mechanisms, essentially subjective and arbitrary, they have reached a state of complete unreality. Where formal logic admits that a class such as chair is a generalisation, which refers to no chair in particular, dialectics has wanted to refer not only to real chairs, but to chairs in their development and movement. Since this is a task only for the physicist, they have instead managed only to describe these circumstances in the most abstract terms: the chair becomes a synthesis of itself and its non-self; it is the negation of the negation. Accordingly we are left not even with the chair but with a host of metaphysical encumbrances that, far from providing us with a clear view of the chair for what it is, prevents us even from thinking of it in its own terms. We get the worst of both worlds: of sheer triviality which in no way enhances our knowledge of the chair—that it is in movement, has a history, a present and a future, and soon—and sheer make-believe—that it is not just a chair but a union of opposites by virtue of which it is both itself and not itself. Yet we are still only confronted with the chair. 'Plus ça change, plus c'est la même chose.' Perhaps this would be a better description of dialectics.

It goes without saying that dialectics stands or falls by the notion of opposites. If, as I have suggested, they represent but one interpretation, which is, of its nature, the work of abstraction, and reflects nothing that can properly be held to stand as a self-evident universal truth, they become reduced to another category. This need not invalidate their truth; and as we shall see there is a strong element of plausibility in the dialectic. But as an account of the laws of development it can hardly be admitted; for the underlying assumption is of an entirely arbitrary and metaphysical progress through struggle. Once again, as taken over by Marxism, dialectics has been betrayed by its antecedents. In its original Hegelian form dialectics was an intellectual process; it described the working out of reality as the pale reflection of the absolute idea. As such it was essentially conceptual in its categories. As Marxists are so fond of telling us, dialectic derives from the Greek as the art of reaching the truth through discussion and the clash of opinions. In this logical form it is, as we have mentioned, quite tenable to talk in terms of thesis, antithesis, and synthesis as a description of the process of reaching the truth. Yet it falls to the ground as soon as it is applied as a universal law of nature or history; for in both cases, while it may be true to describe certain developments as the result of struggle, all point is lost when this is elevated into an absolute truth. Indeed it has led not only to the very reverse of the objectivity upon which Marxism prides itself, but to distortion.

This can be seen in two main respects. Firstly, contradiction and opposition have been made central to everything, with, as we have seen, nonsensical results. This has entailed a standard of judgment which to say the least is arbitrary. Why, for instance, should we be more concerned with a chair or billiard balls as unions of opposites than simply as chairs and billiard balls? What, to use Marxist terminology, are the objective grounds for emphasising their flux rather than their stability? Who is to say that their origin and eventual decomposition are more significant than the comparatively settled century or half century of their existence as chairs or billiard balls? But, it may be objected, billiard balls and chairs are not living things: what about men, or barley, or capitalism? How are we to understand the way in which they change and what is likely to happen to them? The very question helps to provide an answer. It tells us firstly that it is precisely because we approach something for a particular purpose that we emphasise one aspect rather than another. If I simply eat barley, as opposed to growing it, my interest will be very different from that of the farmer who wants to ensure a good crop. Similarly if I am in a remote relation to someone, what he may be in twenty years time will concern me differently from the way in which it will concern his mother. Secondly, and here the fundamental point, it is the very confusion between the importance of something for us and in itself that is the fault in dialectical reasoning. For, in non-human terms, there is nothing to say that one part of a cycle is more significant than another; it is an entirely anthropocentric conception. Who is to say, as a dispassionate fact, that what a man will be twenty years hereafter is more important than what he is now? Or that the interest in a fine June day lies in whether the sun will still be shining in July? Only when we add that we want to take our holiday in July does the future sunshine take on more importance than the present. The same applies to society. If we desire social change and regard the present system as unjust and un-tenable then we seek means of bringing about an alteration. But to assert unconditionally that the future is more im-portant than the present is to succumb to the mystique of change for the sake of change, as we feel when we hear Stalin on the subject: 'The dialectical method regards as important primarily not that which at the given moment seems to be durable and yet is already beginning to die away, but that which is arising and developing, even though at the moment it may appear to be not durable, for the dialectical method considers invincible only that which is arising and developing.'[75] What relation such incantations bear to science it is for Stalinists to explain. Yet Stalin's conclusion is itself only the outcome of the second great distortion wrought by the dialectic and expressed in the negation of the negation: namely that development is a progression from lower to higher. It is to be seen in Engels's discussion which we quoted above; but it became far more clearly asserted with Lenin, who gave it its subsequent dogmatic form: 'But as formulated by Marx and Engels on the basis of Hegel, this idea is far more comprehensive, far richer in content than the current idea of evolution. A development that seemingly repeats the stages already passed, but repeats them otherwise, on a higher basis

75. *Problems in Leninism*, p. 571.

("negation of the negation"), a development, so to speak, in spirals, not in a straight line;—a development by leaps, catastrophes, revolutions;—breaks in continuity;—the transformation of quantity into quality;—the impulses to development, imparted by the contradiction and conflict of the various forces and tendencies existing on a given body, or within a given phenomenon, or within a given society. . . .'[76]

Here in characteristic style we have the law of continuous progress through discontinuity; so that, even when a development appears to be negated, it is in fact a negation on a higher level. The same sentiments—we can hardly call them arguments—are to be found in both the handbooks of Cornforth and Politzer. Cornforth speaks of 'The old going down, fighting against the new. The new grows strong, overpowers and supplants the old. Such is the pattern of development. . . . This pattern of development is the dialectic of forward movement—"in which", as Engels has said, "in spite of all seeming accidents and temporary retrogression, a progressive forward development asserts itself in the end". The process moves forward from stage to stage, each stage being a genuine advance to something new, not a falling back to something already past'.[77] Politzer likewise speaks of 'Le developpement historique ou en spirale', giving as examples, the transformation of an apple into a tree and the yield of 'apples' (*des pommes*) from what was originally a single apple. However high-sounding all this may be, so soon as we examine actual cases we find that the whole conception is illusory. For what we are in fact treated to is a mechanical cycle of growth and decay which can be interpreted in whichever way one cares to approach it. Firstly, it is utterly unfounded to talk of a constant process of development from lower to higher. In nature, to take the examples given, we witness simply the birth and death of individuals within a species and nothing more. Death negates life, but how, in any but supernatural

76. *Selected Works*, Vol. XI, pp. 17–18.
77. *Dialectical Materialism*, Vol. I (London, 1954), p. 106.

terms, is this to be regarded as a higher level of existence? The apple becomes the tree, the tree gives apples which are eaten, or rot, and so it goes on; the grain of barley ripens into the stalk, the stalk yields grains and withers, the grains more stalk and so on. Where is the ever-progressing development, from old to new from advance to advance except as the recurrence of different individuals? Granted it is possible that over many millenia the apple may evolve into something else, but that is quite beyond the process as presented to us. Are we to conclude that each year's apples or grains are better either in quality or quantity than those of the last? The question hardly deserves to be raised. Similarly with men: is every new generation better than its predecessor? If so, one Einstein should produce a family of super-Einsteins but how often does that happen? If we take society and frankly confess that all this refers to the hope and belief in human progress we are no longer confronted with a universal law of nature but with the special case of humanity in which progress depends upon more than the merely automatic process that Engels, Lenin and their disciples have adduced from nature.

Such confusions and trivialities are inseparable from taking essentially anthropomorphic conceptions for universal truths. In natural processes, terms like 'advance' and 'change' are irrelevances. They are value-judgments which have no place where the central fact of life is repetition. Whether in the life-cycle of oaks or men there is no invariable progression from lower to higher nor any inherent modifications from generation to generation. Even in the lands of the dialectic, barley crops and men; have been known to fall off; while, for the rest of the world, failure, of harvests as of everything else, has been one of the constant vicissitudes in human history. It needs more than the negation of the negation to explain how fundamental change occurs.

Quantitative and Qualitative Change

When we come to the law of quantity into quality the

case is somewhat different. No one would deny that difference in quantity does in many instances mean a difference in quality: height, heat, baldness, light, dark, are all states that we can recognise by virtue of the concentration, or lack, of a given quality. Yet how far this is a universal law of development, and, even more relevant, whether the transformation from one quantity to another takes place in a sudden revolutionary leap is another matter. On the first point, as so often in Marxism, there is a looseness of terminology that cannot but give rise to muddled thinking. It arises primarily over what is meant by a quality. The traditional example of the 'law' derives from Hegel's example of water at certain temperatures (boiling point and freezing point) turning to ice or to steam and thereby changing in quality. These 'nodal points' take place suddenly, so that whereas at 211° fahrenheit we are still only confronted with very hot water, at 212° it has become vapour; and the same at the other end of the scale with ice. Another example from the canon is the birth of a child, which after months of gestation in the womb suddenly takes place violently, with the emergence of a new being. Now the problems to be faced are not the same in the instances given. In the first there is the actual transformation of water to another state; in the second there is the emergence of a complete organism which is the child. With water we are merely presented with it in different forms; it nevertheless remains water and, indeed, can only return to water at the slightest increase or decrease in temperature. Accordingly water has not become anything else when ice or steam; the basic molecular composition remains as it was, even if the structure is either more extended or concentrated. Such an instance therefore cannot serve as an example of a universal law of development: for what in effect we are shown are the different states in which water can be found. The definition of quality is accordingly an arbitrary one, in that it refers to one or other of different states peculiar to water, as liquid, solid, or vapour. While in this sense these constitute three different qualities, they do not in the sense that they constitute something that no longer possesses the qualities of water; for, ultimately, we can explain ice and vapour entirely in terms of the behaviour of water. Thus we can argue equally that it is by virtue of water being water that it freezes and vapourises; far from those being different qualities they are subsumed under the very term water. Nor is it good enough to argue as Cornforth does that 'an atom consisting of one proton and one electron is a hydrogen atom, but if another proton and another electron are added it is an atom of helium'.[78] For this is not simple quantitative growth but a change in structure. There is all the difference between increases in quantity and alteration in the structural combination. This is confirmed by the second illustration of the birth of a child. Here, too, we are not in fact dealing with a measurable change in quality, but simply with full evolution of those attributes which we recognise as a child's; even in its first embryo we can say it is of the quality of a child. It is by virtue of its quality, or kind, or other recognisable traits as a child embryo, that the child emerges as a child. The quality of child is there from the beginning; but unlike water this change comes about not through a simple increase or decrease but through the gradual emergence of *new* features inherent in it.

If on the other hand quality is to be regarded in descriptive terms as that which is different from its previous state, we are faced with a number of considerations. Firstly, as Acton has pointed out,[79] 'Strictly speaking every observable change is a change of quality'; and when we say that something is bigger or smaller, hotter or colder, lighter or darker, and so on we are in fact referring to differences in quality no less than in quantity. This applies to almost everything and every experience. We do not therefore have to, nor do we, specify qualitative change only at some nodal point. Secondly, this helps to show us how imprecise the term quality, or

78. *Op. cit.*, p. 94.
79. H. B. Acton, *The Illusion of the Epoch* (London, 1955), p. 92.

qualitative difference, is. It has not one univocal meaning but a number of connotations. Thus to talk of the change from water to vapour or to ice is to designate the changes possible in the state of water: as we have said, in one sense it could be argued that these were not a change in quality at all but simply to be subsumed under water. Then, there is the case of the growth of an embryo into a baby or an acorn into an oak. If the word growth is taken merely to mean increase this will hardly suffice; for the evolution of a baby or a tree is more than simple increase in quantity but is in itself a qualitative process in which *new* attributes continually arise. Thus an acorn does not grow and grow and thereby become an oak; it rather sets in train a process that leads to the appearance of a trunk and branches and leaves. To interpret this quantitatively as pure increase is to beg the question of *what* is increasing. Finally, there is a vast range of cases in which the term quality is merely one of convention or personal judgment: tall, short, soft, hard, and so on, as we have already mentioned in another context, are not measurable states let alone universally applicable. There is no means of verifying that a height of 6 feet is tall or 5 ft. 8 in. is short or that to possess fewer than a certain quantity of hair is to be bald. Yet a great number of our judgements are of that nature. From this it would appear, then, that far from being a universal law the transformation of quantity into quality is at once ambiguous and highly subjective. It depends entirely upon the arbitrary contexts by which we are conveying the differences of degree or kind. At one extreme it can denote different states and conditions; at the other our own reactions. But in any case it is essentially one of interpretation; and as with so much else in dialectics we could as well substitute other terms: in this case, we could either from the outset regard all difference as a difference in quality, or deny that water or an embryo or an acorn are anything other than natural kinds, such that in designating any of them one thereby includes their different attributes. What is untenable is to try to identify qualitative change through quantity with structural alteration, as Cornforth has attempted; for, then, the concept of quality is subsumes a difference in structure.

There remains to be considered the other aspect of qualitative change—that it happens suddenly. To quote Cornforth again: 'If you are boiling a kettle the water suddenly begins to boil when boiling point is reached. If you are scrambling an egg the mixture in the pan suddenly "scrambles". And it is the same if you are engaged in changing society'.[80] It is clearly with the last example that the full import of change lies, and it is precisely on the grounds that the transition from one state to another must be sudden that the Marxist belief in revolutionary change is founded. Yet, while leaving aside for later political considerations, how far is it valid in other respects? Perhaps the first point to be noted is that it conflicts with the other emphasis of dialectics upon being as a state of constant flux. As Cornforth has already told us in an earlier context: 'For example: when is a man bald? Common sense recognises that though we can distinguish bald men from non-bald men nevertheless baldness develops through a process of losing one's hair, and therefore in the midst of this process enter into a phase in which we cannot absolutely say that they are bald or that they are not.'[81]

This passage, as we have seen, is in no way uncharacteristic of the dialectical case against clearly-defined states. How, then, is it to be reconciled with the doctrine of sudden change, whereby something is transformed into something else? Clearly this is one more instance of the confusion of concepts which permeates dialectics; it springs from the belief that it is possible to portray the intricacies of nature in everyday language without giving attention to the order of reality to which we are referring. We have already adverted to this impasse; here it suffices to point out that neither statement can be taken as a universal truth. While things change continuously, the change is often so imperceptible and insignificant that it is merely trivial to consider

80. *Op. cit.*, p. 95.   81. *Ibid.*, p. 75.

it. On the other hand, we do recognise differences between boiling water and ice, but not always as sudden confrontations of a new state. No one can deny that any change, by implication, involves crossing some boundary or nodal point; otherwise it would not be change: ultimately, in order to be tall or hor or dark, the point has to be reached at which we can so describe someone or something; in the same way to pass from one country to another is to have to cross their border. But this is not the same as saying that the whole process is one of sudden revolutionary transformation. If Marxism cannot establish that it is, it has merely presented us with one more tautology, namely, that change entails change; and this in effect is what its doctrine amounts to. To take Cornforth's examples of egg-scrambling or water-boiling: before either state is realised there is an ascertainable preliminary process in which we can recognise the development towards the final goal; at some point (in the case of water at 212° F.) this is reached; but it could as well be so prolonged—if say the water or the egg were on a very low light—that the final stage was almost imperceptible. The same applies to crossing a country's border; true enough there is a final point beyond which it is different territory, but except in cases of recent and artificial political change there will be a noticeable hybrid area in which much of the language and tradition is indistinguishable as between the two states. Even with natural phenomena the same frequently holds: in areas removed from the equator there is usually a prolonged period of twilight between light and darkness, so that even though there is a lighting-up time at a particular instant the state which gives rise to it is not reached suddenly. These are just a few instances in support of a different interpretation of change, namely, that it lies as much, if not more, with the whole process as with the final moment; others can no doubt be adduced for the opposite case—earthquakes, jet propulsion, sudden death— but they are far from constituting a universal law. Nor do we act as if they did: most of our actions, including boiling water and scrambling eggs, are conducted on the assumption that the process is gradual rather than sudden. Indeed, we tend to be shocked when confronted with *faits accomplis*.

It would appear, then, that the law of quantity into quality by sudden change is one more example of the dialectical interplay of truth and falsity: it is half-truth. Where it is true it merely tells what is not in dispute, namely, that things change and change means difference. Where it is false is in seeking one way, and one instant, in which difference comes about. As Lenin with his logic, it has once again abstracted a moment from reality and erected it into a universal—and metaphysical—truth.

Yet for all that, dialectics is not simply another unclad Emperor; stripped of all the pretensions to the non-existent finery of ultimate revealed truth, there remains a core of truth which cannot be gainsaid. It is 'that the world is not to be comprehended as a complex of ready-made *things*, but as a complex of processes'. This sense of movement, and of multifariousness, of combination and recombination, is of the essence of a proper understanding of existence. It constitutes the foundation of virtually all branches of knowledge and the sciences: the realisation that there is no permanent state of hardness and fastness but an almost unending series of chain-reactions that comprise everything, from the cells in our bodies to men's relations with one another. For that reason it must be acknowledged that the dialectical view of existence harmonises with the modern scientific outlook and in this sense it can claim to be pertinent. Similarly it accords with the growing flexibility in our very mode of expression: the realisation that our knowledge, experience, and meaning cannot be subservient to one rigid form, as either true or false, that a problem can be approached from an irreducible number of ways; that in fact there are as many sides to a question, as there are positions from which it is judged. It is this awareness of the indissoluble interconnection of things that is the indispensable contribution of dialectics. It informs all scientific and rational thinking. It is the essential precondition of all true knowledge and understanding. It lies behind the revulsion against the absolute criteria of classical science and thinking: the assumption that there is the truth to be plucked from the empyrean, whether it be the absolute space or time of Newtonian physics, or the perfect goodness or knowledge of the philosopher, or the natural man of the social reformers. In its emancipation from this closed and static world we can accept dialectics. But it is exactly at this point that the dialecticians fail us: not content with freeing us from false gods, they seek to set up others in their stead. Movement is all, they say, but it can only be conceived in one way—as struggle; everything is in flux but only because it is a union of opposites; change is the law of existence but only as an ever-rising spiral; what is today will not be tomorrow, therefore we must focus our gaze on what is to come; and forget the present. As so often, the means have supplanted the end: what began as an aspect of truth has become the truth. Its categories have engulfed the reality they were designed to explain. The result is nonsense, but dangerous nonsense because it is believed and acted upon.

II. MATERIALISM

When we come to examine materialism in the light of this enquiry we can hardly fail to notice a startling discrepancy between precept and practice. Although, as we have previously said, dialectics and materialism were conceived by its founders as a unity, a materialist dialectics, in fact they are mutually exclusive. The reasons are not far to seek. In the first place, in general terms, dialectics as we have found are a highly abstract and arbitrary set of preconceptions, permeated by a schematic a priorism which has little or nothing in common with a truly scientific attitude. If it is anything it is metaphysics, and while this is not necessarily reprehensible in itself, it can hardly be more damning when applied to Marxism. There is no connection between the Hegelian categories of Marxist dialectics and the criterion of materialism laid down by Engels: 'to comprehend the real world—nature and history—just as it presents itself to everyone who approaches it free from preconceived idealist fancies'.[82] Whether or not one defines the interpenetration of opposites, the negation of the negation, quantity into quality and the rest of the dialectical impedimenta as idealist fancies, they can hardly be regarded as simply the burnt offerings of the sacrifice of truth. On the contrary, it would be more accurate to call them the idols before whose altar truth has had to bow. From this point of view alone, dialectics and materialism are contradictory.

In the second place, however, over and above this general consideration, materialism as preached by Lenin and subsequent Marxist orthodoxy is unfitted for the attainment of Engels's aim. It is devoid of those very qualities prescribed as dialectical: it denies reciprocity (between knower and what is known); it takes no account of the interaction between perception, on the one hand, and what we may call preconception, on the other—that is to say, the difference between a mere sensible experience and the knowledge and ideas which arise out of it and which are brought to bear upon every percept; it fails to recognise qualitatively different levels of reality and hence of knowledge. Let us consider each of these in turn.

The failure to recognise the indispensability of personal experience in all knowledge is, I think, the most fundamental blind spot in Marxist materialism; it is at the root of its failure to appreciate, let alone incorporate, the revolutionary advance in twenieth-century knowledge, whether of post-classical physics, or in the new fields of psychology and social studies. It helps to explain the almost ludicrous solemnity with which we are treated to explanations of reality in terms of 'motion' and 'matter' and the truly awesome spectacle of being presented, in the posthumously published lectures of Georges Politzer, published in the year 1946, with the same three great discoveries (the living cell, the transformation of energy, and the evolution of the species) which Engels gave in 1884 as evidence of the truth of dialectical materialism: it is hard to conceive of more

82. *Ludwig Feuerbach, Selected Works*, Vol. II, p. 349.

damning evidence for the 'dialectical' thinking of his successors.

The cause of the trouble lies above all with Lenin, although, as we have seen, its germ can be traced back to Engels, in his statement in *Ludwig Feuerbach*. In particular the word 'image' has bedevilled any attempt to take Marxism out of the very rut from which it claims to have rescued the older materialism. There can be all the dialectics in the world when applied to nature or history, but it is unavailing if it does not extend to human thought as well; and this is precisely the case with Marxist materialism. From the time of Lenin it has become a central tenet of orthodoxy, echoed and re-echoed in the official handbooks, that thinking is the reflection of being. This, too, has its origin in Engels's oft-repeated quotation about the two great camps: 'The great basic question of all philosophy, especially of modern philosophy, is that concerning the relation of thinking and being . . . The answers which the philosophers gave to this question split them into two great camps. Those who asserted the primacy of spirit to nature, and, therefore, in the last instance, assumed world creation in some form or other . . . comprised the camp of idealism. The others, who regarded nature as primary, belong to the various schools of materialism.'

'These two expressions, idealism and materialism, originally signify nothing else but this.'[83]

Once more one can only regret that a characteristically loose generalisation has been taken as the literal truth. It has led to a wholly artificial split between what are two artificial categories and has helped to keep Marxist thinking focused upon what is, in effect, an unreal problem. The very term, 'being', begs most questions; for the whole of the Middle Ages, and beyond, the primacy of being was accepted without demur; the question was what constituted being? Or more accurately, where was true being to be found? In contemplation, turning away from this world, as the Augustinians generally held, or through abstracting the

83. *Ibid.*, p. 334–5.

true essence of reality from the objects given to us in sensory experience? There was here no bifurcation between thinking and being; all agreed that being was primary. Yet its thinkers would be called Idealists in virtue of their conception of being. It was with Descartes onwards that the distinction came about, but this was itself a concomitant of the new classical physics in which space, time and movement were all absolute, with no place for an observer. In adhering to this position Marxism reveals its own datedness, for what was a justifiable and transitory mode of regarding reality has become outmoded as the assumptions on which it was based have been supplanted.

This was already the case when Lenin wrote *Materialism and Empirio-criticism* in 1908, the source book for all that is most dogmatic and retrograde in Marxist philosophy. We leave aside the declamatory, hectoring style, and the marked absence of what can be called logical, as opposed to emotive, argument. The main thesis can be expressed in the following propositions: 'Materialism, in full agreement with natural science, takes matter as primary and regards consciousness, thought and sensation as secondary, because in its well-defined form sensation is associated with the higher forms of matter (organic matter)', while "in the foundation of the structure of matter" one can only surmise the existence of a faculty akin to sensation'.[84] This assertion of the dualism between matter and consciousness is the core of Lenin's argument; he judges a philosophy as reactionary or truthful according to its standpoint over their relationship. Only those who unswervingly adhere to the primacy of matter are in grace; nothing can save the others from damnation. Thus the entire burden of the book is to reduce every philosophical position to a confrontation of this stark alternative and to judge it accordingly. The pointlessness of this procedure needs scarcely to be stressed except in so far as it shows the tenuous premises on which Marxist materialism is founded. Once deny the antimony between being

84. V. I. Lenin, *Materialism and Empirio-Criticism, Selected Works*, Vol. XI, pp. 112–13.

and thinking and there is no means of advancing further; and this unfortunately is what has happened. Marxist philosophy has stood still, or rather regressed, through sheer inability even to recognise that there might be other problems and other solutions; its exponents still tilt at metaphysical windmills in an age that has forgotten that they exist. They seem oblivious of the fact that their enemy against whom they are still hurling their thunderbolts was quietly taken from behind some fifty years ago and that all that remains to them are their own obsolescent weapons.

This is apparent as soon as we seek to test the validity of Lenin's position. He defines matter as 'a philosophical category designating the objective reality given to man in his sensations, and which is copied, photographed, and reflected by our sensations, while existing independently of them'.[85] We are thus confronted with three inescapable implications. The first is that reality is identical with our image of it; second that therefore it is as it appears to us, regardless of whether we are there to perceive it or not; and third that knowledge owes nothing to the knower beyond passively receiving ready-made what is already there to be known.

The first, apart from the enormity of flouting the canons of dialectics, is palpably untrue. It takes our macrocosmic view of the world as the one and only world. For us, the chair or the flower or the hand 'given to us in our sensations' is a chair or a flower or hand and not an assemblage of atoms and cells. It is only on investigation, when we manage to pass beyond what is given to us in sensation, that we become aware of another, microcosmic, world to which we cannot penetrate at the level of perception. By means of scientific calculation and experiment, we are enabled to know that what our senses take to be brightness or smoothness or redness are not such in terms of physics; they are qualities which describe our reaction to certain physical stimuli. Thus, as Lenin himself acknowledges, albeit inconsistently: 'If colour is a sensation only depending upon

85. *Ibid.*, p. 192.

77

the retina (as natural science compels you to admit), then light rays, falling upon the retina, produce the sensation of colour. This means that outside of us, independently of us and of our minds, there exists a movement of matter . . . which, acting upon the retina, produces in man the sensation of a particular colour'.[86] We need not labour the undeniable discrepancy between this passage and the definition of materialism quoted above. If our sensations literally 'copied, photographed, and reflected' reality, then when we saw a colour, red, for example, our awareness would not be simply the effect of light waves acting upon the retina but of red being 'copied, photographed, and reflected' in it. In either case, the question to be faced is whether we can regard our sensations as providing a fair copy of the external world such that they enable us to know things as they really are. If there is held to be a direct correlation between sensations and objects, we are presented with what is tantamount to the denial of objective knowledge; for, in contradiction to the Marxists' ceaseless reiteration that this is the one guarantee of reality, it makes the attainment of truth impossible.

In the first place, let us consider what the consequences would be if we were to regard our perceptions of any object, for example, the sun, to constitute knowledge of it as it exists. If the sun were really the same as we saw it we should at once be confronted with the insoluble problem of reconciling all the different aspects of the sun: by what means would we determine whether it was more true to regard it in terms of the experience of an inhabitant of the equator or that of an eskimo? How would we arrive at its true colour as between its zenith at noon and its setting at night? Each different perception of it, if a true reflection of it, would have as good a claim as the other. In the second place, it is of the nature of our preceptions that they are in terms of sensible qualities; we think in terms of things, not processes, as we have abundantly learned from our discussion of dialectics. For us the sun is not the astronomer's sun, but a

86. *Ibid.*, p. 121.

bright, round, hot object suspended above us; our sensations can tell us nothing about its constituents; indeed, to take them as sovereign is to be denied any access to what Marxists, in good scholastic terminology, call the essence of things, but on the contrary to be misled. Thus the sun as it appears to us is a little larger than a football; but while there is no doubting this as a sensation, to refuse to doubt it as a matter of fact would be a denial of the very scientific knowledge which through non-sensory processes enables us to know the size and distance of the sun. The dilemma is apparent but it is also a false one, and only arises from the indefensible position which Marxist materialism has taken up. Lenin himself in the passage quoted above shows that when it comes to actual matters of fact it is not possible to exclude the subject from consideration. But it is simply to beg the question to conclude, as he does, that 'This means that outside us, independently of us and of our minds, there exists a movement of matter, let us say of ether waves of a definite length and velocity, which, acting upon the retina produce in man the sensation of a particular colour . . . This is materialism: matter acting upon our sense-organs produces sensation. Sensation depends on the brain, nerves, retina etc., i.e. on matter organised in a definite way. The existence of matter does not depend on sensation. Matter is primary. Sensation, thought, consciousness are the supreme product of matter organised in a particular way'.[87]

While no rational person will deny that light waves exist independently of our mind, as a matter of scientific fact, this does not explain how our sensations of colour can be anything but in terms of our own awareness; and how, if we did not ourselves have the experience of lightwaves, they would exist for us. For, ultimately, it is the acme of futility to look for primacy in what is essentially an indissoluble reciprocity. It is no more meaningful to ask whether sensation or matter come first than whether the football or the footballers come first in a game of football. Without a subject to experience sensation, however many lightwaves

87. *Ibid.*, pp. 121–2.

acting alone will not produce the sensation we call colour. A new-born baby is at first quite unable to focus upon objects or to distinguish colours even though lightwaves act upon his retina; later when he is able to do so he then becomes aware of colour. But he only understands what he is seeing through receiving a conceptual framework from his elders by means of which he is able to identify his perceptions. It is quite as legitimate to conclude from this that the subject is primary and matter is secondary, in that the subject is not only the starting point in any act of perception, but can only comprehend it through placing it according to a pre-existing conceptual order. If put this way, no denial of 'objective reality' is entailed; and this, of course, is where Lenin and his disciples have been blinded by obsession. They have been so convinced that only by safeguarding the primacy of matter can the world be saved for materialism that they have omitted to ask themselves *how* we came by knowledge in the *first place*. Thus Cornforth, in what is a more flexible interpretation of the doctrine of reflection, is forced into an essentially vague and contradictory position, in attempting to counter the charge already advanced, this time by means of the example of a penny. 'If you look at this penny from a distance it looks small, while if you hold it close to your eye it looks big . . . while the material object, of which your perceptions are alleged to be images in your mind, does not change at all'.[88] 'The philosophers who argue in such a way', he replies, 'have simply forgotten that reflection is an active process, conditioned by the actual relations between the organism and its surroundings. Thus if we look at the same thing from different distances or from different angles, then of course it will be differently reflected in our perceptions—its size or shape will differ'.[89]

Quite so; a man's language is usually a reliable guide to his state of mind, and whether this cloudy form of expression

88. M. Cornforth, *Dialectical Materialism*, Vol. III, *Theory of Knowledge*, pp. 36-7.
89. *Ibid.*, p. 37.

is simply the conditioned reflex of years of Marxist phraseology, or whether it reflects a certain lack of clarity in the author, it remains sheer equivocation. If, by calling reflection an active process, is meant that it does more than merely copy, or as Lenin put it, photograph, then it should not be so designated; in that case we should be told clearly what relation our perceptions bear to reality. If, on the other hand, Cornforth adheres to the accepted Marxist usage and really does regard our perceptions as reflecting reality then his qualification that it is an active process is mere word play; the onus is upon him to explain how if we mirror reality as it is, different perceptions can be reconciled with one and the same reality. To say that our reflection 'will necessarily be altered by the actual state of our sense-organs' is in effect to acknowledge that it is as dependent upon them as upon what it reflects. On the other hand, if to look at the same thing from different angles is for it to be 'differently reflected in our perceptions', how are we to decide between the different aspects and arrive at a universally accepted specification of a penny? Were we to follow Cornforth in giving sovereignty to our reflections we should be plunged back into the very subjectivism, indeed solipsism, from which Marxism claims to be saviour.

The bitter truth must be faced: all knowledge begins, but does not end, with the knower. This is not the same as saying that it bears no relation to anything outside him. It means simply that not only our perceptions but also our conceptions are but the starting point for what is to be known. The great fault of Marxism, and indeed of classical materialism, has been to turn the process upside down: to make an illicit jump over this indispensable preliminary direct to what is known and then erect the latter into an inviolable truth; it has thereby been confronted with the object ready-made, as it were, as a sovereign independent entity, the source from which our knowledge is derived. The result has been the distorted 'metaphysical' attitude for which Marxists attack the rest of mankind. Instead of recognising that the very act of knowing is relationship between knower and known, both equally necessary, they have become bifurcated; each has been made into a separate entity, with clearly demarcated functions; and where we should be able to see 'interpenetration' we are presented with a rigid dichotomy.

Inevitably this has led to the distortion of the whole concept of knowledge. Marxism looks upon it as a series of truths simply to be found, grasped, and utilised. Thus Cornforth quotes Mao Tse-Tung: 'The task of knowledge is to start from perceptual knowledge and actively develop it into rational knowledge, and then, starting from rational knowledge, actively direct revolutionary practice so as to remould the subjective and objective world.'[90] In the first place, it should be noted that many forms of knowledge, including dialectics, are not perceptual in origin; they are simply artifacts that could as well be otherwise. Thus latitude and longitude are not perceptual facts, but an arbitary arrangement of numbers that could have been ordered differently—there is nothing in experience that makes the longitude of Greenwich 0°. The same applies to a vast segment of our knowledge that owes nothing to an initial perceptual impulsion. Theoretical science and matters of logic, for example, have their own dynamic that is the inverse of the Marxist sequence from practice to theory: far from invariably receiving its impetus from external facts, that strict adherence to Lenin's assertions would entail, a process of reasoning can lead to a new awareness of facts, however abstract. How can an equation that led Einstein to relativity be meaningfully accounted for in terms of Lenin's formula of consciousness as the reflexion of reality, a mere photographic copy? Or even in terms of the primacy of matter? If it is replied that ultimately Einstein's pre-occupation with relativity is a reflexion of external problems confronting him this is like saying that my taste in clothes utlimately reflects my need to wear clothes at all. It is so true as to be trivial, although in fairness, such an approach is of the utmost importance when applied sociologically and

90. *Ibid.*, p. 197.

historically to elucidate the development of ideas; and, as one of the main elements in historical materialism, we shall consider it in the next chapter. Nevertheless it does not meet the gravamen of the charge here, that in Leninist terms thinking is secondary to being and should therefore only come about as the result of practice. The fact that it does not, and that men continually arrive at knowledge and hypothesis, subsequently verified, without first having had practical experience of what they know, is in no way a refutation of reality but only of the rigidity of Marxist materialism; provided that thinking follows an intelligible order of correct implication and is related to our experience of what we take as reality, it fulfils the necessary precondition of truth. The primacy of matter or the derivatory status of consciousness is irrelevant to the simple requirement that ultimately there must be a sense in which our thinking is meaningful. That this can often only be logically demonstrated or empirically established by practice is not the same as making it dependent upon practice any more than that every expression must have its correlative in an actual entity to which it corresponds. Thus to say 'dogs are animals' or that 'sin is evil' does not entail their depiction in reality. It suffices that these terms have an intelligible meaning which can be inferred from experience. It is abundantly possible to accept the reality of the world and its independent existence without having to embrace Lenin's view of reflexion.

This leads us to the other two features of Marxist materialism: the failure to take account of the different elements in knowing and the different kinds of knowledge. In the first case the absurdity of Lenin's position is due to the confusion between sensation and idea; he appears to identify the former with knowledge and makes no allowance for non-sensory understanding of the kind to which we have just adverted. One does not have to be a Kantian to recognise that ideas, abstractions, analogy, classifications, generalisations, are an indispensable part of our cognitive equipment; yet Lenin gives them no attention because, in his preoccupation with asserting the reality of what we know, he omits to consider how we know or the nature of our knowledge. Yet only thus, in tracing the formation of our knowledge, can we be in a position to assess its scope and validity. This has two aspects. The first is that sensation in itself does not constitute knowledge, even when what we experience is neither distorted nor illusory—which it frequently is as, for example, in the case of a stick which in water appears bent, or of the sun, which is to us a small round shining ball. If a baby hears thunder for the first time the act of perception does not explain that it is the result of electricity in the atmosphere; conversely, we do not say that we do not know that deserts or Australia exist because we have not perceived them. Above all, were we to depend upon sensation our knowledge would always be in the form of a reflex to what had gone before; what we had not experienced we could not envisage or anticipate, and our intentions would be mere reflex actions. Thus, if a river had not previously overflowed, we should not know how to take precautions against it until it had done so. In fact, of course, knowing is a qualitatively different activity from sensing. It relies upon memory, abstraction, analogy, deduction, and induction, all of which are mental processes that owe nothing to any counterparts of the external world. They enable us to build up a pattern of events that is based not upon photographing what exists but upon selecting and rejecting. If practice is the starting point, the deductions to which they give rise become our guide. We live by precepts like 'fire burns', 'rain wets', 'cars run over', without necessarily ever experiencing more than a fraction of them ourselves. They are inferences from the facts, which although, as Hume showed, do not provide any logical certainty that they will continue to hold, are in practice so overwhelmingly probable as to be taken for granted. Thus we believe all men are mortal though we can never prove this to be so in fact; we assume that fire burns although it may not. In this way all our conceptions are the result of inference, experience, instruction, and analogy.

For example we speak and think of 'human beings' or 'animals' where in fact we only perceive individual men and dogs and cats. We attribute certain properties to different classes in virtue of correlating the characteristics of individuals, as when we say that elephants have a trunk and camels a hump. Our very use of language is in terms of such universal classification, as we have already discussed. Despite a welcome if belated recognition given to such non-sensory knowledge, or judgement as it is called in Mao Tse-Tung's *On Practice* and Cornforth's *Theory of Knowledge*, there has been no attempt by Marxists to face up to the implications of this position.

This constitutes the second aspect. It is that knowledge, even at its most precise and objective, is never entirely impersonal. All that we know is an amalgam of what we have been taught and what we are able to deduce. From birth we receive an ever-growing body of beliefs, assumptions, and pre-suppositions that, stored in the memory, govern all that we do. Thus, with the possible exception of the first man, there has never been a time when knowing was not as much the product of our habits and beliefs as of what was directly experienced. If we grow up to believe that thunder is a god, or that fire burns, these associations will colour all our judgements about them, unless we come ultimately to reject either or both: they will influence our ideas about them and we shall examine their properties in the light of our presuppositions. Now it is precisely this personal/social element that Marxism ignores; its entire account of the development of knowledge whether by Lenin or by Cornforth is of some irresistible super-human progress—history—to which men appropriately submit, so that each phase in the growth of our knowledge is in keeping with what the epoch has demanded. No one, as we shall discuss in the next chapter, could deny the importance of circumstances, but this is not the same as there being nothing but circumstances. There still has to be the Newton or the Einstein who has the personal intuition that leads to a new conception; and he does so not merely by reflecting upon what has been brought to his perceptions, nor by an impersonal act of judgement, but through an interaction between what he has been taught to believe and what he has discovered, so that he comes to doubt the accepted assumptions. That is to say, advance in knowledge is a complex of believing, knowing, doubting, and rejecting, and to aspire to explain its growth in its own terms without reference to the factors that make new discoveries necessary and possible is both nonsensical and undialectical, as we shall discuss in the next chapter.

Finally, there is the question of the nature of knowledge. Marxists are not alone in omitting to define knowledge, and in treating it simply as a comprehensive term; but in their case this vagueness enables them to evade what would otherwise be almost insuperable difficulties. Their entire case rests upon the assumption that knowledge corresponds to verifiable facts, so that although, as Cornforth and Mao Tse-Tung imply, this need not be interpreted as perception, our consciousness must reflect material being. Now just as we do not gain our knowledge exclusively in one way, so we are not confined to only one kind of knowledge. Traditionally knowledge has been divided into that which we know intuitively and immediately through direct perception and that which comes about through mental judgement. We adverted to this earlier in connection with our criticism of Lenin. We suggested that it is only by ordering our experiences conceptually that we can make the connections which alone render possible an understanding of the properties in things. But this does not imply previous perceptual experience. The entire distinction between non-sensory and sensory knowledge is largely irrelevant to the problem of knowledge. To begin with it concerns only a limited part of it. There is a whole realm of knowledge that is independent of perception, whether in the formal sciences, like mathematics and logic, or in social and personal phenomena. Neither the State nor the square root of two can be directly perceived as physical entities, but they are no less real than hot buttered toast or measles. To demand for them all the same kind of direct verification would make nonsense of what we know to be the case. Rather we have to recognise that there are different orders of knowledge according to what is being known. Just as only a fraction of what we know can be logically entailed so much of what we know empirically cannot be established perceptually. It is precisely according to the different objects to which it is directed that there are different modes of knowledge. The very fact that these differ means that they cannot all be treated as the same. Now this is just what the Marxists, like the Logical Positivists, attempt to do. But whereas the latter disqualify as knowledge all that cannot be reduced to direct perception, the Marxists denote it as idealist. In each case both assume that knowing is synonymous with direct experience. The consequences are similar; for in denying the diversity of knowledge they also deny its unity. Or rather they fail to see that that is where the real distinction in knowledge lies. If, on the one hand, knowledge differs according to what is known, the process of knowing is universal. It consists not only in those common mental attributes which we possess in virtue of being men; but also in coming through the activity of the knower. Neither is bounded by sensory experience. As the mystic can have a vision of God's presence which is seen or felt by no one else, so the physicist or the astronomer can have an hypothesis about something which he does not yet know exists. Moreover he seeks to establish it by manipulating existing reality. If successful he discovers what is not already given; and he does so because he has broken away from what does exist, even if it is only to look at it in a new light. All new developments in thought or imagination have happened throughout the ages as a jump, deliberate or accidental, from the given to the not given. What makes the physicist's knowledge scientific, as the mystic's is not, is less the way he comes to his knowledge than in his ability to relate it to what is already established by corroboration. If he succeeds, it can then stand independently of his own intuition. But he is no less dependent initially than the mystic, or indeed the child, upon the set of assumptions which make his intuitions intelligible. It is here that he joins all knowers. We all work within a framework of beliefs, habits, values, experiences, which we bring to bear upon what we know and seek to know. Only a fraction of it is ever gained by direct perception and it in turn colours all our perceptions. Once we have learned that a particular object is a house or a cow we no longer think of it perceptually as hard and red or as moving on four legs but as belonging to a particular class. We thereby substitute a concept for a thing, by which we place it within our framework.

In that sense all knowledge of whatever kind is a conceptual system. It is a world of references in which we relate what we encounter to what we already know or think or believe or have experienced. As such we are the arbiters of what we know.

This however does not lead to the dissolution of all objectivity but rather to what Popper has called inter-subjectivity,[91] in which our knowledge in referring to common experiences, has a public character. Such a notion is at once more realistic and flexible than the Marxist one of an inexorable objectivity to which we must all submit.

That Marxists should have been so haunted by the spectre of a mental world is indicative of their inflexibility. It can be directly ascribed to their insistence that knowing must reflect being. In the world of quantum physics, explicable only by mathematical formula, they have lost their bearings. The prospect, fed by the speculations of scientists like Jeans and Eddington, that our knowledge of the world is a mere mental construction has terrified them. In fact, if modern science has shown anything it is the utter unreality of making a hard and fast division between the subject and the object. It has shown the indispensability of the 'this-sidedness' of man's thinking which Marx spoke of in his Second *Thesis on Feuerbach*; perhaps had Marx himself pursued these questions, instead of leaving them to Engels, there might have been a different outcome. As it is, while

91. K. R. Popper, *The Open Society* (London, 1962), Vol. II, pp. 217 ff.

Marxists expend their energy needlessly in asserting the importance of activity, when it concerns society, they fall back upon a passivity indistinguishable from mechanistic materialism when confronted with individual knowledge. Perhaps the contradiction is a dialectical one too subtle for those not versed in its arts; if so, it awaits its resolution, which will enable it to make the qualitative leap from the nineteenth to the twentieth century.

Our examination of dialectical materialism has been, of set purpose, negative and critical. For too long it has been made to appear as the acme of enlightened scientific thinking among all those seeking a philosophical basis for their socialism. It has caused untold confusion in its adherence to a scheme which insists upon outworn categories and has branded those who have tried to look ourselves and our meanings in the face as reactionaries, idealists, fainthearts, shamefaced materialists, and so on. Above all it has put itself outside the mainstream of new knowledge and new thinking. To this day dialectics is contraposed to a 'metaphysics' which is, to say the least, antiquated. All the official texts from Stalin to Cornforth and Politzer, give the same dreary recital of the two opposing standpoints, substantially unaltered since Engels first made the comparison in *Anti-Dühring*. Yet it may well be questioned how many people still, if they ever did, regard 'nature as an accidental agglomeration of things, of phenomena, unconnected with, isolated from, and independent of, each other'[92] or 'that nature is in a state of rest and immobility, stagnation and immutability'.[93] Surely the opponents whom Marxists should be combating are those who accept interconnection and movement in existence but without feeling the need to adopt the dialectic to support them.

With materialism, equally, the days of the battle royal with idealism are past. Marxists may rail at and vilify the different schools of philosophical analysis as 'reaction in its modern guise' but in doing so they only show their own lack

92. Stalin: *op. cit.*, p. 570.   93. *Ibid.*

of awareness of the problems that helped to call these schools forth. Even if many of the latter are trivial, arid, and unadventurous, the same can be said of Marxists in their insistence upon the voice of authority. They have failed to recognise the validity of the problems thus raised: of how with our knowledge in such an acutely specialised state, in which inference plays a dominant part, we are to verify the principles on which our knowledge is founded. The crude juxtaposition of matter to mind not only evades the issue but does not approach to understanding it. Marxist materialism is less to be regarded as a philosophy than as a part of a wider campaign, in which the individual issues are important not for themselves, but for their overall implications. For that reason it is quite as a priori as the idealism which it condemns; ultimately its positions are determined by the dictates of an orthodoxy which, unfortunately for it, received its final stamp from Lenin.

Meanwhile it is not only possible but essential to break with these dogmas to retain a rationalist standpoint. Engels's words that that 'there is no longer the need for any philosophy standing above the other sciences', apply nowhere more than to dialectical materialism. At least we should begin from what can be known before going in search of ultimate truths. But knowledge consists in more than what is presented to us. It is governed by a process of understanding that has nothing to do with dialectics. There is no simple and schematic order of knowledge that is reducible to the 'laws' of dialectical materialism. According to Lenin agnosticism equals 'shamefaced materialism'; but it is better to make uncertainty our starting point than impose our conceptions upon the world in the belief that they have all along existed independently of us. All knowledge as representing the experience of the knower is arbitrary and partial in the sense that it is 'this-sided' and incomplete. What we call knowledge is not an absolute standing outside us; nor is it, except in the most general terms, unitary. It is rather the product of diverse modes of envisaging the world and hence, as we have said, is itself diverse. The initial failure by Engels and then Lenin to accept this has been the source of the sterility of dialectical materialism. Far from its having led to emancipation from old dogmas it has imposed a new tyranny of concepts—with the difference that its adherents have not even recognised them as concepts. The inflexible sequence from being to thinking, even with dialectics thrown in, makes their materialism virtually indistinguishable from the older mechanical materialism that they were attacking. Both have failed to admit man to full status in the process of knowing; they share the same mistrust of the mental and have sought to circumscribe it, while themselves remaining caught up in the self-imposed dichotomy between mind and matter. Were we to confine ourselves to the truths of dialectical materialism we should have no means of understanding how man has succeeded in imposing his own pattern upon much of nature precisely by his ability to distrust the findings of his senses and to pass beyond their images which Marxism insists are reflected in his head. Foresight and imagination, to envisage and seek what does not yet exist, those are the attributes that have enabled men to pass from savagery to some degree of civilisation. One would not know it by following dialectical materialism.

In the end, then, it is dialectical materialism that is not realist enough; imprisoned by its own preconceptions and misled by its pretensions it has signally failed to fulfil Engels's precept to approach reality just as it is. Instead of humility towards the facts and flexibility in their interpretation something nearer to dogma reigns. Dialectical materialism does not represent a new scientific outlook on the world; it only impedes its understanding, and must be set aside by those who seek to understand.

II

HISTORICAL MATERIALISM

———◆———

I. HISTORICISM

To turn from dialectical to historical materialism is to leave
the misty realms of abstraction for the real world of men. If
both reality and men are sometimes lacking in fulness, at
the least they are recognisable. For in the Marxist conception of history we are presented with what, when all the
qualifications have been made, is the perhaps most
challenging attempt conceived to comprehend human
development. Allowing for the exaggerations, rigidities, and
distortions that are inseparable from any orthodoxy, it
remains an unassailable fact that the insights of historical
materialism have entered into our assessment of all social
phenomena. That it has unfortunately led to the enthrone-
ment of a new deity in the shape of history, with the blind-
ness and fanaticism inherent in doing any god's bidding,
does not alter the fact; nor that Marx himself derived
from his theories a messianic belief in the historical
destiny and the mission of the proletariat. To paraphrase
Marx, just as we do not judge an individual by his own
opinion of himself, so we cannot be confined to the conclusions he draws from his own work; it is perfectly possible
to accept the main tenets of the materialist conception of
history without subscribing to its prophecies or the means
needed for their realisation.

This must be emphasised at a time when it has become the
fashion to decry any theory of history as historicism because
of the excesses and wrongful attitudes that can result from it.
Yet it is to misconceive the nature of history to imagine
that it can be written with no standpoint; and it is better

that it be avowed than remain unacknowledged, since it will nevertheless almost certainly be present. The very act of writing history, the simplest task of assessing characters or events, entails some canons of judgement. They need not be moral judgements but judgements they remain. Thus we are interested in the Barbarians who settled the Roman Empire because they succeeded it: had they been driven out our treatment of them would have been in quite other terms; we select Innocent III as worthy of greater consideration than Innocent II because we judge him to be the more important Pope; we regard Luther as of greater significance than Hus, for he precipitated the Reformation whereas Hus was burned at the stake; we are more interested in Holland than in Spain in the seventeenth century and more in France than either, in the eighteenth, because of their differing degrees of importance. We assign all these priorities according to definite criteria by which, wise after the event, we are able to distinguish the greater consequence from the lesser. Had we been contemporary to any of these examples, and closely involved in them, our attitudes would necessarily have been different; at the very least they would have not been determined by the same standards. We reach our judgements on reality by abstraction, as when we designate men human beings in virtue of recognising that their collective similarities outweigh their individual differences. So with history. We select and reject, include and juxtapose, subordinating what we consider trivial to what we consider important. But with this difference: that in history the entire operation is one of classification and reconstruction; for in dealing with nothing as it actually exists, in the here and now, we cannot test our conclusions in experience, as with the sciences;[1] even the status of a fact must be frequently the result of a complex process. It is therefore idle complaisance to imagine that

1. For this reason I do not accept Collingwood's contention that history is science on the ground that 'Science is finding things out: and in that sense history is a science', *The Idea of History* (Oxford, 1948), p. 9. So are a baby's movements, but that does not make them scientific.

history can be otherwise than by means of interpretation; however multifarious the evidence, and however strictly we adhere to it, it rests with us to impose order, to recognise connections, to draw parallels, to interpolate from our experience as historians where knowledge is lacking, to recognise the arbitrary nature of the evidence, and above all to ask the questions which alone can give coherence to the material available and direction to our enquiries. Without these activities there would be no history, and because of them it must continually change from generation to generation.

This is recognised by Professor Karl Popper when he speaks of history as an interpretation; yet it is he who has been largely responsible for the widespread attack upon patterns in history. However laudable his motives in combating the irrationalism which he believes to have been bred by conceptions of historical destiny, it has led to a self-defeating distrust of history that has harmed the study of society in recent years. There have also been strong attacks upon historical inevitability in the apparent belief that there is no discernible coherence in history; whereas in fact to dispense with patterns in some form or another is ultimately to attack history itself. It is among the most vulgar errors to believe that only those who adopt an avowed point of view are interpreting or that only an explicit pattern is a pattern. Destiny and necessity, it is true, are the stock-in-trade of those who look to history for guidance and they can lead only too easily to irrationalism and excess. Yet they are no more attitudes than their contraries: chance and contingency equally betoken a point of view and imply equally large assumptions. To deny that history can be a vehicle of planned change is not thereby to dispense with interpretation, for, when broken down, it says in effect that the present order is better than any other likely to be attained; that man's condition cannot be improved by human agency; and that there is no meaning to be derived from the endless flux and succession of events, which can be used to improve man's lot. It is essentially a doctrine of

94

acceptance, and as such expresses a definite view of history and human development, be it that human nature is weak and cannot be improved; that it is invariable; that it is prey to unfathomable instincts; that we are all subject to the inscrutable workings of God's will. In any event, whether it rests upon cynicism, scepticism or fideism, such an outlook must colour history as surely as that of so-called historicism, and men and their actions will be judged accordingly. Nor will their ultimate position be so different from that conceived by determinism; for if man is the slave of his own follies, or instincts, or nature, or subject to the play of the contingent and unforeseen, or God's creature in a state of original sin, he remains bounded by insuperable obstacles as surely as if he were the prisoner of history. The difference is that where the historicist points to a route which he can take, the anti-historicist denies that there is any course to follow.

I have naturally oversimplified the case, but it emphasises the groundlessness of the attack upon historical interpretation. It derives largely from a misconception of history in its attempts to confine it simply to a record of specific topics. This is particularly apparent in the case of Popper whose two works, *The Poverty of Historicism* and *The Open Society and its Enemies*, besides constituting the most formidable and penetrating attack on what he misterms historicism, are actuated by a love of reason. Since they are directed primarily against the Marxist conception they raise issues of fundamental importance, which it is necessary to discuss at the outset.

Popper describes historicism as 'an approach to the social sciences which assumes that *historical prediction* is their principal aim, and which assumes that this aim is attainable by discovering the "rhythms" or the "patterns", or the "laws" or the "trends" that underly the evolution of history.'[2] Such an approach to history he believes to be misconceived and illicit, since it is based upon the false belief that there can be a theoretical history and hence historical prediction.

2. K. R. Popper, *The Poverty of Historicism* (London, 1958), p. 3.

Now the core of Popper's case rests upon his avowed belief that history, *in se*, as a body of truths, has no meaning and therefore the facts of history will not furnish a scientific understanding of its laws and underlying evolution: 'But in history we have no such unifying theories; or, rather, the host of trivial universal laws we use are taken for granted; they are practically without interest, and totally unable to bring order into the subject matter.'[3] Accordingly, he calls historical theories, 'in contradistinction to scientific theories, *general interpretations*'.[3A] They are important because they are unavoidable, but since they cannot be tested they cannot be scientific; hence there can be no single interpretation of history, although some are more plausible and more fertile than others. Popper therefore concludes that 'there can be no history of "the past as it actually did happen"; there can only be historical interpretations and none of them final; and every generation has a right to frame its own'.[4]

We may accept this; and had he abided by such latitude we could have followed Popper's own injunction and treated his conclusion as just one more interpretation; but since his two books are largely designed to debar the historicist interpretation, this is hardly possible. The grounds for his attack are two: first that historicism embodies dangerous fallacies which cause it to mistake the nature of truth and second that the false sense of understanding which it engenders leads to prophecy and, ultimately, irrationalism.

It should be stressed at the outset that these are two quite distinct problems and that they have no immediate bearing upon one another; indeed the very definition of historicism given above is largely a figment of Popper's imagination. In the first place, there is no a priori interdependence between historical laws and prediction, and Popper at no point attempts to establish that there is; he simply takes it for granted. But this is to beg the entire question upon which Popper's avowed case against historicism rests. Contrary to his contentions it can be plausibly argued that it is quite

3. K. R. Popper, *The Open Society*, Vol. II, p. 264.
3A. *Ibid.*, p. 266. 4. *Ibid.*, p. 268.

possible for an historian to believe that history has a guiding law—say nationhood or representative institutions—as with so many nineteenth-century English historians, without any impulsion to make prediction a major part of his outlook. This is not a matter that can be decided by fiat, but depends upon specific circumstances. Thus in the stable upper reaches of English nineteenth-century society, the goal of history was regarded as contemporary England. Far from looking into the unforeseeable future, they took the present as a consummation and read all history in that light. This was the essence of the so-called Whig Interpretation of history. In Germany, on the other hand, in a nationalist ferment, history was made to justify German self-determination. What moral are we to draw if not that the 'laws' of history are a secondary consideration, and that, like drugs, their effects depend upon their use, a contingency quite independent of their intrinsic properties? The fact is that in periods of crisis anything can be turned to account and thereby distorted. One has only to think of Coke's interpretation of *Magna Carta* in the seventeenth century. But are we on that account to regard *Magna Carta* as a paradigm of English liberties? In the second place, however, what Popper understands by prediction is merely a special case, which is harnessed to attempts to change society *in toto*. It is in this sense that he opposes what he calls the 'holistic' conception of society that regards it as a totality and not in terms of its actual parts. Yet it is as much a prediction to deny the efficacy of these wholesale changes; the emphasis is simply upon the status quo, and, in upholding it, its adherents are in effect implying the same things that we mentioned in connection with historical inevitability. Thus Popper has not heeded his own warnings of the need to be aware of one's point of view; prediction, and an attitude to history, are implicit in his very rejection of revolution.

Thirdly, as he develops his arguments, it cannot be said that Popper has really done justice to any actual historicist point of view. No doubt he had Marxism mainly in mind, but, even allowing for its strong messianic elements, prediction in the sense that Popper uses it does not occur: there is simply a goal that must be reached by struggle, but the route to it is anything but predictable; hence the expedients adopted in the name of the revolution. Similarly it is hard to believe that Popper really believes that the arguments used by social scientists in support of an historical approach to their concepts can have the same goal as those of the Marxists, or that they can be meaningfully bracketed together with Mill, Comte, Mannheim, and Plato as basically sharing the same outlook. Yet this is what Popper's historicism ultimately amounts to. The result is a bloodless artifact.

Let us begin by agreeing with Popper that history for reasons which I shall discuss,[5] is not a science, with its own laws, and that it does not therefore enable us to make predictions in any strict sense. Let us also agree that to all intents and purposes historical events are unique in that they never take place in exactly the same context, if only because, however similar events may be, the participants are usually different. But this does still not preclude any kind of comparison between them from which conclusions may be drawn and prognoses made. Popper's analogy that 'the most careful observation of *one* developing caterpillar will not help us to predict its transformation into a butterfly' while true as an argument against prediction based upon universal conditional laws is hardly apposite to an understanding of social evolution. In the first place history is, in one sense, repetition, the unending succession of men and their civilisations; and their study will enable us to make some distinction between what is constant and what is variable, between certain universal characteristics of human behaviour that distinguish men as social beings and what is peculiar to them at different epochs. In the second place this enables us to impose some order upon human development. That it is conceptual, and to that extent arbitrary through the selecting and isolating of what seem to be the

5. I have since developed them in *History and Social Theory*, Part One.

significant elements, and so is ever liable to revision, does not make such a task any less indispensable. Through our classifications of history into different civilisations and eras, such as paleolithic, neolithic, feudal and so on, we render history intelligible in terms of a pattern of development; and by applying it to a specific society we can place it and define it in relation to other societies. From this, thirdly, we are able not only to identify the guiding factors, such as nationalism or industrialism, in a particular area or epoch but also to posit an order in which they occur, and even to infer, so far as the present is concerned, the most likely future course of development. Without a knowledge of the part played by industrialism and nationalism over the past two centuries much of the present would be unintelligible; and it is just because we have such knowledge that we have some kind of awareness of their importance, which in turn helps to colour our future attitudes. Such understanding, it is true, is not scientific in the strict sense; but as deriving from the deductions from past knowledge it is as indispensable to intelligent human conduct as knowing that a bend in the road leads to a drop of 400 feet is to an individual's survival.

Viewed in this light the question of prediction in history is largely irrelevant; and while we can share Popper's abhorrence at the irrationalism that a belief in historical destiny engenders, to attempt to exclude history from social discourse can produce its own, scarcely less dangerous, irrationality. History is indispensable to social and human understanding just because human conduct is not predetermined. The characteristic of human history is change and the repeated emergence of the new: not only new individuals but also civilisations and their attributes. It is precisely for that reason that human history cannot be subsumed under universal laws. The coming of a Socrates or a Galileo, of the watermill and the internal-combustion engine, not only cannot be causally predicted but leads to a transformation of what previously existed, setting in train a new sequence that is discontinuous with what held before.

The omnipresence of change distinguishes human history from the workings of nature, and prevents the study of society being reduced to the same static model as the study of nature. Far from their following similar methods, as Popper holds, the social and natural sciences should be distinctive. Human knowledge must be comparative and qualitative. It can be based neither upon invariable laws nor quantification because men both change their lives and their values. Human behaviour is regulated by norms which vary from epoch to epoch and society to society. For that reason they can only be related comparatively, that is historically. In the absence of social uniformity, history as the record of human society resumes the totality of social experience. It is therefore the medium of all social knowledge.

Paradoxically it is his recognition of social change which underlies Popper's whole case against historicism, in his denial that the causes of these changes can be understood or their course predicted. Yet this notwithstanding, for all practical purposes he leaves it out of account. Consequently he appears oblivious to the consequences. These are, firstly, that in examining society we are not examining something that is structurally constant; indeed to plagiarise Popper we are examining societies, not society; and these may have virtually nothing in common beyond the fact that they are social groupings: the very word 'man' can become largely a question-begging term when comparing say, a cannibal with a member of a twentieth-century industrial civilisation. Accordingly, the social sciences cannot apply the same criteria as the natural sciences. In science, for all practical purposes, the object of study, whether atoms or mammals, can be regarded as structurally constant, enabling its regularity of behaviour and ultimately its predictability to be established, at least in theory. With mankind, however, variability and change are the operative factors. Social and material life, knowledge, techniques, and attitudes, all undergo constant development in such a way as to render it impossible meaningfully to talk of them or of man or o society except in terms of generally recognised phases

Where is the ground for the common approach of which Popper speaks when he says: 'the significance of our analysis lies in the fact that it draws attention to a really fundamental similarity between the natural and the social sciences'?[6] The attempt to do so can end only in capitulation to irrational and unscientific attitudes; for so soon as we omit to examine the pedigree of any stage of society, and to ask how and why it came to have the features it has, and to assess it both against its own antecedents and other societies, we lose all perspective; we come to accept it as given; we fail to discern what is common to man down the ages, and what is peculiar to him at different epochs; we have no yardstick by which to distinguish between what is innate in human nature and what is the product of circumstances; we shall judge—and probably judge wrongly (as when we say 'men love war', or 'all men desire power'). We shall thereby have abdicated the dual responsibilities of truth and morality. In the first case, we shall court certain error in failing to recognise the central role of change and in implicitly assuming that our own state is fixed; in the second we shall, by the same token, accept the prevailing injustices and iniquities as part of an unalterable dispensation, instead of being in a position to recognise that we need not bow to them in the same way as we must accept, for example, the molecular structure of a crystal.

It is precisely for these reasons that history is indispensable to the social sciences: for they become meaningless without reference to place and time. That it will not be the precise understanding of the natural sciences; that such knowledge that we gain can never be fully tested; that, as Popper so strongly emphasises, it can hardly be more than an interpretation which will change with the emphases of every generation: all this is not in question. On the contrary it is a different kind of knowledge firstly in being concerned with contingent as opposed to necessary events. So long as there are alternatives to a particular course of action, its outcome, whether intended or unintended, cannot be regarded as

6. Popper, *The Poverty of Historicism*, pp. 61-2.

inevitable. That is not to say that there were not determining factors which help to explain why what happened at any given time did happen, but rather to recognise that it need not have happened at all or could have happened differently. Thus unlike a scientific law, such as that of the boiling point of water, the operation of which, given certain conditions, is invariable, there is no such law that holds to explain why it was Harold and not William who was killed at the Battle of Hastings in 1066. The event could have happened the other way round so that we can only explain it by the contingent factors that led to Harold's death, which, until it occurred, was only a possibility, not a necessity. In the second place all social knowledge is value-charged. On the one hand it is concerned not only with what was the case but what men took it to be. Many social and historical events have been the result of men acting upon what turned out to be misconceptions, such as the belief of the Flagellants in 1348 that Jews had poisoned the wells or the panics that have periodically led to financial collapse. But these false valuations do not make the events to which they led any less real. Moreover even where there is no such discrepancy between fact and value, they remain inseparable in all that concerns social events. The very act of accepting a bank note as currency is to invest it with a worth which derives not from any intrinsic property but from the social system to which it belongs. Consequently to understand social phenomena entails going beyond the object or event itself to the meaning that it held at the time. It is this dependence upon meaning that sets the procedures of the humanities and social sciences apart from the natural sciences. To study society is to grasp the complex of intentions, assumptions, ideals, and interests that went into the making of any set of events.

On the other hand this can only be by means of the anthropomorphic categories that are common to all men. In that sense all social and historical categories are themselves value-charged because they are applied to human conduct. We use terms like 'rise', 'decline', 'beauty', 'murder', 'progress' to describe historical events because they are the ones appropriate to men's actions. For that reason, however scrupulous we may be in passing judgement, to do so is in the very nature of historical and social discourse. That we can be too confident in our reading of the past and too ruthless in drawing our conclusions for the future does not alter the case. The answer is not to deny the place of history in the study of society but to seek for what Popper calls the most 'fertile' interpretation. Never was the need for it more imperative at a time when our very existence is at the mercy of correct historicist prognoses; for who would deny that our attempts to control nuclear weapons or to help the underdeveloped areas are in essence the result of a recognition of the past and an attempt to regulate the future? And who would deny the indispensability of these tasks?

It is my contention that we not only cannot escape what Popper calls historicism but that we also need it, and that far from this necessarily entailing the irrationalism and messianism that Popper ascribes to it, to deny it is to court these very consequences. This can be seen in two examples of Popper's method. The first is his advocacy of what he calls 'nominalistic methodology' in the social sciences, which he opposes to 'essentialist methodology'. By 'essentialism' he means the same as the realism of the middle ages, the belief in the reality of universal essence such as whiteness, goodness, and so on: 'Essentialists deny that we first collect a group of single things and then label them "white"; rather, they say, we call each single white thing "white" on account of a certain intrinsic property that it shares with other white things, namely, "whiteness". This property, denoted by a universal term, is regarded as an object which deserves investigation just as much as the things themselves. . . . Thus universal terms are held to denote universal objects, just as singular terms denote individual things.'[7] 'Nominalism', on the other hand, regards universal terms such as white 'to be nothing but

7. Popper, *The Poverty of Historicism*, pp. 27–8.

a label attached to a set of many different things—snow-flakes, tablecloths, and swans, for instance.'[8] 'Instead of aiming at finding out what a thing really is, and at defining its true nature, methodological nominalism aims at describing how a thing behaves, and especially, whether there are any regularities in its behaviour. In other words methodological nominalism sees the aim of science in the description of the things and events of our experience . . . words it considers rather as subsidiary tools for this task, and not as names of essences. The methodological nominalist will never think that a question like "*What* is energy?" or "*What* is movement?" or "*What* is an atom?" is an important question for physics; but he will consider of importance a question like: "How can the energy of the sun be made useful?" '[9]

Now while methodological nominalism is largely the method of the natural sciences, that of essentialism still dominates the social sciences—and with pernicious consequences; for it has led them to follow Aristotle in searching for 'the essence of things in order to explain them',[10] instead of realising with the physicists that names are only arbitrary descriptions and could be otherwise. Hence they ask questions such as 'What is force?' or 'What is justice?' in the conviction that only thus will they attain to a true understanding of institutions. It leads to the belief that in society there is an unchanging essence that underlies all institutions, and hence that history is the means of exhibiting this essence in its different aspects. Accordingly essentialism is one of the main props of historicism, for the latter provides the key to the different forms that institutions can take.

Popper's treatment of essentialism shows very clearly the shortcomings of his standpoint. In the first place, he does not, as we have already argued, differentiate between society and nature. But in the second place, and even more germane here, he has allowed his own terminology to obscure a fundamental difference. It is not more essentialist to talk of

8. *Ibid.*, p. 27.
9. Popper, *The Open Society*, Vol. I, pp. 26–7.
10. Popper, *The Poverty of Historicism*, p. 28.

the state than to talk of the bile duct; true both, unless we are referring to specific cases, will be abstractions, but they will not be universals in the sense that whiteness or goodness are, for the simple reason that with both state and bile duct we can point to specific examples. Where they differ is in their structure and therefore in their attributes and ultimately in the questions to be asked. The state has not the palpability of the bile duct: it is an abstraction, what he calls a 'social whole', which can only be adequately perceived through its operations over a period of time. Its attributes, such as justice, describe social relations and are not physical definitions. Above all, since they are social relations they are not eternally fixed, as indeed the most elementary survey of the history of terms like 'justice' or 'law' will show. Inevitably therefore the first question in the social sciences will be 'what' and 'why', for there is no ultimate appeal to an eternal and constant order. Thus it is not a matter of endowing the universal, or the essence, with an independent reality; it is that rather we are dealing with a different form of reality that demands different terms for its elucidation.

Were we to follow Popper's injunction to ask only 'how' questions we should be confining ourselves to the status quo; for in not asking 'what do we mean by justice?' and 'why need it be in the way in which it is?', we should have to accept what we found. This would be the ultimate degree of obscurantism; we should have forfeited rational enquiry and criticism because we should have abandoned historicism.

The same applies to the second example that is taken from *The Open Society*. There Popper attacks both Plato and Marx for 'posing the problem of politics by asking "who should rule the state?" ' 'It is high time for us to learn', he says, 'that the question "who is to wield the power in the state?" matters only little as compared with the question "*how* is the power wielded?" and *how much* power is wielded?'[11]

Here we see the outcome of confusing two quite distinct

11. Popper, *The Open Society*, Vol. II, p. 162.

fields. While it would be otiose to frame the question in any other way than 'how is so and so to be utilised?' or 'how does so and so behave?' if we are referring to physical objects, it becomes meaningless when applied to men. Here there is no natural order that enables us to take their condition for granted, and hence no warrant for making a distinction between 'how' questions, on the one hand, and 'who' and 'what' and 'why' questions, on the other. To uphold it is not to be scientific and objective, but, on the contrary, partial and circumscribed from the outset. It becomes both futile and servile to ask how power is wielded if we are not also to ask by whom, by what right, and to what effect; for the object of our enquiry, if it has any meaning, is not simply to know and leave it at that, but to modify if necessary. We do not hesitate to utilise our scientific knowledge for our benefit; why should we not do likewise with our institutions? But unless we first know all that is relevant to them, unless that is to say we do not take them for granted but question their very foundations, we cannot do so. To follow Popper would be to accept this disability.

Ultimately, then, Popper's failure to recognise the essentially different nature of human society has led him to attempt to impose upon its study the *schema* of the classificatory sciences. Therein lies the fallacy. He has denuded society of its dominant traits—change and values—with the inevitable result. History has been banished and in its place has come an eternally fixed order, to challenge which is to sin against reason. In the end the effect is not so different from the totalitarianism that Popper attacks: his 'piecemeal social engineering' is at most a safety value, designed to uphold the prevailing social structure; so are the five-year plans of his opponents. With neither rests the initial alternative of another dispensation. Where Popper differs from his opponents and from Plato is that he wants history to stand still where it is, or at least not to be harnessed to further change. But, when all is said and done, he accepts its verdict as fully as they do; and his choice has been as little actuated by scientific considerations as theirs.

It is my contention, then, that history is a matter of attitudes and that it cannot have a consistently scientific basis. But whereas this leads Popper to attempt to banish it from the study of society, I believe the converse to be true: namely, that we must study it as searchingly as we can in order to reduce to a minimum the play of our own predilection. So soon as we reject the study of history we do not thereby free ourselves from arbitrary preconceptions, but on the contrary give them full rein. We cease to look critically at the present or flexibly at the future; we turn from historical categories to fixed categories and thereby circumscribe ourselves intellectually and morally. We take for granted what we should question; we accept uncomprehendingly where we should compare and contrast; we submit where we should choose. That we incline against such a course in effect makes most of us historicists; and any system which helps to further us in our understanding should be welcomed regardless of the uses to which it may have been put.

II. Historical Materialism as Science

It is in this light that I shall consider historical materialism. My concern will be not to argue for or against it as a philosophy of history, since I have already given my grounds in favour of such an approach, but to assess its efficacy as such.

We may perhaps take as our starting point the paradox that through historical materialism we are able to discern the fallacy of dialectical materialism. For whereas the latter assures us that our consciousness is a true reflection of reality, historical materialism is concerned to show the essentially incomplete and transitory nature of our awareness: its 'false-consciousness'. Where dialectical materialism, as expounded by Engels and Lenin, affirms the direct correlation of what is to what we experience, historical materialism shows the complexity of the connection; where the one seems to imply that the world is an open book, the other points to the need to pass beyond appearance to reality; above all, where dialectical materialism emphasises the derivative nature of our knowledge, historical materialism points to its active nature. Now these divergences cannot be argued away. They have their source, I believe, in the discrepant origins of the two doctrines. As I attempted to show in the last chapter, the perfunctory growth of dialectical materialism through the reflections of Engels, contrasts with the systematic study of society pursued by Marx. From the outset dialectical materialism lacked the firm foundation in reality that characterises historical materialism. Its very presence is testimony to orthodoxy rather than rationality, as with so much of present-day Marxism.

Historical materialism, in contrast, was the starting point for all Marx's main investigations and he never forsook it. Throughout all the writings of his early, philosophical, phase, the *Economic and Philosophic Manuscripts of 1844*, *The Holy Family*, *The German Ideology*, *The Theses on Feuerbach*, *The Poverty of Philosophy*, we are aware of the same theme: '*just as* society itself produces *man as man*, so is society *produced* by him. Activity and consumption, both in their content and in their *mode of existence*, are *social* . . . the *human* essence of nature first only exists for *social* man; for only here does nature exist for him as a *bond* with *man* . . . Thus *society* is the consummated oneness in substance of man and nature . . . the naturalism of man and the humanism of nature both brought to fulfilment.'[12]

This passage offers a striking insight into what we may call the Hegelian genesis of Marx's thinking about society. It helps to explain the processes which underlay the 'standpoint of the new materialism', which he declared in the Tenth *Thesis on Feuerbach* to be 'that of human society or social humanity'. By society Marx envisaged not simply an association of men but the condition of men's existence as human beings; both man the individual and man as part of nature are subsumed, as it were, under social man: 'Society is the consummated oneness in the substance of

12. Karl Marx, *Economic and Philosophic Manuscripts of 1844* (Moscow, 1956), pp. 103-4.

man and nature.' Accordingly, the very humanity of man, or as Marx yet put it, the human essence, was in virtue of his being social man. The implications of this conception scarcely need to be stressed. In the first place, for Marx, man is human because he is social; there can be no false dichotomy between the individual and the group: 'What is to be avoided above all is the re-establishing of "Society" as an abstraction *vis-a-vis* the individual. The individual is *the social being*'.[13] He can only be considered, therefore, in terms of his social existence. This means, in the second place, that not only are we not concerned with man as an abstraction; we are not even concerned with men, but only with men as they exist in society. And since society changes, so do men. Accordingly man is to be known not in his individual psyche, but through history, the record of man's nature: 'It will be seen how the history of *industry* and the established *objective* existence of industry are the *open* book of *man's essential powers*, the exposure to the senses of human *psychology*. Hitherto this was not conceived in its inseparable connection with man's *essential being*. . . .'[14] As Marx was to state it so succinctly in his Sixth *Thesis on Feuerbach*: 'But the essence of man is no abstraction inherent in each separate individual. In its reality it is the *ensemble* (aggregate) of social relations'. Thirdly if man cannot be abstracted from his social relations, neither can nature. We have already alluded to the essentially human character of nature in the last chapter, and it suffices here merely to recall it.

Finally, and this in many ways was the most profoundly original element in Marx's thinking, human consciousness is equally a social product, expressing (I refrain from saying reflecting) 'the ensemble of social relations', that is to say, his social condition. This is perhaps the source of Marx's entire outlook; it is apparent already in his *Contribution to the Critique of Hegel's Philosophy of Right*, written in 1843, where he writes: '*Man makes religion*, religion does not make man. In other words religion is the self-consciousness and self-feeling of man who has either not yet found himself or

13. *Ibid.*, p. 104.   14. *Ibid.*, p. 109.

has already lost himself again. But *man* is no abstract being squatting outside the world. Man is the world of man, the state, society. This state, this society, produce religion, a *reversed world-consciousness*, because they are a *reversed world* . . . It [religion] is *the fantastic realisation* of the human essence because the *human essence* has no true reality'.[15] Similarly in the third of his *Economic and Philosophic Manuscripts* there is a sustained discussion of the social nature of consciousness. There he says: 'In his *consciousness of species* man confirms his real *social life* and simply repeats his real existence in thought . . . Thinking and being are thus no doubt *distinct*, but at the same time they are in *unity* with each other'.[16] We have only to ponder this passage to realise how little the dialectical materialism of Lenin and Stalin has in common with Marx's new materialism; for him the categories of being and thinking were essentially social, referring not to lifeless antitheses, but to man's actual condition in society. In this sense it would be true to say that none of Marx's successors was Marxist enough: they succumbed to abstractions—untenable ones at that—where Marx never forsook the social framework of all things human; he had no place for the banalities of his successors in their endless reiteration of the independent existence of the world; for, if man was not social, he was nothing. It was this conviction in man's sociality that drove Marx to look to society for the explanation, and history for the record, of man's development. He made history, not philosophy, the key to this understanding because the truth about man was not to be found in his consciousness but in his existence; and his existence was not timeless but rooted in a specific set of circumstances, past and present. As Marx put it in the First *Thesis on Feuerbach*: 'The chief defect of all materialism up to now (including Feuerbach's) is that the object, reality, what we apprehend through our senses, is understood in the form of the *object or contemplation*; but not as *sensuous human activity*, as practice'. This is the defect epitomised by Lenin and his followers, as

15. *Marx and Engels on Religion* (Moscow, 1957), pp. 41–2.
16. *Ibid.*, p. 105.

we saw in the last chapter; it is the defect of the dichotomy between subject and object, thinking and being; it is the defect which has its roots in Engels's *Ludwig Feuerbach*, where he said that, 'The great basic question of all philosophy . . . is that concerning the relation of thinking and being'[17]; and unlike Marx he did not go beyond this division, but took his stand as the protagonist of the primacy of being. He was duly followed into this blind alley by the Marxist cohorts who to this day are still enclosed in it. It represents not simply a reversion to 'the contemplative materialism of separate individuals' (Tenth *Thesis on Feuerbach*) but misconceives Marx's intentions, which were to explain the forms men's consciousness took, not to enunciate the truth in set terms. It was the difference between asking why men believe something to be true and asking what is truth. Marx, in addressing himself to the former question, was in effect more concerned with falsity than with truth: that is to say, with tracing the source of men's illusions and locating them in their conditions of life, rather than criticising them and amending them in the light of an absolute truth. This was the core of his materialism: it was essentially a social doctrine directed to man as a social being. Consequently categories like thinking and being were outside its terms of reference, or rather irrelevant, in that they were comprehended in social activity. That this does not dispose of them is only evidence that Marxism is not a universal methodology of unlimited applicability; but that, on the contrary, it was designed to answer the questions, so abhorred by Popper, of how and why. The failure of Marxists to recognise this limitation has meant the imposition of dogma upon what can only legitimately be the realm of empirical enquiry.

Having emphasised the social foundation of human nature, activity and thinking let us now consider more precisely its import. This can be expressed in the general proposition that it is the way in which men have to combine together to live that ultimately determines their social and

17. *Ibid* p. 24.

spiritual life. Or as Marx put it in the famous passage in the preface to *The Critique of Political Economy*: 'In the social production of their life, men enter into definite relations that are indispensable and independent of their will, relations of production which correspond to a definite stage of development of their material productive forces. The sum total of these relations of production constitutes the economic structure of society, the real foundation on which rise a legal and political superstructure and to which correspond definite forms of social consciousness. The mode of production of material life conditions the social, political, and intellectual life process in general'.[18]

Now in this process four main aspects can, I think, be discerned. First there is what Marx and Engels, in the *German Ideology*, called 'the first premise of all human existence', namely, 'that men must be in a position to live in order to be able to "make history" . . . The first, historical act is thus the production of the means to satisfy these needs [of self-preservation], the production of material life itself. And indeed this is an historical act, a fundamental condition of all history, which today, as thousands of years ago, must be daily and hourly fulfilled merely in order to sustain human life'.[19] Production therefore is the starting point of men's social relations. It is this which characterises man's human existence: 'Men can be distinguished from animals by consciousness, by religion or anything else you like. They themselves begin to distinguish themselves from animals as soon as they begin to *produce* their means of subsistence, a step which is conditioned by their physical organisation'.[20] Moreover, and this is par excellence the distinguishing feature in the Marxist notion of production, 'This mode of production must not be considered simply as being the reproduction of the physical existence of individuals. Rather it is a definite form of activity of these individuals, a definite form of expressing their life, a definite

18. Marx and Engels, *Selected Works*, Vol. I, pp. 328–9.
19. Marx and Engels, *The German Ideology*, p. 39.
20. *Ibid.*, p. 31.

mode of life on their part . . . What they are, therefore, coincides with their production.'[21]

Accordingly we cannot view men apart from their productive activity, for the process of production engenders the form of organisation and outlook appropriate to it: 'The nature of individuals thus depends on the material conditions determining their production.'[22] Now what are these material conditions? They are what Marx, in the preface to *The Critique of Political Economy*, calls 'the mode of production',[23] which is synonymous with the way in which men earn their living. It comprises the forces of production, instruments, and men with the skills to work them, on the one hand, and the relations of production, that arise from these productive activities, on the other. As Marx says, 'In production men not only act on nature but also on one another. They produce only by co-operating in a certain way and mutually exchanging their activities. In order to produce, they enter into definite connections and relations with one another, and only within these social connections and relations does their action on nature, does production, take place'.[24]

Now as men's power over nature increases, or, in Marxian terminology, as the forces of production improve, their social relations correspondingly change; the latter are therefore dependent upon the former, and it is to the productive forces that we attribute the development of society. 'Social relations', said Marx, 'are closely bound up with productive forces. In acquiring new productive forces men change their mode of production; and in changing their mode of production, in changing the way of earning their living, they change all their social relations. The handmill gives you society with the feudal lord; the steam mill, society with the industrial capitalist.'[25]

That 'men establish their social relations in conformity

21. *Ibid.*, pp. 31–2.   22. *Ibid.*, p. 32.
23. *Selected Works*, Vol. I, p. 329.
24. Karl Marx, *Wage-Labour and Capital, Selected Works*, Vol. I, p. 83.
25. Marx, *The Poverty of Philosophy*, p. 92.

with their material productivity'[26] is therefore the law of social development; and all history thereby becomes the study of men's changing productive activity. As Marx's aphorism on the handmill and the steam mill illustrates, a given social order is distinguished by the prevailing mode of production; and the difference between one stage of society and another is the difference between one mode of production and another.

This leads us to the second aspect: the emergence of classes and the subsequent domination of society by their struggle. They arise from the division of labour which is itself the effect of the growth of the productive forces: 'How far the productive forces of a nation are developed is shown most manifestly by the degree to which the division of labour has been carried. Each new productive force, in so far as it is not merely a quantitative extension of the productive forces already known (for instance the bringing into cultivation of fresh land), brings about a further development of the division of labour'.[27]

The division of labour begins with the separation of agricultural labour from industrial and commercial activity, and 'hence to the separation of *town* and *country* and to the conflict of their interests', and then to further division and sub-division. To these different stages belong different forms of ownership, beginning with tribal ownership, that 'corresponds to the undeveloped stage of production, at which a people lives by hunting and fishing . . .',[28] through ancient and feudal societies to capitalist society. They arise from the 'unequal distribution, both quantitative and qualitative, of labour and its products, hence property';[29] with the result that there arises a conflict between 'the particular and the common interests'. 'For as soon as labour is distributed, each man has a particular, exclusive sphere of activity, which is forced upon him and from which he cannot escape. He is a hunter, a fisherman, a shepherd, or a critical critic,

26. *Ibid.*, p. 93.
27. Marx and Engels, *The German Ideology*, p. 32.
28. *Ibid.*, pp. 32–3.   29. *Ibid.*, p. 44.

and must remain so if he does not want to lose his means of livelihood'.[30] Accordingly society will be so regulated as to sustain the state that arises 'out of this very contradiction between the interest of the individual and that of the community'.[31]

The antagonism between the interests of the individual and society is the characteristic of class society, for it is in effect only the sign that society is controlled in the interests of a class and not all its members: 'The social power, i.e. the multiplied productive force, which arises through the cooperation of different individuals as it is determined by the division of labour, appears to these individuals, since their cooperation is not voluntary but has come about naturally, not as their own united power but as an alien force existing outside them'.[32] This 'estrangement' of man from the control over his own activities and the products of his labour is central to Marx's thought.

Marx took over from Hegel the concept of alienation; it underlies his first excursion into political and social theory in his *Critique of Hegel's Philosophy of Right*, where he treated the state, democracy, and the proletariat in terms of man's separation from his own human essence in society. The overcoming of alienation lay in abolishing the social and property divisions among men. A year later in the *Economic and Philosophic Manuscripts of 1844*[33] Marx carried his analysis beyond political and constitutional forms to political economy. He now came to see men's property relations as the source of their social relations, and alienation as the outcome of private appropriation of the producer's product, at once dividing one from the other and man from his fellows. In Marx's own words:

'What, then, constitutes the alienation of labour? First, the fact that labour is *external* to the worker, i.e. it does not belong to his essential being; that in his work, therefore, he

---

30. *Ibid.*   31. *Ibid.*, p. 45.   32. *Ibid.*, p. 46.

33. I have used the English edition published in Moscow, 1956. They have also been translated by T. B. Bottomore in *Karl Marx, Early Writings* (London, 1963).

does not affirm himself but denies himself, does not feel content but unhappy, does not develop freely his physical and mental energy but mortifies his body and ruins his mind. The worker therefore only feels himself outside his work, and in his work feels outside himself. He is at home when not working, and when he is working he is not at home. His labour is therefore not voluntary but coerced; it is *forced labour*. It is therefore not the satisfaction of a need; it is merely a *means* to satisfy needs external to it. Its alien character emerges clearly in the fact that as soon as no physical or other compulsion exists, labour is shunned like the plague. External labour, labour in which man alienates himself is a labour of self-sacrifice, of mortification. Lastly, the external character of labour for the worker appears in the fact that it is not his own but someone else's, that it does not belong to him, that in it he belongs, not to himself, but to another . . . it is the loss of his self.'[34]

The consequences are that man is estranged from nature, himself, and from what Marx calls 'his species being'—that is from his own nature—and from other men.[35] The whole order of man's real life is thus reversed, instead of labour being regarded as man's very essence as a conscious active being, it becomes degraded into a means of existence. The relation between essence and existence is inverted, or rather they become separated, when in reality they are inseparable.

This conception of labour as man's 'life activity, productive life itself', and alienation as man's loss of control over it, remained Marx's fundamental premise. Although the term alienation disappeared from Marx's published writings in his own lifetime[36] it informed the whole of his

34. Marx, *Economic and Philosophic Manuscripts*, pp. 72–3.

35. *Ibid.*, pp. 74–7.

36. It continued to be used in *The German Ideology*, written in 1845 and 1846, and reappears in his *Gründrisse zur Kritik der Politischen Ökonomie*, his draft of *Capital*, written in 1858–9, but unpublished until 1939. There is now a German edition (Berlin, 1953), as well as an English translation of certain chapters under the title of *Pre-Capitalist Economic Formations* (London, 1952). For a brief account of alienation see D. Bell, 'The Debate on Alienation' in L. Labedz (ed.), *Revisionism* (London, 1962), pp. 195–

subsequent thinking; indeed his study of capitalism, as has frequently been pointed out, is only a development of the positions already reached in 1843 and 1844. The essential continuity in Marx's thought, and with it its Hegelian cast, can no longer be doubted.[37] But this is not to deny either its other influences, above all from English political economy and French socialism, or Marx's own evolution. 1848 marks the watershed. From then onwards there is a gradual hardening of Marx's categories. If one can still discern the humanism of his youth, his earlier conception of man as separated from his own human essence as a species, through the division of man from his work, his product, nature, and society, becomes crystallised into the antagonistic personifications of capital and labour. If the ultimate objective of man's reintegration with himself still remains through his reintegration with society and the proletariat still continues to be the instrument of his transformation, the mode becomes more narrowly defined in a causal order from economic basis to instituional and ideological superstructure. Man as an abstraction is superseded by the abstractions of classes, and human activities are translated into the mechanisms of a class divided society. It was a change that shifted the emphasis from society measured as a deviation from man's nature to man subsumed under society. If in each case it was the same notion of man that was striving to be set free, in Marx's later works it became increasingly impersonal and denuded of specific human content, an attitude that orthodox Marxism has enshrined. But the source lies in Marx's own abstract conception of man; from the outset he treated man as an indifferentiated human essence who was defined through his productive activities. In seeking to go beyond the political and ideal forms in which man expressed his real condition Marx set

---

211, which should however be read in the context of Avineri's correction (*op. cit.*, pp. 96–8).

37. Although it has again been recently denied by I. M. Zeitlin, *Marxism, a Re-examination.*

up the new abstraction of man as *homo faber*,[38] who only needed to be allowed to realise his true nature in labour to be restored to himself. Nevertheless for Marx, unlike Lenin and subsequent orthodoxy, the future lay open in that the mode of man's transformation was secondary to the transformation itself. Man, not the party, remained the measure of man's destiny.

Marx arrived at his notion of alienation through Feuerbach's transformative method earlier alluded to, namely of inverting Hegel's categories and making man their subject. For Hegel[39] alienation meant the spirit's separation from itself and its objectification in the external world; through spirit's externalisation of itself (the result of its creative activity) it appeared in the form of nature and history. As such it appeared as what it was really not. But whereas nature is spirit that is unconscious of itself, man is spirit that, through history, gradually becomes conscious of itself as spirit. To achieve this return to his source in the absolute spirit, man had to transcend the world in which spirit was embodied; he had to recognise the illusory, alien nature of all that was not spirit, for so long as he remained conscious of objects he was bounded by the material and finite. Emancipation from the 'sorrow of finitude' thus lay in passing beyond consciousness of the world as object to self-consciousness of spirit as subject. It was this search for self-knowledge that was the driving force of history; its epochs were so many stages leading to man's gradual ascent from the world to the spirit, which was about to have its consummation in Hegel's own time.

This debased form of Neoplatonism, with its Eckhartian phraseology,[40] was distinctive in seeing human history rather than human nature as the medium of the spirit's activity

---

38. As Kamenka, *The Ethical Foundations of Marxism*, p. 99, has justly observed, Marx conceives the human essence 'as universal in a qualitative and intensional sense'.

39. For a good account of Hegel's doctrine see Tucker, *op. cit.*, chap. 2.

40. Meister Eckhart, c. 1260–1327, was the first to employ the term 'negation of the negation' to describe God.

in man. But no more than Eckhart can Hegel be said to have integrated nature into spirit.[41] On the contrary his dialectic was designed to transcend the natural world. The latter as the negation of spirit had its own negation in self-consciousness. This final resolution (*Aufhebung*) was achieved through the denial that the objective world was real. Its attainment meant man's freedom.

Hegel's position therefore rested upon two assumptions. The first was that alienation was a state of consciousness that could only be resolved through self-consciousness. The second was that the object was identified with what was alien. Hence objectification was the same as alienation, to be overcome by denying the object. The practical effect was quietism, leaving the world to its non-existence and turning to contemplation.

These were the grounds upon which Marx opposed Hegel.[42] By reversing Hegel's order between object and consciousness Marx made man the subject of alienation; it lay not in man's separation from spirit but from the object he himself created. Man is of his nature a '*corporeal*, living, real, sensuous, objective being; full of natural vigour . . . he has *real, sensuous objects* as the objects of his being or of his life . . . he can only *express* his life in real sensuous objects.'[43] Accordingly it lies in his definition as a being that, far from alienation residing in objects, 'a being which does not have its nature outside itself is not a *natural* being'.[44] Hegel's failure to see this led to a double error:

'The first emerges most clearly in the *Phenomenology*, the Hegelian philosophy's place of origin. When, for instance, wealth, state-power, etc., are understood by Hegel as

41. As Avineri does, *op. cit.*, p. 6.
42. Especially in the last of the *Economic and Philosophic Manuscripts*, 'Critique of the Hegelian Dialectic and Philosophy as a whole', pp. 142–71. Marx directs his critique to Hegel's Phenomenology, in which Hegel stated his view of alienation. I am indebted to Avineri, *op. cit.*, p. 6, for stressing the importance of this manuscript and Marx's own position on this issue.
43. Marx, *Economic and Philosophic Manuscripts*, p. 156.
44. *Ibid.*, p. 157.

entities estranged from the *human* being, this only happens in their form as thoughts. . . . They are thought-entities, and therefore merely an estrangement of *pure*, i.e. abstract, philosophical thinking. The whole process ends therefore with Absolute Knowledge. . . . *The philosopher* sets himself up . . . as the *measuring rod* of the estranged world. The whole *history of the alienation-process* and the whole *process of the retraction* of the alienation is therefore nothing but the *history of the production* of abstract (i.e. absolute) thought. . . .

'*In the second* place, the vindication of the objective world for man—for example, the realisation that *sensuous* consciousness is not an *abstractly* sensuous consciousness but a *humanly* sensuous consciousness—that religion, wealth etc., are but the estranged world of *human* objectification, of *man's* essential powers given over to work and that they are therefore but the *path* to the true *human* world—this appropriation or this insight into this process consequently appears in Hegel in this form, that *sense, religion,* state-power etc. are *spiritual* entities, for only *mind* is the *true* essence of man. . . . The *humaness* of nature and of the nature begotten by history—the humaness of man's products —appears in the form that they are *products* of abstract mind, and as such therefore phases of *mind-thought entities*.' [45] Nevertheless, despite the mystifying inverted form in which Hegel expressed it, the notion of alienation as man's estrangement from the real world, formed the point of departure for a critique of the real world. To quote Marx again:

'The *Phenomenology* is, therefore, an occult critique—still to itself obscure and mystifying criticism; but in as much as it keeps steadily in view man's estrangement, even though man appears only in the shape of mind, there lie concealed in it *all* the elements of criticism, already *prepared* and *elaborated* in a manner often rising far above the Hegelian standpoint. The "Unhappy Consciousness", the "Honest Consciousness" the struggle of the "Noble and Base Con-

45. *Ibid.*, pp. 149–50.

sciousness", etc., etc.—these separate sections contain but still in an estranged form the *critical* elements of whole spheres such as religion, the state, civil life, etc. . . .

The outstanding thing in Hegel's *Phenomenology* and its final outcome—that is, the dialectic of negativity as the moving and generating principle—is thus first that Hegel conceives the self-genesis of man as a process, conceives objectification as loss of the object, as alienation and transcendence of this alienation.'[46]

It was this insight into alienation as an historical process representing man's loss of control over his own objects that Marx took up and made the basis of his materialist conception of man as *homo faber* deprived of the products of his labour. He thereby also went beyond Feuerbach. Feuerbach had treated alienation as man's own alienation from himself as subject; it expressed a division within man, between his essence and his existence, which he objectified into the distinction between God and man: 'But if it is only in human feelings and wants that the divine "nothing" becomes something, obtains qualities, then the being of man is alone the real being of God—man is the real God. . . . The true statement is this: man's knowledge of God is man's knowledge of himself, of his own nature.'[47] The result is 'the disuniting of man from himself. God is not what man is—man is not what God is. God is the infinite, man is the finite being. . . .'[48] Feuerbach was therefore reduced to seeing God as the projection of man's own ideal self. Self-alienation in consequence was not an historical phenomenon, as Hegel and Marx had in their different ways conceived it; least of all did it owe anything to man's sensuous activity; rather it arose from a false conception of man's own essence, which he wrongly attributed to God. Feuerbach's solution was for man to recognise himself in his conception of God and so to substitute reverence of man

46. *Ibid.*, pp. 150–1.
47. L. Feuerbach, *The Essence of Christianity* (New York, 1957), p. 230; quoted in Tucker, *Philosophy and Myth in Karl Marx*, p. 86.
48. Feuerbach, *op. cit.*, p. 33 (*ibid.*, p. 88).

for worship of God. But as Marx saw this was also to sub-stitute one abstraction for another.

For Marx, on the other hand, religion was but one aspect of man's alienation. It had its source not in the human essence but in human activity and could be only overcome by praxis not contemplation. That is the standpoint that Marx expressed in his *Theses on Feuerbach*. He had reached it through following Feuerbach in transposing alienation into human terms, while—unlike Feuerbach—retaining Hegel's dialectic of man's self-activity. Marx was thus able to treat alienation as an historical phenomenon that be-longed to man's process of 'the loss of the object, as alienation and transcendence of this alienation.' Already in the *Economic and Philosophic Manuscripts* this served to express what was taking place under capitalism. 'Labour produces not only commodities; it produces itself and the worker as a *commodity*—and does so in the proportion in which it produces commodities generally.

This fact expresses merely that the object which labour produces—labour's product—confronts it as *something alien*, as a *power independent* of the producer. The product of labour is labour which has been congealed in an object, which has become material: it is the *objectification* of labour. Labour's realisation is its objectification. In the conditions dealt with by political economy this realisation of labour appears as *loss of reality* for the workers; objectification as *loss of object* and *object-bondage*; appropriation as *estrangement*, as *alienation*.'[49] In other words where the product is alienated, including labour itself, it becomes an alien object, standing outside and above those who produce it. Alienation becomes expressed in objectification not because of any inherently alien property in the object as such but because of the system of appropriation which endows it with an inde-pendent power and to which the producer is himself subject. As Marx later distinguished, 'What is being underlined is not objectification, but the process of *alienation*, externalisa-

49. Marx, *Economic and Philosophic Manuscripts*, p. 69.

tion, estrangement, the fact that the immense objective power belongs not to the worker but to the objectified condition of production, i.e. capital.'[50] It was this that Marx in *Capital* called the 'fetishism of commodities': commodities come to be treated as objects in their own right when in fact they reify social relations between men; they do so because men are themselves separated from their products, which therefore appear to them alien objects. As such fetishism is one aspect of alienation in which objects rule men through other men.

Alienation was therefore the driving force in Marx's critique of capitalism and his interpretation of class society. It represented the 'very contradiction between the interest of the individual and that of the community'.[51] As formulated in *The German Ideology* it has now become a conception of history: 'The social power, i.e. the multiplied productive force, which arises through the co-operation of different individuals as it is determined by the division of labour, appears to these individuals, since their co-operation is not voluntary but has come about naturally, not as their own united power, but as an alien force existing outside them, of the origin and goal of which they are ignorant, which they cannot control, which on the contrary passes through a peculiar phases and stages independent of the will and action of man, nay even being the prime governor of these.[52] Its elaboration constitutes Marx's system. As it later came to be expressed it represents the exploitation of the producer by those to whom he is subject, whether a slave owner, a feudal lord or a factory owner. It is common to all class society just because men do not enjoy the fruits of their labour, but, owing to the prevailing productive relations, have it appropriated by those who control the productive forces. 'In the social production of their life men enter into definite relations that are indispensable and

50. Marx, *Gründrisse der Kritik der Politischen Ökonomie*, quoted in Avineri, *op. cit.*, p. 105.

51. Marx and Engels, *The German Ideology*, p. 45.

52. *Ibid.*, p. 46.

independent of their will'.[53] So long as the handmill pre-
vailed, so long were the productive relations those of
feudalism; and until these were superseded men had to
submit to them.

But there comes a time when the productive forces change,
when the handmill is displaced by the steam mill; and here
we have the third aspect of social development. Once this
change takes place a conflict is set in train between the new
forces of production and the old relations of production,
which were based upon the previous forces of producton.
That is to say, 'the forms of intercourse' connected with a
previous form of producing the wherewithal of life are
rendered obsolescent by the changed methods of production.
From having previously been in harmony with the latter
they now become a fetter. As Marx put it in the preface to
The Critique of Political Economy: 'At a certain stage of their
development, the material forces of production come into
conflict with the existing relations of production—or what
is but a legal expression for the same thing—with the
property relations within which they had been at work
hitherto. From forms of development of the forces of production those relations turn into their fetters. Then begins
an epoch of social revolution. . . . No social order ever
disappears before all the productive forces for which there is
room in it have been developed; and new higher relations
of production never appear before the material conditions
of their existence have matured in the womb of the old
society itself.'[54]

This is the motive force of all history within class society;
it is generated by the contradiction between the forces of
production and the relations of production, and the need
for the latter to be brought into alignment with the former.
Since, however, these relations are enshrined in a particular
social order that serves to maintain them, and since, in
class society, this means the maintenance of the exploiting

53. Marx, Preface to *The Critique of Political Economy, Selected Works*,
Vol. I, p. 328.
54. *Ibid.*, p. 329.

class, any such change entails the overthrow of that class. This can only be achieved by the exploited classes. Hence 'not criticism but revolution is the driving force of history';[55] hence, too, 'the history of all hitherto existing society is the history of class struggles',[56] for it is by the agency of classes, expressing the different interests of society, that the needs of society are furthered. Within the wider conflict between man and nature, expressed in man's increasing mastery of his environment, goes the struggle between men over the appropriation of the products of their control. But, although it has dominated all written history, it is a transient phase, to be ended with supersession of capitalist productive relations by socialist productive relations, which will abolish private property and with it exploitation.

Finally there is the role of consciousness or, more exactly, the relationship of ideas, whether political, legal or philosophical, to material life. This was stated by Marx as follows: 'The mode of production in material life conditions the social, political and intellectual life processes in general. It is not the consciousness of men that determines their being; but, on the contrary, their social being determines their consciousness'.[57] Consciousness is therefore essentially a social product, expressing the prevailing state of society at a given time. It reflects not man as an isolated individual, but as belonging to a particular form of society. As such, it has two peculiarities. The first is general to all consciousness, namely, that it arises from the material conditions in which men live at any given time. It is the reflection of their state of development and will be framed in terms of the problems, achievements, hopes, and fears that confront them in real life. That is to say, men's consciousness is not simply consciousness but consciousness *of* something; it is neither timeless nor universal: 'The production of ideas, of conceptions, of consciousness, is at first directly interwoven

55. Marx and Engels, *The German Ideology*, p. 50.
56. *Communist Manifesto* (London, 1948), p. 1.
57. Preface to *The Critique of Political Economy, Selected Works*, Vol. I, p. 329.

with the material activity and the material intercourse of men. . . . Conceiving, thinking, the mental intercourse of men, appear at this stage as the direct efflux of their material behaviour. . . . Men are the producers of their conceptions, ideas etc.—real, active men, as they are conditioned by a definite development of their productive forces. . . . Consciousness can never be anything else than conscious existence, and the existence of men is their actual life-process'.[58] Thought, therefore, whatever it forms, is to be regarded as the superstructure that corresponds to the 'economic structure of society'—the mode of production—as its basis. Its character, or more accurately, content, is determined by the problems that confront men in their actual material existence. As Marx put it, 'Therefore, mankind only sets itself such problems as it can solve; since, looking at the matter more closely, it will always be found that the problem arises only when the material conditions for its solution already exist or are at least in the process of formation'.[59] This accounts for the origin of all forms of consciousness and all institutions. Their validity lies essentially in their consonance with the social order of which they are the expression, and once its economic foundations are changed 'the entire immense superstructure is more or less rapidly transformed',[60] to accord with the new economic structure.

The second peculiarity is that, since all hitherto written history is the history of class society, so ideas have a class character. 'The ideas of the ruling class are in every epoch the ruling ideas: i.e. the class which is the ruling *material* force of society is at the same time its ruling *intellectual* force. The class which has the means of material production at its disposal, has control at the same time over the means of mental production, so that thereby, generally speaking, the ideas of those who lack the means of mental production are subject to it.'[61]

58. Marx and Engels, *The German Ideology*, p. 37.
59. Preface to *The Critique of Political Economy, Selected Works*, Vol. I, p. 329.
60. *Ibid.*   61. Marx and Engels, *The German Ideology*, p. 60.

Now 'these ruling ideas are nothing more than the ideal expression of the dominant material relationships, the dominant material relationships grasped as ideas'.[62] They therefore depict only that aspect seen by the ruling class: and since this reflects its own desire to sanctify the existing order, their ideas are naturally self-interested and distorted. They suffer from what Engels called 'false-consciousness'.[63] Thus, in dealing with ideas, we are not dealing with truth minted in pure metal, but with an alloy, compouned out of a specific viewpoint and a specific time. In order to test its validity we must inquire into its components: by whom it was formulated and when, and in what circumstances; we cannot take it at its own valuation: 'Just as our opinion of an individual is not based on what he thinks of himself, so we cannot judge of such a period of transformation by its own consciousness.'[64]

Accordingly we may say that man attains to ever greater knowledge as he attains to ever greater control over his surroundings, and to increased social justice through the different partial, limited, and self-interested phases of society. Ultimately those same productive conditions which make for a classless society will make for a classless ideology.

Such, then, are the main elements of the materialist conception of history. It would be hard to deny that its signal contribution lies in the very offence for which Popper arraigns it, namely, an historical interpretation of society: the recognition that to understand men and their ideas we do not go to human nature and philosophy but to the circumstances in which they were formulated; and that this entails considering men as active members of society engaged in the pursuit—or the rejection—of a given mode of life. In that way, as suggested earlier, we are enabled to break down abstractions, like man, society, nature, religion, into living men, societies, aspects of nature and religion; in Marx's words, we are able to pass beyond 'the opinions men have of themselves', to the reality they express. In this sense

62. *Ibid.*   63. See p. 130.
64. Preface to *The Critique of Political Economy, Selected Works*, Vol. I.

Marxism has endowed thinking with a new insight, which, properly applied, is the strongest antidote to self-delusion, fatalism, and obscurantism.

Yet this is far from making it a science or of universal application; and I wish to consider some of the objections to treating the materialist conception of history as if it were the key to an understanding of mankind, rather than a particularly fruitful interpretation of history. The first point to note is that it is essentially concerned with the study of society; even when we admit that man is a social being, the product of the society into which he was born, we are still not compassing every aspect of his nature, or knowledge. It is one thing to explain the circumstances of something: it is quite another to explain it in itself. To confuse the two is tantamount to the crudest of all forms of reductionism: in this case breaking down everything, no matter what its peculiarities, to expressions of economic and class situation. It is to invite specious parallels, begged questions, and weighted verdicts, the diametrical opposites of a scientific attitude. Unfortunately, these have not been resisted, and official Marxism abounds in such explanations for most phenomena, whether Shakespeare's plays or present ills. It is easy to see the temptations of resolving a problem by such a methodology; and it becomes almost too easy to perform once the principles have been learned. Thus Cornforth on Aquinas: 'In the heyday of feudal society the greatest philosopher of the Middle Ages, Thomas Aquinas, represented the entire universe as being a kind of feudal system. Everything was arranged in a feudal hierarchy, with God surrounded by the chief archangels at the top'.[65] It is hard to know what to marvel at most: Cornforth's view of Christianity, feudalism, or Aquinas, but in any case it represents a piece of meaningless juxtaposition in which a superficial parallel has been made into a causal relation. Even so subtle and original a thinker as Georg Lukács comes near to the same position, when he seeks to explain

65. Cornforth, *Dialectical Materialism*, Vol. II: *Historical Materialism*, p. 17.

the emphasis in modern philosophy upon isolated elements, and the lack of an overall unity, in terms of the essentially isolated, contractual nature of relations under capitalism.[66] To do so is to substitute dogma for empirical investigation, omitting any consideration of the increasing exactitude of scientific knowledge that leads to the ever more precise isolation of the elements composing an object. Such an approach inevitably means the introduction of arbitrary and extraneous presuppositions, with the result that what should be explained is explained away. This approach is the inverse of scientific method, where the starting point for analysis is what happens to be the case in all its complexity and irregularity. Society is as comprehensive a term as nature; yet where study of the latter has given rise to a dozen distinct disciplines—in the natural and biological sciences—Marxists appear to believe that for society only an historical assessment of the mode of production at any given time is required: psychology and sociology in their different aspects have never been officially accepted, presumably because they were not acknowledged by Marx.

This brings us to the second point, namely, that the Marxist interpretation of history is not a science. There are two reasons against acceding to such a claim on behalf of historical materialism. The first is the general one, to which we earlier alluded, that history lacks the requirements of science.[67] There is no means of subsuming its events under universal laws or of verifying conclusions by experiment or of treating the material except by the most arbitrary forms of selection (when there is too much) and reconstruction (when there is not enough—the common case in pre-modern history); there is no unifying agency other than that of the historian; and finally there can be no means of establishing by proof positive the priorities. If one person holds that Shakespeare's plays are self-explanatory, without the need for historical background, and another that his

66. *Op. cit.*, pp. 112 ff.
67. I have since discussed the nature of historical knowledge in *History and Social Theory*, Part One.

significance lies in their historical implications, where is the final decision to lie? Similarly, if one person regards men's ideals as the most noble and worthwhile feature of history and another as false-consciousness, however sincerely held, who is to demonstrate scientifically the falsity of one or the other? We are back at our earlier proposition that history can never be more than an interpretation, and what Marxists call historical laws are generalisations from tendencies.

The extent to which history is a matter of interpretation will be known by anyone who has been confronted with hitherto unworked material: the lacunae, the allusions, the emphases, the sequence of events, present an irreducible number of alternatives, that can rarely be reconciled with certainty or regarded as more than suppositions. In such a situation it rests with the historian to arrive at a working hypothesis; or rather the way in which the facts are ordered will depend upon the questions that the historian brings to them. This is the governing consideration. At no time, in any science, do the facts speak for themselves in the sense that the observer merely registers what is to be observed and presents it accordingly. On the contrary, with everything that we approach we do so with presuppositions and intentions, that are inseparable from our upbringing and the social heritage that has been transmitted to us; yet, at the same time, the intuitions that we have, the questions that we ask, the objectives that we set ourselves are personal to ourselves. Certainly they will be coloured by all that has gone towards making us conscious, but the actual point at which we act, in giving them expression, rests with us. We may agree with Marx that 'mankind only sets itself such problems as it can solve', but they are individual men who reach these solutions; and they do so by first becoming aware of the problems for which answers must be found. Many besides Newton had seen an apple drop to the ground, but only Newton formulated the occurrence in terms of a problem; it thus became qualitatively transformed from an apple dropping to the cause of the apple dropping and thence to the nature of gravity. The same applies to knowledge of all phenomena. As we discussed in the last chapter, to observe is not the same as to understand; and therein lies the fallacy of a purely inductive view of science. We can live a lifetime among regularities—the rising and setting of the sun, the dropping of apples that are ripe, the association of hunger with the need for food—but these alone will not give us any precise knowledge of their causal relationship. For that we must first frame questions and seek answers; and to do so we must first want reasons.

Such procedure is only a systematised and directed extension of our everyday activity. Gestalt psychology has shown that perception is the result of the ordering of different clues into a whole; and while I agree with Polanyi[68] that in this case it is an automatic rather than a deliberate process it nevertheless points to the essential element in all cognition, namely, the ability to arrive at coherent pictures of reality by selection. Our knowledge of reality is viable only because it is a construction; were it to embrace everything it would mean incoherence through the inundation of the significant by the trivial. Animals can only survive by their capacity to react against danger; and this entails taking account, not of all the possible kinds of threat, but of those to which they are specifically prey: if the mouse were to worry as much about elephants and dogs as it does about cats it would be far less able to cope with the latter and so would be infinitely more exposed to destruction. Similarly in our knowledge we do not have to know the molecular structure of water to know that it is wet, or the cause of fire to realise that it burns; and indeed it is precisely because our perception of an event does not entail knowledge of its structure that we can only arrive at such knowledge by investigation. But this in turn is possible only because we desire to know, and so pose the problem in the first place. I leave aside for the moment the question of the circumstances that give rise to the demand for such knowledge: for whatever these may be, and however instrumental they are in initiating such activity, they cannot determine the

68. M. Polanyi, *Personal Knowledge* (London, 1957), p. 97.

precise way in which it will take place or the means by which a solution is arrived at. That is essentially an individual matter. I submit, therefore, that the systematic acquisition of all knowledge is not a mere generalisation from experience, which anyone trained in the relevant techniques can accomplish; but that it depends upon the personal insights and what Polanyi calls the 'intellectual passions'[69] of the investigators; that knowledge only advances because it is conceived in terms of problems that demand a solution; and that these are not there for the asking but arise in as many different ways as there are individuals for whom they arise. The personal element is therefore indispensable to all knowledge, and the problem is not to deny it or purge it, but to adopt methods by which we can establish its non-personal, inter-subjective worth.

Now in the exact sciences this personal quest can ultimately be corroborated by experience and experiment. As Popper says, 'It is irrelevant from the point of view of science whether we have obtained our theories by jumping to unwarranted conclusions or merely by scrambling over them (that is, by 'intuition') or by some inductive procedure. The question, "How did you first *find* your theory?" relates, as it were, to an entirely private matter, as opposed to the question, "How did you *test* your theory?" which is alone scientifically relevant'.[70] There is therefore a definite yardstick by which to measure the validity of a scientific hypothesis. The same does not apply to history, since, while fundamentally the same intellectual processes are at work in the attainment of conclusions, there is no means ultimately of verifying them. It is idle to pretend otherwise; at the very most there can be agreement by what we may call plausibility, in which the trustworthy consensus accepts one interpretation rather than another. But this cannot attain to the status of scientific truth, for it lacks certainty.

It is in this sense that it can be said that there are no laws in history. In the first place, a law is a statement of universal

69. *Op. cit.*, p. 135.
70. Popper, *Poverty of Historicism*, p. 135.

conditional form such that we can say that, given A, B will follow. Yet the whole nature of the subject of history belies any such estimates, unless, as Popper has pointed out, they are so general as to be utterly trivial: that the victor in battle is stronger than the vanquished or that war is the outcome of conflict. The reason has already been adverted to in the earlier discussion on historicism. Human society, the subject of history, is an abstraction; what we really study when we examine it are many different kinds of society comprehending a multitude of different practices. What, then, are we to understand by the laws of historical development? That the nature of society is determined by its economic activities? That as these become more complex so society becomes more advanced? That ideas represent the real problems confronting men in their daily lives? All of these may be valid, but they can hardly be called laws, just because they lack any of the precisions and causal regularities that distinguish strict scientific laws. Not only are they too general to be of application in the investigation of specific features of society, but they beg questions that invalidate them as laws: What do we mean by determining the nature of society? Is it to be a strict correlation? If so, then we are in fact reducing all social phenomena to one kind of activity and negating the very complex structure that we call society. More than that, we are specifying that men always act in a certain way, which is sheer determinism, and indeed must be if we are to attempt to designate their activities in terms of laws at all. Above all if there were laws for society, society would have always to conform to them in its movements and its phases. How then would we account for the fact that societies in the same stage of development evince different literatures or forms of art or outlooks or institutions? If, on the other hand, the very futility of these questions makes us look away from any rigid determination, we are outside any measurable terms of regularity. For so soon as we grant that there is no direct correlation between one form and another, such that if one is given, we can specify the other, we accept that there is no such universality. We are then thrown back upon parallels, metaphors and analogies, which at most constitute indirect influences. These are in fact the stock in trade of Marxist historians, where a given situation is explained through its association with certain characteristics as, for example, the rise of science or the novel with the rise of the bourgeoisie, or catholicism with feudalism. Valid they may be, but parallels they remain.

It is hardly surprising, then, that laws cannot be adduced from history. Quite apart from the absence of verifiable criteria there is the nature of society: firstly what is its common denominator if not men, and where are we to look for the universal law that describes men? Do we begin with what is loosely called human nature, and reckon in terms of man as a species? Do we think of man as the creator of societies? Or man as the bearer of consciousness? In short what is our criterion, if not an arbitrary one? We are thus reduced to the fundamental question, who is to say what is the peculiar trait of man amongst all his different attributes? For none of them is in itself complete. Man is producer, thinker, warrior, and each must be taken into account if we are to do justice to him. Secondly, equally characteristic of man as his manifold activities is the fact that, as a social being, he changes. We have already considered this aspect and it remains but to note that, to all intents, we are describing different social beings when we refer to man in different epochs: the values and activities of stone age society and industrial society are, what Marxists would call, too qualitatively different to make any direct identification between them meaningful. A man who thinks it both permissible and desirable to eat his enemies is a different being from one who believes that he should love his neighbours; and although no one would pretend that the latter attitude overwhelmingly preponderates it yet expresses another order of conduct: to call both attitudes human is to render the word empty; it has no more relevance than to subsume the actions of all mammals under the same term.

From this it follows, finally, that the mistake of historical materialists is to believe that there is a universal law that sums up all human development. Cornforth expresses this view when he says: 'If, then, as we say that society develops according to objective laws, we mean (1) that social events take place only when the conditions causing such events have come into being. If, say, a movement starts up in which people put new social objectives before themselves, then that movement arises when and only when the conditions for it exist. It occurs at a definite time and in definite circumstances, and could not have occurred at another time and in other circumstances when its causes were not present. . . . We mean (2) that once certain events have taken place their effects will follow independently of people's desires or intentions. . . . For example, the invention of the mariner's compass set in motion a whole train of events which went far beyond what anyone had intended or foreseen; so did the invention of the steam engine, the spinning jenny, and so on. . . . We mean (3) that, though circumstances never recur, nevertheless the same causal connections are discoverable in different sequences of events. . . . If, for example, three hundred years ago there was a movement to get rid of capitalism, these movements, different as they are, repeat the same process—they both arise because an existing system has become a fetter upon economic development.'[71] This passage has been purposely quoted at length in order to show the triviality and imprecision into which the attempt to formulate laws for history leads. Any of these three 'laws' is so unexceptionable that it is tautological. No one, it would seem, without being self-contradictory, could possibly disagree that social events take place only when it is possible for them to take place any more than we sleep only when we can go to sleep or it rains when there are rain clouds to make rain possible; nor can it be confuted that one event leads to another, whether we like it or not: if I throw a stone and it hits someone he will be hurt even if this was not my intention; but then no one would doubt

71. *Dialectical Materialism*, Vol. II, pp. 2–42.

that we are not entirely masters of the consequences of all our actions, simply because they involve others over whom we have no control. H. A. L. Fisher used the same argument to discount all laws in history when he talked of 'one emergency following on another'.[72] This could equally be inferred from Cornforth's explanation that the effects of certain events 'will follow, independently of people's desires and intentions'. The third point is a parallel that is so general as to explain nothing beyond what it says; it is as enlightening as to say that men died three hundred years ago from old age and they still do so today. It is true to the point of being a truism; and it could apply to anything else as well as to historical epochs.

What is common to all of these 'laws' is that they lack intrinsic connection with history. They are generalisations of the same order that 'if you walk you are able to walk' and of the same value: they will do no harm, but they will not do any good.

That Cornforth is reduced to such triteness is not a reflexion on historical materialism but on the inflated claims made for it; and indeed he himself in common with most Marxists shows that what is really implied is that it is a methodology. In Lenin's words: 'By examining the *ensemble* of all the opposing tendencies, by reducing them to precisely definable conditions of life and production of the various *classes* of society, by discarding subjectivism and arbitrariness in the choice of various "leading" ideas or in their interpretation, and by disclosing that all ideas and all the various tendencies without exception have their *roots* in the condition of the material forces of production, Marxism pointed the way to an all-embracing and comprehensive study of the rise, development and decline of social-economic foundations.'[73] If we allow for Lenin's over-statement in the use of the word 'disclosed' this is a succinct summary of the emphases in the materialist approach to the study of history;

72. H. A. L. Fisher, *History of Europe* (London 1936), p. vii.
73. Lenin, *The Materialist Conception of History, Selected Works*, Vol. XI, pp. 19–20.

what pass for laws constitute in fact an order of procedure: the deductions remain to be made.

It has been necessary to stress the absence of laws since it is to misconceive the nature of both history and the materialist conception of history to imagine that history is an open book waiting simply to be read aright. No one would deny the much greater degree of accuracy with which the economic conditions of a given society can be examined as compared with its institutional and ideological super-structure. But it is precisely in assessing the latter that different techniques are required; and in that sense there is not one historical method but several, corresponding to the different aspects under investigation. No one would suggest that a banker and a philosopher practise the same skills, or that by understanding how the banker operates one *thereby* has an insight into that of the philosopher. Why therefore should one do what is tantamount to the same thing in history? What can be said is that, as products of the same age, they will both be absorbed in the problems and practices of their age; and to recognise their interconnection with their society is the prerequisite to a proper understanding of them. But to say this is to point to a prerequisite of investigation not to a law; for it is hardly worth stating, 'That if two men live in the same society at the same epoch they are members of the same society': and this is the only hard and fast demonstrative statement that can be made in this connection; any further conclusions will be the result of study not laws. I conclude, then, that history cannot be considered a science.

The second reason for rejecting a like claim for historical materialism is specific to Marxism. It is that, whatever its exponents say to the contrary, Marxism is a teleology: the words 'inevitable', 'mission', 'historical destiny', constantly recur in relation to the supersession of capitalism by socialism; they form a continuous theme from the writings of Marx to the present day. Thus we read in the *Communist Manifesto* that, 'All preceding classes that got the upper hand, sought to fortify their already acquired status by subjecting society at large to their conditions of appropriation. The proletarians cannot become masters of their productive forces except by abolishing their own previous mode of appropriation, and thereby also every other previous mode of appropriation. They have nothing of their own to secure and to fortify; their mission is to destroy all previous securities, and insurances of individual property'.[74] Likewise *The German Ideology* talks of 'a class [which] is called forth, which has to bear all the burdens of society without enjoying its advantages . . . and from which emanates the consciousness of the necessity of a fundamental revolution'.[75] Of course, no one can deny that the historical role of the proletariat was derived from the study of past and present society. As Marx put it in the preface to *The Critique of Political Economy*: 'The bourgeois relations of production are the last antagonistic form of the social process of production . . . at the same time the productive forces developing in the womb of bourgeois society create the material conditions for the solution of that antagonism. This social formation constitutes therefore the closing chapter of the prehistoric age of human society'.[76] This is the necessary outcome of bourgeois society of which the proletariat is its 'special and essential product', engendered by 'the formation and augmentation of capital': 'the condition for capital is wage-labour. Wage-labour rests exclusively on competition between the labourers. The advance of industry, whose involuntary promoter is the bourgeoisie, replaces the isolation of the labourers, due to competition, by their revolutionary combination, due to association. The development of modern industry, therefore, cuts from under the feet of the bourgeoisie the very foundation on which it produces and appropriates products. What the bourgeoisie therefore produces, above all, are its own gravediggers. Its fall and the victory of the proletariat are equally inevitable'.[77]

This passage exemplifies the logic of the proletarian

74. *Ibid.*, pp. 24–5.   75. *Ibid.*, p. 85.
76. *Ibid.*, p. 13.   77. *Communist Manifesto*, p. 26.

revolution. In considering it, the issue is not the validity of its analysis, but the attitudes that it expresses. They entail, I think beyond doubt, a particular interpretation that puts the emphasis upon the condition of the mass of the people. They stress its exploitation, its antagonism to the ruling class, its periodic eruptions and their inevitable failure, since it is only with the full development of capitalist society that the material conditions for proletarian revolution and socialism exist. Inevitably, therefore, the entire products of successive societies will be seen not merely as transitory but as a 'pre-human', expressing men's technological inadequacy to control nature freely and thereby their inability to live, save through the exploitation of one class by another. What achievements there have been must be seen in the light of class privilege, as the product of man's inhumanity to man; the really fundamental change issues in the progressive elimination of such elemental conditions, and the new era which will open with the victory of the proletariat.

We need not disagree with this position to see that it constitutes but one of many approaches to history. It may be argued that it is the correct one, the only one that will lead to a rational and proper understanding of the development of society, but this does not alter the fact that it is concerned with a particular aspect of history; that this interest is bound up with its belief in a definite outcome; and that its questions are framed with this in view. It implies a conception of progress as surely as the so-called Whig interpretation; it views the past by hindsight as much as other historians; its criteria are as much the result of judgements, priorities, and preconceptions; and they are incapable of verification.

We must conclude, then, that neither history in general nor the materialist conception of history in particular can properly be called a science. At best we can have methods of studying history, and if we consider Marxism in that light it has, I believe, every claim to be regarded as a particularly fruitful methodology. Yet to say this is not to say that the key to an understanding of any and every epoch, or activity, is to hand; rather we have been made aware of some of the indispensable prerequisites for their study. As such they can help us to frame our questions in the most telling way, but they do not provide the answers. Having argued that Marxism is not a science, it still remains to be considered how far it can be held to be of universal application to all departments of society; and here there are, I suggest, four main areas: the structure of society; human nature; the products of consciousness, or, in more technical Marxist phraseology, the superstructure; and the realm of the contingent and unforeseen.

III. Society

The Marxist analysis of society rests on the distinction, already quoted from *The Critique of Political Economy*, between the economic structure and the legal and political super-structure that rises upon it. Each of these is in turn sub-divided into a further causal relationship. The economic structure, or basis, as it is most commonly called, com-prises the forces of production and the relations of produc-tion, which together make up the mode of production. In Marx's words men's relations of production 'correspond to a definite stage of development of their material productive forces. The sum total of these relations of production constitutes the economic structure of society'.[78] The super-structure is in turn composed of the legal and political institutions and the forms of consciousness, 'the ideological forms', that correspond to them. We shall leave for the fifth section a disussion of the validity of this latter distinc-tion. For the moment we are concerned to adumbrate the notion of a tiered society: from productive forces to pro-ductive relations—the mode of production—that constitute the basis; and from the mode of production to the institutions and the ideas to which it gives rise—the superstructure. Marx describes this causative order as follows: 'The mode

78. Preface to *The Critique of Political Economy*, *Selected Works*, Vol. I, pp. 328-9.

of production in material life conditions the social, political and intellectual life process in general. It is not the consciousness of men that determines their being, but, on the contrary, their social being determines their consciousness. At a certain stage of their development, the material forces of production in society come into conflict with the existing relations of production, or—what is but a legal expression of the same thing—with the property relations within which they had been at work hitherto. From forms of development of the forces of production these relations turn into their fetters. Then begins an epoch of social revolution. With the change of the economic foundation the entire immense superstructure is more or less rapidly transformed'.[79]

Accordingly the different societies are to be judged in relation to their different modes of production, of which Marx enumerated four—'the asiatic, the ancient, the feudal and the modern bourgeois'[80] and to which must now be added socialism. This conception is amplified by Stalin who says: 'The basis of the relations of production under the slave system is that the slave owner owns the means of production: he also owns the worker in production whom he can sell, purchase or kill. . . .[81] The basis of the relations of production under the feudal system is that the feudal lord owns the means of production and does not fully own the worker in production—the serf. . . . The basis of the relations of production under capitalism is that the capitalist owns the means of production, but not the workers in production—the wage labourers . . . [who] are personally free, but who are deprived of the means of production'.[82]

Now, confining ourselves for the present to the economic structure of society, three considerations arise from the foregoing account. Firstly productive relations are to be distinguished from the forces of production; secondly it is the clash between the two that is responsible for social change which, by implication, comes about by revolution; thirdly the mode of production determines the 'social formation':

79. *Ibid.*, p. 329.   80. *Ibid.*
81. *Problems of Leninism*, p. 588.   82. *Ibid.*, pp. 588-9.

hence the record of different societies is to be sought in changes in the mode of production.

Perhaps, to begin with, it would be as well to discount as carping the oft-repeated criticism levelled against Marx's views, that they are not a consistently materialist interpretation, since they are dependent upon the importation of non-economic criteria, namely productive relations and the skills that go to make up the productive forces. For example the *Communist Manifesto* speaks of the creation by the bourgeoisie of 'more massive and more colossal productive forces than all preceding generations together. Subjection of Nature's forces to man: machinery, application of chemistry to industry and agriculture, steam navigation, railways, electric telegraphs . . .'.[83] That these clearly refer to techniques and labour as well as mere resources and instruments —the means of production—is not to be denied; yet it is carrying criticism to absurdity to labour the discrepancy, as Plamenatz does, between what he terms Marx's 'economic determinism' and the non-economic factors which are subsumed under it.[84] Not only is it a mere verbal quibble to restrict the word 'materialist' to non-economic categories (Marx himself, in his *Critique of Hegel's Philosophy of Right*, talks of ideas becoming a 'material force', when they have 'gripped the masses'), but it in no way confirms or invalidates the interpretation in question.

More germane, it would seem, is to ask whether there is any tangible way in which productive forces can be meaningfully distinguished from productive relations such that each can stand alone as a separable category in its own right. That is to say, are we when we speak of a productive force able to regard it as an entity that is distinct from the social organisation with which it is associated? Now we have already observed that a productive force is more than a mere instrument; it involves precisely the organisation of labour and the application of human skills. Thus Marx talks of 'the

83. *Ibid.*, p. 18.

84. J. Plamenatz, *German Marxism and Russian Communism* (London, 1954), p. 53.

productive forces resulting from cooperation and division of labour'[85] and of science as 'a productive force distinct from labour'[86]. Accordingly we are driven to ask what is a productive force if not at one and the same time also a social relation that includes people, their skill, and their knowledge? How, for example, do we separate capitalist sheep farming in the sixteenth century from that by the Cistercians in the twelfth and thirteenth centuries, if not by the different forms of organisation that they engendered: the relations in ownership, the presence or absence of enclosures and so on? Similarly the technological differences between a large manufactory in fourteenth-century Ghent and a modern factory lie not merely in the machinery but in the different productive organisation—division of labour, technical skills, contractual relations—inseparable from its working, and without which it would be meaningless to talk of productive forces. Marx himself recognises this when he says that 'machinery is merely *a* productive force'.[87] To consider it on its own would be to treat as only an instrument, of itself inert, what it is in fact the active power determining the entire life and development of society, as when Marx says that the 'division of labour in manufacture creates a qualitative gradation . . . in the social process of production; it consequently creates a definite organisation of the labour of society, and thereby develops at the same time new productive forces in the society'.[88] Above all, we have no less an authority than Stalin to tell us that, 'The *instruments of production* wherewith material values are produced, the *people* who operate the instruments of production and carry on the production of material values thanks to a certain *production experience* and *labour skill*—all these elements jointly constitute the *productive forces*'[89].

If we accept this, it seems impossible to conceive of a productive force which is not also a productive relation. Organisation then becomes as inherent in the forces of

85. *Capital*, Vol. I, p. 382.   86. *Ibid.*, p. 355.
87. *The Poverty of Philosophy*, p. 113. My italics, G. L.
88. *Capital*, Vol. I, pp. 358–9.   89. *Op. cit.*, p. 583.

production as the instruments around which men group and which they direct. As Marx and Engels put it in *The German Ideology*: 'a certain mode of production, or industrial stage, is always combined with a certain mode of cooperation, or social stage, and this mode of cooperation is itself a "productive force" '.[90] The consequences of this interpretation are far-reaching, for they entail nothing less than the invaliditating of Marx's other main propositions. The first is that if there is no actual distinction between the forces of production and productive relations the contradiction between them is not the motive force of change; if a productive relation is inherent in a productive force they are no more entities to be juxtaposed than are the heart and the brain; they are each inseparable from the ensemble which they compose. The implication is not, as Plamenatz would have it,[91] that since Marx says one is determined by the other they must always correspond; for to determine is not necessarily to entail automatic correspondence in a one-to-one correlation: it could equally be by means of a struggle. It is rather that the clash is not simply an economic clash, since they cannot be regarded as self-subsisting entities, let alone as constituting antagonistic elements. Where, for instance, is the contradiction in, say, the application of the division of labour to the spinning mule? Or to the productive organisation engendered in car manufacture? These are at once social relations but not of such a kind that they can be regarded as hostile, for they are (a) unlikes, inanimate material and human beings, with no meeting place other than their mutual harnessing to production; and (b) neither is viable as a productive force without the other, as we have mentioned. Yet together they both serve an economic function and are subject to an overriding direction in the production of values. Hence to gain a proper insight into their role at a given time we must look beyond the simple economic categories to those forms of social control—that is the property-relations—governing them: and this immediately involves the political and legal superstructures which, according to Marx arise on the economic bases

90. *Ibid.*, p. 41.   91. *Op. cit.*, pp. 28–32.

and which in themselves are only 'more or less rapidly transformed' after the clash between the productive forces and property relations. That is to say, where Marx distinguishes productive or property[92] relations, as part of the economic structure, from the legal and political superstructure, they are in fact inseparable. As they stand in the Marxist scheme they occupy a third position between productive forces and the superstructure; but this is untenable as the most cursory review will show. According to the Marxist view we should be able to distinguish (a) the forces of production, (b) the relations of production (or property relations) to which they correspond, (c) the legal and political institutions to which (a) and (b) give rise, and which (d) are in turn expressed in ideology. To follow this we should have to say of productive relations what we have previously seen we could not say for productive forces, namely, that they could stand in themselves devoid of political and legal elements, and that so stripped of all extraneous attributes they would still constitute a recognisable entity. But is this so? Let us take, for example, feudal property relations. Where is their foundation if not in the legal and political forms that define them and give sanction to them? There is nothing in petty peasant production which of itself gives rise to the property relations of serf and lord. In terms of productive forces alone, the level of techniques, the instruments utilised, the working of the land, are not substantially different from Roman (slave) society. It is the social organisation based upon it that differs: the differences between the directly forced labour of slavery and the small scale individual farming of the dependent tenant; between the slave as a

92. I have treated them as synonymous on the grounds, firstly, that this is what Marx's own loose wording in the above passage would suggest; and secondly that, otherwise, the concept becomes meaningless and there is then no point in pursuing the matter further. This seems to me to be both unwarranted and futile, as is only too plain from the case of Plamenatz who adopts such a course. In doing so he confounds Marxism with such a degree of incoherence that we are left to wonder how it could ever have met with any acceptance, let alone the degree which it has enjoyed.

chattel, and thereby treated as the property of the slave owner, and the serf as able to work the instruments of production himself and rendering compulsory surplus value to his lord as an independent operation. As Marx himself says, one form of society is distinguished from another by the way in which surplus value is extracted. Ultimately, then, the distinction between slavery and feudalism is in the property relations; and these far from being a unique expression of the prevailing forces of production, as Marx's preface to *The Critique of Political Economy* would imply, are superimposed upon it, by legal and political means. For what compels the peasant to render his due to the lord if not the sanction of society? And what is this if not the power that the lord can bring to bear upon the peasant, through politics and law (the custom of the manor, the rights of work days or other tribute, the power to try him at court, to impose arbitrary fines, the lack of legal standing of the peasant in his unfreedom)? And what in turn do these rest upon if not the military and coercive power that the lord can deploy and their enshrinement in the teaching of the Church, that each man is called to a certain station in life and must follow his calling? What indeed is the agreement between peasant and lord but a political and legal compact by which service is given in return for protection? These are the factors that combine to create the feudal bond; it is essentially a series of non-economic compulsions, in no way inherent in the actual economic activities of peasant cultivation: there is no a priori reason why a peasant should have a lord rather than be free; and none that in having a lord he should be thereby dependent and personally unfree, compelled to render his tribute in a certain way. Such exigencies depend firstly upon non-economic external factors: the particular course of development that leads to unfreedom—wars, famines, unequal conditions, and so on;[93] and secondly upon 'superstructural'

93. Engels appears to recognise this when he describes feudalism as the outcome not of a contradiction in the mode of production between the forces and the relations of production, but through extraneous causes like war, theft, impoverishment, the advent of the Germanic tribes, and

elements: the particular application of custom, law, politics, and morality given to these relations. Take away these and we should be left with nothing that could meaningfully be called a property relation. Accordingly it must be concluded that property relations far from constituting a separable entity distinct from both the forces of production and the legal and political superstructure belong to both: or put another way, there can be no such distinction between forces and relations, and relations and superstructure; for the very concept of productive forces, such as men earning their living, or, if preferred, their skills being applied to their operations of gaining a livelihood, entails social organisation —division of labour, relations of authority, and so on. This calls for the recognition of accepted practices, and their enforcement; hence of politics and law; and this in turn implies the prevalence of a particular outlook, of customs, of values, of taboos, and so on. In short there cannot be activity as between men unless there is a social cement that binds them; and this is as much political, legal, and moral as it is economic. Otherwise men would be primarily mere technological automata, who worked and ate first and talked and thought about their work afterwards. In fact, of course, man produces as he does because he acts consciously from knowledge and experience, and so with foresight. To build a bridge, say, is to plan socially and legally: it is to enter into contract with other men for labour and for materials; it is to fulfil a requirement that has some sanction from the community; it is from the first to direct the means of production in particular ways for a particular end. In such an activity men are guided as much by their values as by their stark economic needs, or rather the two are inseparable, embodied in the scales of payment, the conditions of employment, their mutual obligations and so on. In capitalist society they are contractual; but they are no more and no less potent under feudalism, where custom was the arbiter; in neither case could the prevailing canons be flouted with impunity.

so on. *The Origin of the Family, Private Property and The State* (London, 1943), pp. 170 ff.

We must look away, then, from purely economic categories to explain the laws of motion of society. Instead of seeking for a conflict between productive forces and productive relations, as understood by Marx, we have to think in more directly political terms that do not stand for two economic aspects, the progressive and the regressive. Thus in seeking for the transition from feudalism to capitalism there is nothing that corresponds to *new forces* of production displacing *the old relations*. The great technical innovations that came with industrialism constituted, as Marx himself acknowledges, the second phase in capitalism: the first, as has been pointed out,[94] was essentially a period of regrouping in which what Marx described as primitive accumulation and the displacement of the peasantry provided the two prerequisites for capitalism, capital and an army of unemployed labour.[95] These led to the breakdown of the old feudal relations so that the new forces of capitalism could act unfettered by the former.

Now it will be observed that the whole process is in terms of changes in the social organisation of production: different property relations, different dispositions of labour, the replacement of fixed hereditary tenure by contract and social mobility. These were the preconditions of capitalism. Hence the motive force has come from new relationships both in the utilisation of material resources and knowledge and as between men; there is nothing within the feudal mode of production that gives rise to an asymmetry within the economic basis itself. 'With the polarisation of the market', said Marx, 'the fundamental conditions of capitalist production are given.'[96] The change is essentially a totality in which base and superstructure are equally involved; indeed only through the active political and legal re-alignment of productive relations, as in the expropriation of the customary tenant in sixteenth-century England, do changes in the mode of

94. See M. M. Bober, *Karl Marx's Interpretation of History* (Cambridge, Mass, 1948), especially chapter IV.
95. *Capital*, Vol. I, part VIII.
96. *Ibid.*, p. 737.

production become possible. Thus the contradictions that give rise to the change are between economic practice and political and social aspirations; the superstructure is the active agent in that it gives expression to the inadequacies of the economic basis and transforms it.

Such a juxtaposition, I submit, shows how unreal the distinction is between these two elements of society. In fact men acting in a certain way gradually find the need to modify their practice; and this is as much a product of their legal, political and ideological, as of their economic activities.

This brings us to the second great consequence of the inadequacy of the Marxist conception: it does not explain the changes from one form of society to another; for if this does not, as I have argued, come about through a clash between new productive forces and the old relations of production, how is it caused? For example, if the difference between the slave and the feudal modes of production was in the social organisation of basically the same forces of production wherein lay the contradictions which caused the downfall of slavery? As Bober[97] has said it is hardly to be found in the conflict between those in favour of slavery and those representing the new anti-slavery forces. There is certainly no record of a revolutionary struggle between the two, leading to the supersession of the former by the latter. Indeed there seems to have been no revolutionary break between slave and serf status at all; and it is in this status—essentially a social, legal and political as much as an economic concept— that Marxists discern the crux of the differences between the two forms of society. If this is so we are at best introducing an arbitrary criterion to distinguish them, and it may well be doubted how meaningful it is to talk of feudalism as a period of nearly one thousand years any more than it is to describe all slave society from the Roman Empire to India as 'asiatic society'. Even more germane, history does not change through the simple dialectical struggle between exploiting and exploited classes. To take feudalism again, the 'victors' were neither the exploited nor a new rising class; indeed there do

97. *Op. cit.*, pp. 52 ff.

not seem to have been victors at all. What in effect occurred was either the gradual change in relationship between what had often, but not everywhere, been slave owners and slaves into lords and dependent peasantry; or the gradual stratification of those who had been members of some kindred or tribe into rulers and ruled. But the whole process took place over centuries. What then are we to call the intervening period: a transition? In that case, the transitions in history are greater than the states to which they lead! The same anomaly of who triumphs over whom arises in the development to capitalism. The peasantry are the exploited class but they do not overthrow the feudal aristocracy: they still have to wait their turn for the next society but one. The bourgeoisie are the triumphant class, but the older form of land-owning continues throughout, retaining its privileges even when, as in nineteenth-century England, by all the laws of class struggle its members should have been expropriated by their victors, the manufacturers. Consequently the Marxist rhythm of social revolution breaks down. History is full of every kind of revolution except that in which the exploiting class is overthrown by another class in accordance with the requirements of the forces of production, thereby ushering in a new mode of production. This cannot be said of any revolution before the advent of capitalism—whether of the Greek City tyrants, Caesar, Augustus, or the wars of the Italian Cities; or if it can, we have still to learn of it. Those that have taken place in the era of capitalism do not present any coherent sequence. Thus the English Revolution took place, we are told, in the 1640s, yet England was essentially a landlord state until the 1830s. In France the revolution did not come until the end of the eighteenth century yet once again the nobility return to many of their privileges, if not power, for the greater part of the nineteenth century until their disappearance. Above all, capitalism, in Marx's own analysis of England, comes before any revolution and is in existence for the best part of three centuries before the corresponding political revolutions engulf the greater part of Europe. Even when they have come how transformed is society? Or put another way, if there could be a revolution in science in the seventeenth century, if in eighteenth-century France the Enlightenment took place when the *ancien régime* was still in being, what part did the struggle of classes—let alone the victory of the bourgeoisie— play in all these developments? Can we in fact correlate progress with the triumph of a new class? And is the struggle of the new class against the old the great dynamic of social change? The answer does not receive favourable confirmation from history.

We are forced to conclude, then, that the materialist conception of society and its development is founded upon an over-rigid scheme, which, when analysed, does not give a true likeness to society and, even less, explains the motive force of change. By centring this upon the antagonisms that arise between the productive forces and the productive relations the whole interpretation founders; it is made to look to artificial divisions that in fact cannot be sustained and that are inadequate to explain what distinguishes one epoch from another and how they succeed each other. As we shall shortly see the same failure is apparent in the Marxist explanation of knowledge and forms of consciousness, and will likewise have to be revised.

IV. Man

The problem of human nature, or more accurately of individual men, is one that Marxism almost entirely avoids. It does so by regarding men as essentially the products of the particular class into which they have been born and therefore as personifying its practices and precepts. '. . . The human essence is no abstraction inherent in each separate individual. In its reality it is the *ensemble* of social relations'.[98]

Now this is to subsume man as an individual under man in his social relations; more specifically, it implies that as men combine socially in their productive activities so they will be as individuals. In the words of Marx: 'This mode of reproduction must not be considered as being the reproduction of the physical existence of the individuals. Rather it is a

98. Marx, Sixth *Thesis on Feuerbach.*

definite form of expressing their life, a definite *mode of life* on their part. As individuals express their life so they are. What they are, therefore, coincides with their production, both with *what* they produce and *how* they produce. The nature of individuals thus depends on the material conditions determining their production'.[99] By thus explaining man in terms of a given society, human nature becomes a variable that changes as society changes. If this is a dynamic conception it is also one-dimensional in that it takes no account of man other than as a social cypher, or rather it treats of man by means of a set of social criteria. That is to say, his concepts, institutions and self-consciousness are explained as the result of his relationship to production: if he is a member of a primitive tribal community his attitudes will be governed by its practices; if he is a member of the exploiting class under capitalism he will regard men, truth, justice, and so on in a manner consonant with his class position.

Now I submit that, while as a statement pointing to the conditions from which a mode of conduct arises, this attitude may be accepted, it cannot be regarded as an adequate treatment of human nature. In the first place it is not necessary to believe in an immutably fixed category to hold that there are certain constant features that distinguish man as man. Secondly there is much that cannot be explained purely by reference to a man's economic and class position. To do so is to practise reductionism once again, and to deny the multifariousness of personality and society.

So far as the first point is concerned, there is an entire realm of personality that does not respond to Marx's macrocosmic social criteria. Even if we grant that a great part of a person's make-up is determined by upbringing, the moral standards of his parents, the social group to which he belongs, the kind of education he receives, and the social and political atmosphere that prevails, there is still a large element that escapes such analysis. He may have digestive trouble, his parents may not be compatible, he may be bullied and terrorised, he may feel unloved, he may not respond to school discipline,

99. Marx and Engels, *The German Ideology*, pp. 31–2.

he may be hypersensitive, or introspective, or in some other way unable to adjust himself to his surroundings. These can have a traumatic effect upon him. Many of the attitudes which thus arise are entirely a personal matter upon which the materialist conception of history can throw no light. The same applies to differences in temperament and in responses to a similar situation: no such theory as Marxism can explain why one person will be hopeful while another is pessimistic, nor can any order of society, however perfect, eradicate the tensions that come from feelings of inadequacy as compared with others, whether over physical, mental, or social attributes. Such factors can have a decisive influence upon a person's conduct and attitude; and recourse to some kind of individual analysis, or case history, can alone explain the variations that in fact occur. How otherwise in, say, a period of upheaval should people of the same social stratum react differently: why do some members of the working class support communism and others conservatism? If the answer lies in the different degrees of political awareness, the question is only put back one remove to why this should be the case. In the end, once we have left the broad highway of the spirit of an age, we are reduced to examining the individuals that make it up.

It is at this point that the materialist conception of history fails, or rather, stops. In itself this is to be expected, for just as the general and special laws of relativity are concerned with the macrocosm and do not pretend to explain atomic structure, and quantum theory refers to statistical distributions not individual particles, so historical materialism is directed to the general laws of social development and not to specific events. The difference is that Marxists have resolutely refused to recognise this as a limitation that inevitably demands the aid of other disciplines. In the case of man this applies particularly to the findings of psychology, especially psychoanalysis, which has usually been treated with rabid hostility by official Marxism.[100] It regards the notion

100. See, for example, the attack upon Freud by M. Cornforth in *The Modern Quarterly*, Winter, 1950–51, pp. 16–33.

of the unconscious, with its instinctual drives, as reactionary and abhorrent, and seeks instead to explain men simply 'as living conscious organisms in their active relationship with their surroundings'.[101] But men are not ants, and such a doctrine, even with the addition of the word 'conscious', is tantamount to treating them as mechanisms whose entire natures can be explained in terms of their social activities. The inadequacy of such a conception is twofold.

In the first place, it is a fact confirmed not only by clinical findings but from our own experience (if we care to look for it) that many of our attitudes are coloured by associations of whose import we are unaware. We may identify a particular person or tune or smell or idea with a happy or unpleasant event and react to it accordingly; and many of our likes and dislikes derive in this way. Similarly we may often be unaware of our own state of mind, or project our feelings onto external objects; it is a commonplace that a sick and disillusioned man will tend to look at the world with different eyes from one who is buoyant: compare, for example, the earlier and the later H. G. Wells. Equally our anxiety for others may be the result of the anxiety we feel for ourselves. Whether we recognise the sources of such feelings or not, whether, that is to say, we are prepared to try to trace back our attitudes and not simply to take them at their face value, it remains, I believe, incontrovertible that many of our feelings exist in spite of us and that we can remain unconscious of them.

It is in this sense that we can designate as unconscious those feelings and instincts that operate independently of our awareness of them. To do so is not to posit an entity, a region of the psyche as such, but to recognise that what Marx calls 'consciousness of being' must begin with ourselves. Nor is this in any way unwarranted, or metaphysical. We do not doubt that we digest our food, replace our cells, react to changes of temperature, grow old without conscious direction on our part (that we may help to facilitate these processes is a different matter and only evidence of their autonomy); nor

101. Cornforth, *Dialectical Materialism*, Vol. III: *Theory of Knowledge*, p. 29.

that it is not our consciousness of hunger that makes us hungry but on the contrary the pangs of hunger that impinge upon our consciousness and drive us to action. Why, then, should we deny the role of instinct upon personality? That man has consciousness, the capacity for conceptual thought and speech, does not alter the fact that he is an organism whose existence depends upon functions that are not conscious; as with any organism he is subject to certain instincts without which he could not be or survive. If these are frustrated or imperfectly satisfied he will react to seek satisfaction. But, and this is where man differs from other animals, this will not necessarily be an overt and automatic expression of his needs. If a lion is hungry or wants a mate, he looks for food and a mate. In the case of man, he grows up into a particular ethos with its standards of conduct, morals, and taboos that cannot be flouted with impunity. Over and above the individual needs that distinguish Smith from Jones, there is the social order of which not only are they each part but a product, reared in the prevailing social psychology. It is here that the role of personality becomes apparent; for it is in accordance with the assimilation of an individual's personal needs to the demands of a society that his own balance is determined. If he is brought up to feel shame or fear over the satisfaction of a particular need, whether sex or in writing poetry, he can either try to suppress the feelings or sublimate them, turning them to some other object; or he can succumb to his state of dissatisfaction; or he can try to remedy it. Which of these different alternatives is followed will depend upon the individual—and here, I suggest, we have reached the furthest point of explanation, since to ask why one man is stronger or braver than another and will react differently in similar circumstances is like asking why is he taller or has different coloured eyes or is more intelligent. But short of making an open avowal of one's needs, and of the conflict between them and social morality, a man is bound to adjust himself to his circumstances; and in doing so he is unconsciously rationalising his position, imposing an order upon them in conformity with the requirements of society.

It is this discrepancy between the conscious forms a man's thinking and activity may take and the assumptions and interests often unconscious or at least unarticulated that underly them which must be investigated if we are to gain any proper understanding of human conduct. A man's consciousness is not just the product of social values; it is the outcome of all the experiences that have been registered by him as an individual. Naturally these will be of the kind peculiar to his social milieu: a twentieth century intellectual is precisely that and not a witch-doctor because of the society to which he belongs.

We are thus led to the conclusion that human nature cannot be regarded as either exclusively invariable or variable. On the one hand there is man the species, an organism distinguished by those physical attributes in virtue of which he is man. In this aspect he is as much a physical entity as any other creature and as dependent upon the fulfilment of instinctual needs: we have only to take the case of a newborn baby, which is nothing but instinct, to realise this. On the other hand from the very first the infant is trained up in non-instinctual ways, in which the speech, skills, and values of the community are transmitted to it. By these means an individual is shaped; his existence becomes human as opposed to animal; and this is the work of society. In that sense, then, we can say that society is the indispensable condition of a human being. Yet this is not the same as regarding man as a purely social product; his personal traits have not been superseded, but rather incorporated into the prevailing ethos.

Now it is just this compound of instinctual and non-instinctual that is peculiar to man, and from it arises the psychology of human nature. In the first place whatever the circumstances into which a man is born he still has the needs of his species; and if these are overridden, if say, the taboos of sex are so great as to make it something clandestine, or he is instilled with fear, then there is conflict between the outward forms of expression and inner needs. While the pressure of society may make him conform to its standards, their very imposition can lead to constriction and conflicts: how they are resolved will depend upon the individual, as we have already remarked, but whatever the outcome they point to the need to examine the sources of a man's actions and not simply to assume that he is what he professes. Otherwise when men act irrationally or savagely we shall take these actions at their face values and so conclude that men are fundamentally irrational and warlike, whereas the truth would probably be found through examining those feelings as manifestations of a psychological state that had its source not in human nature as such but in the individuals' own histories.

This leads us to the second point, namely, that what we understand by human nature is essentially man at different stages of social development: medieval man was predominantly religious, modern man is predominantly not; some tribes are cannibalistic, the majority of mankind is not; some men in Britain at present favour hanging, others do not. These differences that are all characteristic of certain groups of men only go to show that they are not inherent in anything we call human nature but the result of different milieus. It helps to emphasise that what we frequently take for human nature is in fact human nature at a particular juncture and in particular circumstances, and that if we say, for example, that 'all men are warlike or greedy', we are really making a statement to the effect that 'given the circumstances of tribal society or inflation-ridden, starving post-1918 Germany or the Emperor worship of Japan, man can be brought to believe that war or wealth is the highest glory or duty or necessity, no matter what the cost'. Accordingly we are back at our original position, namely, that human nature cannot be the preserve of a theory of history; it belongs as much to the individuals who make up the human species, in the same way as any species can only be known through the study of its individuals.

From this we come to the second reason for the inadequacy of the materialist conception of man: that man remains at the level of an abstraction. If he is regarded simply as the personification of a specific social order, whether in its aspect of the ruling or the exploited class, he is in effect reduced to little more than a cypher. We therefore see him as neither a fullbodied person, nor as he really is, but as he appears. We fail to penetrate below the surface of his own persona. Now this may be valid if our concern is not with individuals *in se* but simply as agents in an historical process. If this is the case, then let it not be confused with the disclosure of human nature, for they are not the same. We are then viewing men in an exclusively social light and hence only one aspect of them; and it precludes considerations that are indispensable to an understanding of human conduct: their motives, the nature of their feelings, and the forms they take. Without such an assessment there can be not even an elementary insight into the workings of men's minds at different junctures in history.

Nowhere is this more apparent than in the study of social change that is the main interest of Marxism. There the questions of power and of mass human action are paramount. Yet how can we presume to understand them if we do not study their effects upon men? Take the question of power: Marxism likes to pretend that like all such traits this has nothing to do with human nature: that it is merely the product of particular situations. But this is only a further example of its lack of interest in man other than as an abstraction. In fact striving for power and abuse of power have been one of the constant themes in human history uniting Pisistratus to Stalin; nor has it ended with the advent of the Dictatorship of the Proletariat. For that reason alone it must be taken seriously; empirically it is established as one of the social constants to be found wherever men are gathered together, from the local village institute to the highest councils of state. It springs from the need of every individual by virtue of being an individual to establish his individuality and not to be, metaphorically, trodden underfoot. In the same way as any living thing, vegetable or animal, he has to establish his place in the sun. Just as we are born with certain instincts indispensable for survival, so we are endowed with capacities and bents that we desire to realise and that are equally indispensable to our personalities. In seeking to gratify these we are asserting ourselves: did we not do so we should accomplish nothing because we should be nothing. Now it is precisely the reciprocal assertiveness of individuals in society that can lead to the desire for power. No person can normally do all that he desires, because his wishes will conflict with those of others, and therefore, at the very least, there must be some mutual curb upon any one individual's proclivities. But over and above this there are the specific limitations that attach to different societies. If the majority of men are precluded from following their individual bents, either through inadequate opportunity, or class privilege, or social stigma, or parental prejudice, this can only lead to an atmosphere of fear and struggle, of 'the devil take the hindmost', so that self-realisation is transformed into aggressive self-preservation. In these ways the possession of power becomes bound up with individual expression. So far there has always been some kind of social limitation upon self-development and therefore we might say that, given different circumstances, men would not seek power as in the past and that personal expression would not entail the desire for power. But we have still not taken account of the abuse of power that so often accompanies possession.

This is both an individual and a social question. It is individual in the sense not only that individuals abuse power but the nature of the abuse must be sought in the individual; we are thus once again led to a man's own history, since his reactions will be from his own experience. For example, the proverbial incitement to assert himself attributed to the upbringing of George III of England was clearly instrumental in his subsequent attempts at a more personal government; there was nothing in history that decreed that he had to act as he did. The same applies to Stalin or Rakosi; even if they believed that they were really surrounded by enemies, we must seek the causes of their barbarities in themselves as well as in history.

The social aspect of power enters with the general tendency for power to transform a man from his previous self; the ratio of his self-importance to his importance increases geometrically; he tends to becomes less tolerant or considerate of individuals and frequently becomes tyrannous. This is an almost invariable consequence of power. It is so universal that only the exceptional individual has not succumbed to it. The abuse of power has been so much a constant in human behaviour that no adequate view of history can leave it out of account as Marxism has done. It demands stringent institutional safeguards.

The same applies to mass movements in society. Marxism, in its idealisation of the masses, has never, so far as I am aware, considered the nature of mass psychology. Yet it is with the masses that it believes the future to rest; and the whole of communist strategy and tactics are directed to rousing them to revolutionary action. Now everyone knows the vast difference between the mental state of an individual and that of a crowd. With the former, unless he is an exceptional individual, the sanctions of society will tend to prevail. Except when he is drunk or otherwise released from normal constraints he will tend to observe its laws and customs and shy away from doing anything that might mark him out from the rest of his fellows. Far from challenging society, the majority of people are only too content to make their peace with it; and this submission to social convention can, as we have already discussed, be a potent source of tension, as between the satisfaction of personal cravings and the demands of the group. Man's gregariousness exercises a constant pull, often against his own inclinations; it provides him with his sense of social duty, which we call conscience; and although it can take many forms according to the code of society it is inherent in his nature as a social being.

Once however part of a crowd, men feel released from the usual restraints; they no longer take the same responsibility for their personal conduct, since they merge their own personality with that of the crowd and take on its feelings. It is precisely at this juncture that pent-up tensions assert themselves; often it may be over the most trivial incident, and a whole wave of emotion envelops them. This is too much a common occurrence to need stressing. It has occurred throughout history, from Mark Antony's funeral oration to the Hungarian rising of 1956 and the latest Guy Fawkes Night. It takes place on a minor scale every week-end outside many dance halls and public houses. It is ever-present among the rank and file of the army in their disavowal of all the niceties of accepted convention. It need not always be destructive and violent, otherwise football would long since have become the scene of civil war, but it can only too easily be turned to destructive ends. Indeed perhaps the most telling thing about the crowd is the ease with which violence and hatred can supervene, and the rapidity with which it can spread. We have only to think of the War of 1914 and the way in which war hysteria engulfed whole nations of law-abiding, outwardly peaceable citizens; or of Nazi Germany.

Such mass movements evince a definite psychology, akin to paranoia, in which the sense of righteousness takes on abnormal proportions. It is then that men kill and die for what in the harsh light of reflection appears trivial. How else are we to account for the fervour with which men throughout history have been possessed to perpetrate the outrages that they have, outrages that go against their normal life? The pogroms of the People's Crusade or Hitler's Germany are the product of hysteria, of a frame of mind needed for the slaying of one's enemies. The mass leader and the dema-gogue succeed because they themselves are possessed of such an emotional state: in a lesser degree it is present at most meetings and conferences. It no doubt helps to account for the general low cerebral content of political speeches. One has only to read a report of a rousing speech in the aftermath of cold print to marvel at its effect, yet had one been among the crowd when it was delivered one would also probably have been carried away.

All this has an important bearing upon history. In the first place, it points to a definite psychology of revolution: neither its leaders nor its followers can be judged in normative terms. We see men at an unwonted pitch in which their initial intentions can be overborne by the violence of their emotions; hence the instability of the entire process and the rapidity with which it rises and disintegrates; hence the need for constant and ever palpable success if demoralisation is not to set in; hence its destructive force.

In the second place, we may legitimately ask whether mass movements are a desirable way of achieving change, or rather, whether they tend not to be self-defeating, conferring power upon those best able to inflame feeling and making hatred the main driving force. Once such forces have been set in train they are hard to reverse: neither the French Revolution nor the Russian Revolution produced new and shining societies, necessary though they both were. We shall discuss this further in the last chapter.

Finally there is the implication for the materialist conception of history. It seems a flagrant inconsistency to make the discrepancy between reality and appearance fundamental to an understanding of social consciousness and yet to take men's individual actions at their face value; so that if they revolt or proclaim revolution or, as with the Second International, renounce revolution, they are revolutionaries or renegades tout court. If it is superficial and misleading to judge an epoch by its conscious manifestations, it is equally so with men, and the failure to adopt the same criterion for both displays the most glaring inconsistency, to say nothing of the deleterious consequences historically. It is never to go beyond regarding men as units in the onward march of society. It is never to pause to consider whether men might be motivated by more than class interest, but implicitly to assume that they are just social units that differ from ants in being able not only to control nature and to transform their social organisation but also in their ability to give conscious expression to their activities. No one would pretend that these differences are not vast; but as they stand they are inadequate; for, in the last resort, they make the same assumption about men as about ants—that they both build societies, however differently. To do so is to ignore the salient characteristic of man: that his adjustment to society is neither automatic nor uniform and that one of the features of all societies hitherto has been a tension between the demands of society and the needs of an individual through the imposition of constraints.

As a consequence man cannot be judged solely by his external activities or public pronouncements, but by the attitudes he evinces and of which he himself may be unaware. In history these often manifest themselves in sudden outbursts of violence, and may well be motivated by causes other than class feeling or class oppression. Similarly the desire for power, couched though it may be in terms of a social ideal, and representing a particular class, may have quite other causes that lie with an individual's own history. Rather than make his class position the cause of his personal actions, he might well use the former as an instrument to further the latter. Thus it is idle to regard men like Luther or Robespierre simply as personifications of the rising bourgeoisie and to imagine that one has thus explained the wellsprings of their actions, without having first examined them as individuals, to determine whether they did not rather utilise the circumstances to assert themselves. Either is a priori conceivable, but neither is certain; and it is unwarrantable to assume otherwise.

Finally, as corollary, the irreducible differences among individuals preclude any invariable universal explanation of human actions. Even when we have characterised the prevailing habits of society, we have not thereby explained the nature of the men who comprise it. This is particularly apparent the more complex a society is. At the present time, in which, according to Marxists, bourgeois society is in its death throes, there is probably a greater proportion of people performing life-enhancing jobs than ever before: caring for children, refugee relief, cancer research, and so on. Similarly, the range of non-productive, non-class activities in which people are engaged, bird-watching, stamp collecting, games playing, music making and so on, points to the same inescapable conclusion, namely, that men's productive activities and class positions at the most provide only one kind of data — that of the social structure of a given society; they cannot compass the whole of human nature. This however is what historical materialism attempts to do, with the result that it assumes, albeit unconsciously, that man is a

passive product of a given society that he fits in the way a
hand should fit a glove. But in fact far from one being the
precise measure of the other, men revolt continually against
the impositions of society, if not overtly and socially, then in
themselves; and the desire to escape the constrictions of a
particular system, whether at the mere economic level or
from its ethos or mode of thought, provides one of the great
sources of social dynamics.

Only if we are prepared to acknowledge these purely
personal responses to a given social situation, shall we gain
any insight into men's nature. It was in his capacity of a
thinker concerned with the truth and not as a representative
of the rising bourgeoisie that Newton reached his new cosmic
theories. True he was able to do so because the conditions
were such that his interpretation was both possible and
necessary, whereas had he lived three hundred years earlier
he would probably have been a scholastic instead; but this
still does not explain Newton, and his passions, in any terms
but Newton's response to what he found about him. In the
same way, Arnold of Brescia and Lenin were revolutionaries
not because their class was oppressed but because they
reacted as individuals against the social system. Had the
system not been unjust they could hardly have done so and
in this sense circumstances were contributory to their actions;
but this is not the same as saying that they were determined to
do what they did. On the contrary there was no social
rationale that compelled them to adopt the positions they chose
at a time when the vast majority of their class accepted what
they opposed. Theirs was one possible individual response to
a given situation (as we shall discuss below), and it helps to
show that if man is 'the ensemble of social relations', it is
not enough to subsume him under them. At most they are a
starting point for fuller understanding. The proper study of
mankind is man, the whole man. For this, knowledge of
all his facets, not one, is needed. Accordingly historical
materialism is not enough.

V. KNOWLEDGE AND IDEOLOGY

We come next to the role of consciousness, and more especially the forms to which it gives rise and their function.[102] For Marxism this is essentially the problem of relating the economic structure of society to 'the legal and political superstructure to which correspond definite forms of social consciousness'.[103] It proceeds as we have seen from the assumption that, 'The mode of production of material life conditions the social, political and intellectual life process in general'.[104] Now the problem to be faced is twofold. Firstly, how are we to characterise men's intellectual attainments, science, language, writing, art, and so on, that form the heritage of civilisation? Do we regard them as simply the products of particular social orders, the ideological forms in which men express 'their material behaviour'? Or do we regard them as part of the actual productive forces that go to make up a particular mode of production, as instruments of production? Or are they neither? Or a combination of both? Secondly, there is the more general question of the role of ideas in society: how far are they to be regarded as the product of a given social order and how far do they play an active part in all knowledge?

Let us begin with the first group of questions. The very way in which they have been raised is, I think, indicative of the preoccupations of Marxism. They are a further example of the schematic thinking that is engendered by dialectics. In this case it has meant a false model of society, where what were presumably for Marx metaphorical divisions have been taken literally. Marx's own phraseology is very largely to blame; for when he spoke of the 'legal and political superstructures to which correspond definite forms of social consciousness'[105] this was interpreted by Engels and subsequent

102. I have since treated the subject more fully in *History and Social Theory*, Part Two.

103. Preface to *The Critique of Political Economy*, *Selected Works*, Vol. I, p. 329.

104. *Ibid.*   105. *Ibid.*

Marxists to mean that knowledge itself reflected the super-structure of society. Thus Engels in his letter to Bloch says: 'The economic situation is the basis, but the various elements of the superstructure—political forms of the class struggle and its consequences, constitutions established by the victorious class after a successful battle etc.—forms of law—and then *even the reflexes* of *all these actual struggles in the brains of the combatants: political, legal, philosophical theories, religious ideas*[106] and their further developments into systems of dogma—also exercise their influence. . . .'.[107] This is clearly to make knowledge a superstructural phenomenon, not just in the sense that it reflects the economic basis but in that it springs from the institutions to which the basis gives rise. In doing so knowledge was condemned to having its genesis in the self-justification of the ruling class and not regarded as the product of the activities of society as a whole. As a result we are presented, as we have already discussed, with two layers of society that must be harmonised into a definite causal sequence. The effect has been to reduce a complicated body of phenomena—art, science, language, and so on—to certain mechanical components that, as the above questions illustrate, give rise to a serious dilemma. On the one hand, given that men's ideas are the product of 'their material behaviour', they will express their condition: thus in the case of class society they will represent the outlook of the dominant class; they will therefore interpret life and existence in terms of the social order that prevails, accepting it without question as the natural, eternal state of mankind. In that sense these ideas will not be a correct vision of the truth but a false conscious-ness where, said Engels, 'The real motives impelling him [a thinker] remain unknown to him . . . He works with mere thought material which he accepts without examination as the product of thought'.[108] On the other hand, however, it is clearly untenable to regard mathematics, logic, language, and various intellectual techniques as the purely transitory efflux

106. My italics, G. L.
107. Marx and Engels, *Selected Correspondence*, p. 475.
108. Engels, 'Letter to Mehring,' *Selected Correspondence*, p. 511.

of a particular historical and class (false) consciousness. By the very fact that they outlast any particular epoch they are of universal validity. They must therefore represent true knowledge quite independently of the uses to which it is put, or indeed how it originates. Of recent years, especially since the publication of Stalin's *Concerning Marxism in Linguistics* in 1950,[109] this second aspect has come to the fore and the older tendency to think in terms of bourgeois science and bourgeois logic as opposed to science and logic in themselves[110] has been corrected. In his pamphlet Stalin laid it down that language was neither of the base nor of the superstructure, since it is 'the product of the whole course of the history of the society and of the history of the bases for many centuries. It was created not by any one class but by the whole of society, by all the classes of society, by the efforts of hundreds of generations[111]. Yet in doing so he did not alter the rigid division between the two; despite his words on the active nature of the superstructure it still corresponds to a given basis, so that in effect he merely exempted language from the clutches of either.

We need only turn to any other intellectual activities however to see how inadequate such a conception is. Mathematics, logic, the natural sciences can all claim the same exemption on the grounds that when one social system succeeds another they do not suddenly become outmoded. Similarly with great works of art, whether the Venus of Milo, or the poetry of Dante or Shakespeare; or again with inventions like the wheel, the compass, or the theory of the circulation of the blood. If we are to regard all these forms of consciousness as having been called forth from a certain economic structure for the purpose of sustaining the social order to which they belong, then the entire sphere of intellectual activity becomes incomprehensible. In the first place, we should have to be able to relate, however remotely, each

109. See for example, the articles in *Communist Review* (London) for December 1951, January, February and April 1952.
110. Lukács, *op. cit.*, leans towards this view, for example, pp. 129–34.
111. *Ibid.*, pp. 4–5.

such product to the prevailing society—a task that is palpably fruitless and impossible. What grounds are there for characterising Euclid's theorems as upholding or in any way pertaining to the structure of the Greek city state? What is the class content of electronics? What social purpose did Buridan's theory of impetus serve in fourteenth-century France? Who is to say whether Shakespeare or Michaelangelo were supporters of the existing social order or not? And if they were, how does it help to explain the power or the nature of their art in any but circumstantial terms? In the second place, it is the grossest of errors to think of knowledge, or indeed its main branches, science, art, philosophy, as generic terms to be contraposed to productive activities; and herein lies another instance of the fallacy of the basis-superstructure dichotomy. It assumes that certain activities and the men practising them belong to one and others to the other. Thus the philosopher, the artist, the scientist are of the superstructure, while the miner and the steelworker are of the basis. But this is nonsensical. Art, science, philosophy, and so on cannot simply be bandied about as though they were unitary entities that can be located in a specific plane; least of all can they be thought of simply as superstructural products.

To begin with, no intellectual activity that is to carry any weight at all—and the discussion is here directed to those which have a social significance—is simply the product of a superstructure. Let us take the most basic and superstructural of all elements: an idea. For there to be an idea, there must be the techniques of language, of conceptual thought, and observance of the form appropriate to it as an intellectual discipline; and none of these is the property of a specific historical superstructure but part of the indispensable equipment of civilisation. That the idea may be of the most partial and transitory nature does not make it any more the sole product of a given epoch. A poem likewise may accept every prevailing assumption that is peculiar to its milieu—say a belief in demons, in fate, in monsters, yet in order to be a poem it needs the technique of rhythm, of heightened language, or imagery, and so on. A history or a philosophical system may be entirely from the point of view of the ruling class—the present order may be sacrosanct, what happens is the will of God, men must remain in the stations to which they are called, and so on—but it demands the techniques peculiar to it. The same applies to a scientist, who whether he is working to blow the world to pieces or to alleviate suffering, must be master of the (normally neutral) techniques that govern his subject. To look at any or all of these as the property of either the productive forces or the institutions prevailing is, in my view, a profound mistake.

This can be seen from the nature of intellectual activities themselves. When we talk about art and science do we really mean the production of ideas and knowledge in conformity with the basis and superstructure? Let us first take the 'scientist': he is not simply one of a uniform species; if he is an engineer, he may well be in direct contact with the productive forces, building bridges or machinery; if a physicist or a chemist or mathematician, he may be either applying his knowledge to industry, to agriculture, or to medicine, or he may be engaged in theoretical research divorced from any direct practical activity. None of these cases implies a uniform relationship to either the basis or the superstructure; indeed except in cases of the most strictly theoretical kind, in which philosophical assumptions may well enter, it seems incontrovertible that the logic of the subject in question is the sole determinant of activity. If a society changes from one system to another, the second law of thermodynamics does not change with it; it may be put to new applications and new interpretations may result; but these, although called forth by the basis or superstructure, still cannot be called their product; their validity will rest upon conformity with accepted scientific truth, which remains independently of any system.

With art and philosophy the case differs in degree rather than in kind. Language, logic and the techniques of perspective, rhythm, counterpoint, and so on, that form the foundation of such knowledge, stand in the same relation to a particular epoch as the more strictly scientific activities: that is to say, their validity is independent of the class or society that operates them: the law of the excluded middle no more loses its efficacy through the replacement of one system by another than $2 \times 2 = 4$; and even the principles of law—the most susceptible of all forms of knowledge to superstructural influences—are not lightly thrown over as we can see from the preservation of Roman law. Their difference from the exact and formal sciences lies in their criteria. The subject-matter of the human studies and art is human experience. They refer to us and our responses, whether to nature, society, or individual experience. Their evaluations are therefore qualitative and ever liable to change, according to the meaning that the world has for us. For that reason there is far greater variation that can run in a spectrum from myth and pure imagination at one extreme to intellectual disciplines empirically based at the other. But even the most rigorous philosophical system remains an interpretation just because human experience and values are themselves variables and colour our notion of reality. There is no single obligatory way in which we have to regard human conduct or beauty in the way that we have to know the structure of a rock crystal; for where knowledge of the latter is based upon invariable laws, our evaluation of ourselves is contingent upon our system of values. They are therefore more susceptible to change and social pressure.

If this makes for conformity, by the same token it also leads to fundamental divergences from the prevailing outlook. There has always been a Socrates, an Ockham, a Galileo, a Pasternak to challenge orthodoxy; and it is a long standing and deep-rooted fallacy of Marxism to have identified all who are articulate with the ideologists of a dominant class. This has never been true; even in the supposedly intellectual totalitarianism of the Middle Ages one has only to look at the ever-present challenge from dangerous doctrines of one sort or another or to the sermon literature of the fourteenth and fifteenth centuries to see how heterogeneous the intellectual climate was. Moreover, and this is of the greatest importance, the challenge usually was made from within the framework of the then current assumptions. It was not so much to posit an alternative order as to defend the inviolable principles that were commonly held and were being flouted, as for example, in the attacks upon non-Christian practice during the Middle Ages, where the heretics were those who demanded a radical conformity with primitive Christianity. Accordingly it is misleading to regard ideas, even when the direct epitome of the outlook of society, as always buttressing the super-structure.

The mistake of the basis and superstructure model is that it confuses the validity of what we know and experience with how we have come to know and experience it. It thereby makes nonsense of the nature of knowledge and art. On the one hand, the logic of this position is that knowledge must itself vary according to whether it is superstructural or non-superstructural, with absurd results. A composer, say, who, as many twentieth-century composers have done, collected folk tunes would thereby be writing non-superstructural music; but one who wrote an opera for a (capitalist) state opera would be merely producing ideological music. Similarly a painter living in a fishing village remote from government and authority would in depicting fishermen at work be producing non-superstructural paintings and so would a poet non-superstructural poetry who lived in the country and wrote about sheep rearing. Even intellectual disciplines would depend for their validity as knowledge upon whether they concerned the base or the superstructure: indeed a Marxist historian has gone so far as to say that administrative history, in dealing with the state machine, is *ipso facto* reactionary. Viewed in this way, art and knowledge lose any independent criteria by which they can be judged.

On the other hand, it leads to the separation of what is inseparable. In one sense all knowledge is ideological in that it arises out of men's experience at a given time. It thereby develops in the context of what is already known and how it is regarded. But this does not make it reducible to that context. To begin with there is no single standpoint that makes experience the same for all men. What we call an ideology is not a unitary set of values but an abstraction of what we regard the dominant traits of in an outlook. As such it is neither separable into a superstructure nor to be regarded as a universal causal term under which the artistic and intellectual activities of an entire society can be subsumed. In the second place, an outlook that purports to be that of a society must by definition belong to society as a whole. To that extent it must be in some degree common to all its members; as such to plagiarise Marx it is in the very pores of society, not existing above it. It represents the practices, values, and interests that prevail in its system of law, institutions, technology, culture, and conception of man and the world. To some degree these affect all who come within it, even if only negatively in delimiting the area of action and consciousness To that extent no activity can be purely superstructural. A miner is not simply a hewer of coal nor is his outlook simply conditioned by his productive activity. He participates unavoidably in the outlook of his society, both as the recipient of its technology—electricity, television, hygiene, and so on—and the area of values that concern him, such as the right to strike, the expectation of full employment, to say nothing of the common culture that he receives through education and the mass media.

But these represent only the most general level at which ideology can be treated as a universal phenomenon. To pretend that it determines the content of all men's intellectual activities is to fail to recognise its standing. It is a concept that resumes the product of men's different social activities. It cannot therefore either stand independently of them or be made to serve as their material cause. More specifically it bears no relationship to the structure of knowledge and artistic forms. These are governed by their own distinctive criteria that define them. As we have said the principles of mathematics owe nothing to who was ruling whom. On the contrary it is precisely in having their own logic that they develop and remain valid independently of place and time. From this it follows that the practitioners of

any discipline operate within their own autonomous system.
Far from being governed by the prevailing ideology they for
the most part bear no intelligible relation to it; it is a characteristic of knowledge that, unlike the crude Marxist notion of
ideology, it is independent of space-time. Were we to adopt the
Marxist view there would be no means of explaining the
relevance of Aristotle's *Posterior Analytics* or Pythagoras's
theorem to twentieth-century logic or geometry, let alone of
Antigone or Monteverdi's *Vespers*. Their continuing validity
lies in the independent validity of the branches to which they
belong. This is not a matter of ideological theory but of intellectual practice. The motive force in all intellectual development is the tension between assumptions and experience;
between what men have accepted as given and the need to
re-align it with what they come to see differently, whether in
modifying scientific propositions to meet new data or in a
poet's experience. It is therefore the work of individuals and
groups who have refined upon that experience. This is not
the common property of entire classes. Each thinker or artist
interprets a particular segment of the world in terms of his
own vision, compounded of his assumptions, ideals, and
interests, his own position in society, and the time and place
in which he lives. His intellectual activity is therefore more
than a superstructural efflux; it embraces the past as well as
the present—and its efficacy will depend upon its meaning
for the future. Ideology, as the system of values from which
he begins, can only be a limiting factor: it can provide his
orientation and impede or aid the development of his ideas.
But it cannot determine the structure or the significance of
what he produces; least of all can it be evaluated according
to the preponderance of non-superstructural over superstructural elements.[112] If, then, all knowledge is ideological
in that it is partial and rests upon certain assumptions and is
directed to particular ends, this is not the same as the Marxist
belief in false-consciousness. Rather it corresponds to men's
experience at any given time. Far from this making it without

112. As implied for instance by Cornforth, *Theory of Knowledge*, pp.
128-9, in his treatment of science.

value it provides its *raison d'être*. Let us take as an instance the case of Dante: his outlook and assumptions were essentially medieval in every respect and yet he is universally acknowledged to be one of the great poets of all time, even for those who do not share his outlook and for whom hell, with its nine circles, purgatory, and heaven have no meaning. Are we to say, then, as the logic of the Marxist position would have us, that this is because the superstructural elements embodied in his theology are out-weighed by the non-superstructural elements of his poetry? If so how are we to assess the latter? By his use of words, images and rhythms? By his imaginative powers? But by what criterion are we to do so? Who is to say what is a non- or suprasuperstructural use of language? And even if we were to reach such a judgement how should we test its validity? Are we not ourselves the products of superstructure, in which case we should be committing the illogicality of one superstructure judging another for non-superstructural elements. The whole conception, apart from defying rational analysis, overlooks this all-important point that the source of Dante's poetry was the very outlook which was according to Marxism the product of a now outmoded superstructure. In this sense his art was wrought from a false consciousness. The same applies to every work of art; its power and meaning lie precisely in the feelings and concepts which it expresses and which are what they are in virtue of expressing the then prevailing (distorted) outlook. What would *Paradise Lost* be without Milton's Christian fervour? And yet are we to say it lives in spite of rather than because of it? For that is what the Marxist position amounts to. It fails to recognise that Dante and Milton are what they are by virtue of their beliefs, and that these cannot be separated from their work.

Similarly with scientific discoveries and new theories; they have come about, as with Copernicus, frequently for the (scientifically) wrong reasons and yet led to a correct scientific result. We may then say that the result was of value because it transcended its superstructural limitations in denying the assumptions from which Copernicus started. Yet it is equally true that the latter was its cause in providing him with his starting point. Once again we are confronted with an artificial distinction between what are essentially integral elements. It becomes a mere arbitrary piece of scholasticism, when the proper test lies with the retrospective effect of the discovery: it enhanced knowledge and led to a revolutionary and fruitful new way of regarding the solar system: therein lies its validity. Hence knowledge lives not because of some indefinable alchemy as between superstructural and non-superstructural elements that frequently cannot be defined with precision and never with logic, but because it is efficacious for succeeding generations. This efficacy is not of a uniform kind: it may be, as with scientific theories, that it is true or that it responds to some chord in the spirit of the age (as for example the revival of the seventeenth-century metaphysical poets a generation ago) or that they still provide an insight, a beauty, a methodology, a philosophy, and so on that enhance life. To paraphrase Marx, the question whether knowledge is false or true is not a theoretical but a practical question: man must prove the truth.

This leads us to the second part of the problem, the role of ideas; for it is only when we know the nature of the concepts to which men hold at any given time that we can evaluate them. That is to say, what men believe and the truth of their beliefs are two different things and are not to be confused. The theory of basis and superstructure does confuse them with results which we have adumbrated. Instead of taking it as given that at a certain juncture men believe in say demons or slavery, and proceeding to investigate the assumptions that underly these conceptions, Marxism works from the other way. It measures an idea from its ultimate consequences: that is to say whether it enhances or impedes the advance of knowledge. According to its effect it is judged to be super-structural or non-superstructural. Archimedes' Law, say, was progressive and thereby not a mere ideological expression of the outlook of the ancient Greek state, whereas Aristotle's view of slavery, in upholding the interests of the exploiting class, was simply superstructural. Quite apart from the inconsistencies (how, then, to account for the fact that Aristotle also invented logic which was—presumably—non-superstructural?) and the unworkability, examples of which we have already given, such an approach is palpably at variance with the first principles of historical materialism. If ideas are not to be treated as self-subsisting entities but as the expression of a particular way of life, they cannot therefore be allocated to basis or superstructure merely according to their long-term effects; they must be understood in their context. To do this means examining the framework within which they were conceived: how men looked at nature, man, the universe, society, the after-life, and so on; what the state of their knowledge was; how it was practised, for what purposes, and by whom; and to what developments it led. Only thus can we arrive at an adequate characterisation of the intellectual outlook of an epoch. Men's knowledge, like society itself, is only incidentally of a class nature, as we have already argued at length: despite all the ideological distortions—such as a defence of slavery or monarchy or tyranny—it must be *au fond* an adjunct to men's practical life, furthering their activities; otherwise it will perish. The knowledge that $2 \times 2 = 4$ was as necessary to medieval society as to socialist society; and the same applies to all knowledge. It in no way conflicts with the assumption that 'some men are natural slaves'; for each is a valid aspect of life for a particular phase of history. Indeed the same people who accept the latter assumption were also developing mathematical theory as was the case in ancient Greece.

Now this, I submit, is the central feature of all ideology: namely, that there is no invariable correlation between the scientific validity of an idea and the intellectual circumstances from which it arose. On the contrary, far from a scientific idea being the product of a scientific outlook it is as likely to be the outcome of an amalgam of faith, prejudice, intuition, teleology, in short a series of preconceptions that cannot be broken down into anything approaching a consistent scientific attitude. Certainly this is true for all past intellectual development, in which rational activity took place within a non-rationalist framework. The Pythagoreans developed geometry while believing in the mysterious properties of numbers; the great advance in fourteenth-century science took place as a direct reassertion of the unknowability of God's will and therefore of the rejection of the fixed cosmology of Aristotle. Newton for all his explanation in terms of atoms still believed that everything was set in motion by God, and the belief in a supreme architect for the universe remains widespread among scientists. These instances are almost too obvious to be mentioned; but their very triteness reinforces the contention that we cannot judge the nature of an idea solely from its subsequent import. Every idea is the product of specific men living in a certain milieu at a certain time. As such it will bear the impress of all the influences and limitations of which they are the bearers, and hence can never be merely objective: the state of scientific knowledge, the conception of the universe and nature, the personal intentions, theories, and presuppositions of the thinker concerned will all go to determine his thinking. That he may arrive at some quite new theory of the greatest significance for the future in no way alters the nature of his *original* thinking, though it may revolutionise it subsequently; and it is at this point that evaluation enters.

In view of what has been said there cannot, I suggest, be any invariable rule for assessing the ideological nature, or otherwise, of knowledge. It is essentially a matter for individual analysis to discover whether an idea has no intellectual content other than a merely slavish endorsement of the existing outlook. What can be said is that the less palpable an idea, the more it is a matter of values rather than of ascertainable fact, the more it is likely to be ideological, even should it outlast the circumstances in which it arose. Concepts such as Plato's theory of forms or the belief in original sin are clearly of this order as opposed to scientific theories. Their continuing relevance will be in the needs of society, or at least of that group that has a controlling voice, and may well, as Marxists are so fond of telling us, act as a fetter upon further intellectual development. All this seems patent enough. The important point is to assess the role that such an idea plays and its effects upon social thinking and the pursuit of knowledge.

This cannot be done simply in the schematic terms that Marxists are accustomed to employ, namely, as Cornforth puts it: 'The dominant ideology in any period is that of the ruling class. And when this ideology is challenged, that is but the expression of the fact that the existing state of class relations is being challenged by another class'.[113] Even the most cursory study of a period of history will not bear out such stark over-simplification, which indeed amounts to falsification. It takes no account of the internal logic of ideas themselves: that is, the fact that one idea leads to another, frequently with the effect of a chain reaction, often quite as independently of the intentions of the thinkers themselves as the complex of assumptions on which their thinking is based. How else, for example, are we to explain sudden breaches of the prevailing conceptions by some new revolutionary idea? Can we meaningfully regard Newton, Pasteur, Einstein as the representatives of new social forces, who are somehow speaking for the interests of a new class, rather than as the inheritors of a particular line of thinking from which they made new discoveries? The very question seems to reflect a confusion between two distinct things. One is the extent to which the conditions in society make a change in attitude possible; the other is that these changes are the result of a change in the balance of class forces of which new thinking and thinkers are the representatives. The second seems to me to be quite untenable, where it is not fruitless. It assumes firstly that there can be no change in outlook without a corresponding change in social structure; secondly that all such intellectual developments are but a reflection of a specific class position; and thirdly that intellectual progress can only be from the representatives of a rising class. These positions are tantamount to the passivity of ideas; for in the failure to come to terms with the fact that both knowledge and ideology inhere in any outlook, it assumes that all know-

113. *Ibid.*, p. 105.

ledge must serve class interests. This may be so very remotely but any examination of the way knowledge is advanced will show that these are immanent in the structure of the social order rather than active agents. While no one could deny that at certain revolutionary phases, a series of revolutionary ideas arise that directly challenge the old order, this does not explain the development of knowledge during the intervening centuries during which the same social order prevails; nor does it apply to doctrines which are not concerned with society. Let us take as an example the process that leads to a new development in science or knowledge, say, Einstein's theory of relativity: whether or not it received its impetus from the Morley Michelson experiments,[114] it would be hard to deny that his efforts to comprehend the movement of the heavens were made on the basis of the state that physics had then reached. They arose from the need, and the desire on his part, to re-enunciate a theory that would account for the way in which particles of light behaved. What resulted was framed in terms of physics, terms so abstruse that they have no immediate bearing on lay knowledge, and even when they had been translated into more everyday language it is hard to discern their class content. It may be argued, as it has been by certain Marxists,[115] that Einstein's cosmology is that of the static world of the bourgeoisie. Maybe; but it has been on the basis of that world that something like a revolution in physics has been achieved and achieved at a time when bourgeois society had passed its zenith and was already in the last and imperialist stage of capitalism. Nor has their development been noticeably different in the Soviet Union.

The same process is even more apparent in the growth of practical knowledge. Capitalism is ageing, yet its death throes are accompanied by the greatest upsurge in science known to human history: within scarcely more than a half century a series of new sciences have evolved—electronics,

114. Polanyi, *op. cit.*, pp. 9–15, has argued that in fact it did not.
115. See, for example, H. Frankel, in *The Modern Quarterly*, Autumn, 1946, pp. 74–80.

cybernetics, biochemistry, nuclear physics, to name the most outstanding. 'Ah,' we shall be told, 'but these are largely due to the stimulus of war; compared with what man could achieve under socialism, capitalism cripples and distorts science'. To which the reply is that this is even stronger support for the momentum of knowledge in the face of such theoretically insuperable obstacles.

The full inadequacy of the Marxist theory is made manifest when we consider how these changes in knowledge come about. They are not the result of the bourgeoisie suddenly rising up in revolt against feudalism and thereby releasing a new and all-consuming liberation of men's minds, the continuing ripples from which explain the present flow of new knowledge. On the contrary, new developments are the result of individuals working within a common social discipline and following up problems that arise from existing knowledge. They may and do take place without any new class impetus; indeed, as contemporary society shows, they can do so at a time when the existing social order is on the wane. It may be true that there has to be a social impetus to stimulate particular aspects of knowledge but knowledge itself worthy of the name comes from the application of previous knowledge. Thus if linguistics or the study of history or archaeology have undergone vast developments during this century, the direction they have taken and the emphases adopted may well have been influenced by the change in views on society or progress or the scope of knowledge; but they will also be shaped by the techniques that develop and change as well. It is folly to try to divorce the two: we approach a subject with, as we have iterated, a vast number of presuppositions, some conscious, some unconscious, some intuitive, some scientific; we ask certain questions with the intention of solving certain problems and these are largely the expression of our initial attitudes. Yet what distinguishes the entire operation from a mere exercise in prejudice and self-interest is that it must be firmly founded in viable, socially accepted knowledge for it to be of the slightest validity. It is in this sense that knowledge and ideology inhere in any outlook and only changing circumstances sift the one from the other. It is in this sense also that ideas have an active role to play in society.

From what has been said we can formulate this as follows. Firstly, all ideas spring on the one hand from the assumptions and attitudes that at any one time provide men with their outlook and terms of reference, and on the other from the skills and techniques that constitute the different branches of knowledge. Together they represent both the prerequisites and the determinants of further development. They are prerequisites in that they provide the presuppositions and pose the problems; they are determinants in that initially they delimit the scope and direction that such development can take since it is with available techniques that the resources of knowledge lie. Secondly, far from being at the behest of transformations in society, a ferment of ideas can accompany the entrenchment of the old order; indeed the closest correlation between intellectual and social life tends to be found before great social change and not during or after it. We have only to think of the era of the Encyclopaedists in eighteenth-century France, as opposed to the French Revolution or the Empire; of England in the century from 1540 to 1640, as opposed to England from 1660 to 1760; of Russia from 1870 to 1917 as compared with subsequent orthodoxy, to take the outstanding cases. From this it would appear that changes in outlook are not contingent upon changes in society, but on the contrary precede them:[116] a man can reject an idea without rejecting his way of life; he can only reject his way of life when he rejects its concepts. Men have to be aware of their discontents before they can act upon them: Coke comes before Cromwell, Voltaire before Robespierre, for it is they who create the climate from which change springs. With ideas more remote from social activity, such as the theory of relativity, their independence of social change is far greater.

116. This argues strongly against the validity of Marxist periodisation according to the different modes of production—classical, feudal, capitalist and so on. I have since discussed this more fully in *History and Social Theory*, chap. 7.

A theory becomes outworn when it fails to satisfy certain intellectual requirements or when it conflicts with or impedes new knowledge. This can occur as well in capitalist United States as in socialist Russia and does not need to be accompanied by revolution. Moreover the very agents of change can be those most closely connected with prevailing order. A striking example is the intellectual development of the first half of the fourteenth century in North Western Europe. There we witness among the scholastics a growing rejection of the attempts to explain creation by reference to the movements of God's will and instead emphasis upon the autonomy of reason, on the one hand, for the natural order, and of faith, on the other, for the divine. The developments to which this led foreshadowed the modern dichotomy in which belief in God is a matter of faith and knowledge of the natural world is the object of natural understanding and not of first and final causes. Here indeed was a radical change in outlook, but it was the work of friars, monks, and ecclesiastics and not of a revolutionary urban bourgeoisie. Moreover it was accompanied by the spread of mysticism which far from being the work of 'reactionaries' constituted a rejection of the sacramental life of the Church. These were part of a widespread social and intellectual ferment that affected social, intellectual, political, and religious life equally. But he would be a bold man who attempted to diagnose its ills in Cornforth's terms as the result of 'the existing state of class relations being challenged by another class'. True these were not from the challenge of the bourgeoisie, the supplanters of feudalism, but from the peasantry whose conditions in France and England were exacerbated by the effects of the Hundred Years' War. Yet how are we to depict the changes in scholasticism just adverted to? Or the Great Schism in the Papacy? Or even the new political ideas of Marsilius of Padua and Wyclif? All these different events were certainly attacks upon the existing order, but there is not the remotest evidence that they were the work of a revolutionary class, unless we are to believe that it had infiltrated the Church, the Universities, and the Papacy. Surely the more simple and tenable explanation is that the existing institutions and ideas had reached their limits, and could no longer fulfil the spiritual, practical and intellectual functions which men demanded of them. But the reasons for this crisis are not to be found in any one simple explanation, least of all that of class conflict.

Our theoretical starting point then must be the recognition that changes in outlook are not necessarily geared to changes in production or to the emergence of new class forces, but that they arise when men are no longer prepared to accept the existing forms. This is their precondition; their causes must be sought in the circumstances of the time and in general they will be of three main orders; a revulsion against the prevailing outlook or institutions; the incompatibility of the prevailing order of society with the need or the desire for change; and the sheer logic of internal development whereby one concept leads to another. None of these presupposes either a change in the class structure of society or its challenge by a new group, as the history of scholasticism from say 1280 to 1350 illustrates. From it we can see all three influences at work: the rejection of the growing attempts to furnish a natural theology out of something approaching divine determinism; the condemnation of the consequences of this approach as unorthodox and a threat to faith by the university and ecclesiastical authorities at Paris and Oxford in 1277; and the growing emphasis upon the unknowability of God's will that resulted—and hence the lack of any firm knowledge of his actions. It is not necessary to attempt to establish a causal relationship between what are essentially moments in the same process. The *point d'appui* may be one or other, according to circumstances, and can only be discerned by investigation, not metaphysical speculation.

Finally therefore thought and knowledge transcend specific class interests; however strong a component the latter may be they cannot exist to the exclusion of a minimum of objective truth; otherwise any such knowledge would be worthless. In fact, however, ideas are not all of the same genus; men are concerned with other things than narrow class interest, even though it is unconscious. They have a natural curiosity that follows a multitude of different paths, from philosophy to exploration, and that defies any single universal causation. People play games, collect stamps, watch trains, walk 110 miles, and attempt to break all kinds of records not for unconscious class motives, but for as many reasons as there are activities: they may even enjoy doing so. The solemnity of the Marxist analysis forgets that history deals with men, not just classes. It also forgets that life is not simply one long round of deception and self-deception; but that, as Marx said, 'man must prove the truth': if some ideas express class interest, all ideas, to survive, must work. Thus over and above sectional interests there is the communal interest that affects all men: interest of how best to control natural forces, to know the world, and to be happy. It is from these that knowledge springs and is guaranteed, for whatever the distortions that arise from the limitations of an age, they will be balanced by men's need to know at least something of the truth.

VI. INEVITABILITY

We come now to our last consideration: the problem of inevitability in history, or how far all events are determined. From a Marxist point of view the position was stated by Engels, when he said: 'According to the materialist conception of history the determining element in history is *ultimately* the production and reproduction of real life. More than this neither Marx nor I have ever asserted. If therefore somebody twists this into the statement that the economic element is the *only* determining one he transforms it into a meaningless abstract and absurd phrase . . . There is an interaction of all these elements [i.e. 'political, legal, philosophical theories, religious ideas'], in which, amid all the endless *host* of accidents (i.e. of things and events whose inner connection is so remote or so impossible to prove that we can regard it as absent and neglect it), the economic motive finally asserts itself as necessary. . . .

'We make our own history, but in the first place under very

definite presuppositions and conditions. Among these the economic ones are finally decisive. But the political etc. ones, and indeed even the traditions which haunt human minds, also play a part although not the decisive one. . . .

'In the second place, however, history makes itself in such a way that the final result always arises from conflicts between many individual wills, of which each again has been made what it is by a host of particular conditions of life. Thus there are innumerable intersecting forces, an infinite series of parallelograms of forces which give rise to one resultant—the historical event. This again may be viewed as the product of a power which, taken as a whole, works *unconsciously* and without volition. For what each individual wills is obstructed by everyone else, and what emerges is something that no one willed'.[117]

I have chosen this passage rather than the one similar in *Ludwig Feuerbach*[118] in the hope that it may be a little more succinct; but I must confess that for once Engels's coherence of thought seems to have deserted him, and we are faced with sheer confusion as to what is the relation between laws and events: beyond the general proposition that, in addition to the interaction between basis and superstructure individual wills interact upon each other, we are told nothing.

The trouble once again lies in the metaphorical model of society that necessitates plunging below the surface through a series of layers to the source of events (the parallel with Freud can hardly be denied; but whereas Freud was concerned with the practical assimilation of the unconscious feelings to the conscious Marxism keeps them separate for evermore) It is no explanation at all to speak, as Engels does, of the economic motive finally asserting itself as necessary amid all the endless host of accidents; for if they are accidents they cannot be deduced from necessity. More to the point however is that Engels has been once again forced into a metaphysical position in posing necessity and accident as antino-

117. Engels, 'Letter to Bloch, Oct. 1890,' *Selected Correspondence*, pp. 475–6.
118. Chapter IV, pp. 26–7.

mies whereas, in fact, history is not thus divided. Every action has a framework of reference within which, of a number of possibilities, a particular one materialises. One part is not necessary and the other accidental; but rather, if we choose artificially to isolate a particular group of circumstances into an historical event, we have what we may call an historical situation that constitutes the starting point for further events. Now it is this situation, itself the product of previous events, that provides the framework for men's actions; and to the extent that they are compelled to take them into account— whether to accept them or to override them is immaterial— their actions are determined by them; that is to say, every action and event has a context, just as all men have a context, and these must be the starting point.

The real problem is to examine the nature of this context: how compelling it was, the likely consequences to which it could lead, and the effect it has upon the men who found themselves in it. Now clearly there is no universal way of characterising a given situation, and although Engels emphasises this, he nevertheless assumes that it proceeds from the basis via the superstructure to accidental events. Yet when we come to actual situations this advances us nowhere. Take, for example, the case of Frederick Barbarossa in the twelfth century. He was confronted with the inescapable fact that the position of the German king was no longer rooted in the material and social life of Germany. This in turn was the consequence of the growth of feudal power among the nobility enabling them to entrench themselves in the localities and exercise control. We can, if we care, go still further back and speak of the growth of feudal authority as inherent in the feudal mode of production. But when we reach Barbarossa the operative factor for him is the need to re-establish his material position vis-à-vis the nobility; and this involves at once economic and political power. Whatever Barbarossa attempts his actions will have their basis in these circumstances. To that extent they can be called determined, since they are there regardless of his choosing, and cannot be avoided. Yet that Barbarossa attempted to reassert imperial authority in Italy was one possible line of action that was not in any way predetermined; he could have acted differently in, say, concentrating all his efforts in Germany.

It is at this point that Engels's categorisation shows its irrelevance; for beyond seeking to understand the sequences of a series of actions, or rather their circumstances, history cannot meaningfully go. It is as otiose to ask why Barbarossa moved south in any terms but those of Barbarossa, as to seek for sociological reasons why one man likes brown bread and another one white. There are no doubt in both cases good ones but they are not reached except by reference to the people concerned. That is to say, there comes a point in history where the *dramatis personae* take over, when events cannot be broken down beyond their presence as personalities who are themselves the *determinants* in a given sequence of events. The task of the historian therefore is not, as Engels's dicta would imply, to trace back every event to some primal source, but to establish the conditions from which they arose.

The corollary of this contention is that the conditions will vary according to the events, and that these cannot be of a uniform kind. If we are dealing with painting or literature, it is folly to look for the same factors as when we try to trace the causes of Barbarossa's actions. This is particularly the case when confronted with the historian's cliché of a cultural resurgence, or renaissance. The first question not to ask, and which Marxism always asks, is why there were so many great painters in Quattrocento Florence or such great dramatists in Elizabethan England. Neither historical materialism nor any other science can explain why there were great men when there were, least of all why there were so many. Their presence instead of being the object of explanation should be taken as given, and we should seek to know what were the circumstances that caused them to congregate together and to make up a new movement. Here no simple sociological explanation can be adequate: the development in the medium, the chronology of the painters themselves, their mutual influences, the conditions under which they worked, are all indispensable. I can see no justification for invoking the economic factor as the ultimate cause in any more precise relation than if I were to say that ultimately only if men eat and sleep and breathe can they paint. Once we take such universal factors into account we are back at the first and final causes of scholasticism.

There remains finally the charge, levelled by Professor Berlin, that determinism deprives us of the power to make moral judgements, since, to quote him, 'At the very least—if we cannot swallow the notion of super-personal "spirits" or "forces"—we must admit that all events occur in discoverable, uniform, unaltering patterns; for if some did not, how could we find the laws of such occurrences? . . . Our values— what we think good and bad, important and trivial, right and wrong, noble and contemptible—all these are conditioned by the place we occupy in the pattern, on the moving stair'.[119]

The question at issue is whether it is necessary to abdicate all moral judgements in the face of 'the process of history, which in being responsible for providing us with our scale of values, must not therefore be judged in terms of it, and viewed in this light they turn out no longer wicked but right and good because necessitated'.[120]

Now the value of Professor Berlin's criticism lies not in being a valid one of Marxism but for showing the inconsistencies to which a belief in historical laws must lead. It is quite true that only if 'events occur in discoverable, uniform, unaltering patterns' can we subsume them under laws, and if that were the case in history there could then be no place for moral judgements since what happened had to happen. But as it stands Professor Berlin's arguments may be opposed on two counts.

The first is that he has identified determinism with fatalism.[121] To see a causal relation between events does not necessarily imply an invariable sequence. Certainly this is

119. *Historical Inevitability* (London, 1952), p. 11.

120. *Ibid.*, p. 39.

121. As pointed out by A. K. Sen, 'Determinism and Historical Predictions', *Enquiry* II (New Delhi, 1959), pp. 99–116.

not the way in which Marx and Engels regarded history. The
Marxist conception is directed to change; its dynamism has
come from pointing to the historical prizes to be grasped;
they are not simply bestowed upon passive recipients.
Professor Berlin, in juxtaposing the words 'uniform' and
'unaltering' with 'discoverable' has gone beyond the Marxist
contention that there are certain regularities and causal
sequences that enable us to identify and explain any given
historical situation. It may be conceded that Marxists
including Marx himself have exposed themselves to this
charge by calling these laws. In fact, however, they have
never consistently treated them as such; and it is this inconsistency that has saved the Marxist conception of history
from degenerating into mere economic determinism. Rather
it has led as Engels's quotation above shows to a precarious
and self-contradictory balance between wanting all the
benefits of regularity without reducing it to an invariable
sequence of cause and effect. This has meant, on the one
hand, the positing of an ultimate criterion by which to
explain historical events; namely 'the production and reproduction of real life', that comes nearer to a first and final
cause than any scientific law. On the other hand far from
engendering an attitude of submission to an inexorable fate it
has led Marxists to assign a special place to themselves in the
historical process. In that sense they have turned their own
interpretation upside down. For while it is true that whatever they take to be historical necessity is its own moral
justification, as we shall consider in the next chapter, they do
this from their own standpoint outside history. History is the
arbiter in so far as it leads finally to proletarian revolution and
the dissolution of classes. But it is the Marxists alone who
discern its course and are able to act upon it. Consequently
they judge the past and bestow praise and blame not from
history's but the Marxist's point of view. Or rather the two
are identified. In that sense the Marxists are immune from
the vagaries of time and place as agents of the goal to which
history is working. Those who wanted to carry it forward
along its proper path, like the peasants who revolted in 1381

or the Diggers in the seventeenth century, are treated with sympathy; their opponents are denounced even if they could not have acted differently. The Marxists can do this because they alone like God are able to know who is in accord with destiny; those who impede it are not to be pitied or explained away but treated as part of the 'muck of the ages'. It is no accident that the slogan of Marxist studies from the time of Lenin has been 'partisanship'. History, indeed life itself, is to be judged from the point of view of the working class; what is not germane to the victory of the proletariat is only of secondary interest. To this we owe, until recently at least, an attitude of disdain for much of the past and the concentration upon periods of revolution. History from a Marxist standpoint is studied and written as much for the future as for the past. The shortcomings to which such an outlook have led are well enough known. But they spring not from a belief in determinism as something inexorable but as providing an intelligible sequence. From that standpoint it is nearer, as we mentioned in section one, to an intelligent extrapolation of trends.

This leads us to the second criticism of Professor Berlin's contention: that to understand is to accept and so to abdicate judgement. 'To know all is to understand all; it is to know why things are and must be as they are; therefore the more we know the more absurd we must think those who suppose that things could have been otherwise, and so fall into the irrational temptation to praise and blame'.[122] This is to confuse acceptance of a particular situation with moral neutrality. But one does not entail the other. As we shall discuss in the following chapter it is both logically and empirically possible to have to accept what we do not approve. Even if there are no alternatives within a particular situation there are different ways of evaluating it. Human actions are distinguished from the workings of natural phenomena precisely in being contingent.[123] There is an

122. *Ibid.*, p. 38.

123. I have discussed this notion at length in *History and Social Theory*, chapters 1 to 5.

irreducible difference among individuals that provides an irreducible number of alternative responses to the same situation. What these are rests with the individuals themselves, their values, and their ability to act upon them. For that reason there is no invariable manner in which all men behave at all times. No law can explain why for every hundred men who choose life to honour, the hundredth and one prefers death to dishonour, just as no law can account for the variations in human values throughout history. Professor Berlin in his laudable desire to show the moral bankruptcy to which determinism can lead has fallen into the very position that he has been combating. He has assumed 'unalterability' and 'uniformity' in human affairs. In fact, as he himself has rightly said, we assume moral responsibility in human conduct, as when, say, we condemn as irresponsible a driver who under the influence of drink runs down a pedestrian. Only when something occurs that is quite outside a man's control do we absolve him. But this is not the general rule either in daily life or in history. Barbarossa may have had every reason to vanquish the Lombard League but nothing compelled him, to the point of excluding alternatives (and so of absolving him morally) to raze Milan to the ground in 1160.

Professor Berlin's attempt to reduce the logic of historical determinism to that of natural determinism has also led him to the inconsistency of at once attacking determinists for having their values determined by history and from being precluded from holding values. Thus he says it is 'an irrational temptation to praise and blame' and yet that 'we praise and blame, worship and condemn whatever fits the interests and needs and ideals that we seek to satisfy'.[124] The answer is not the vindication of determinism but the recognition of the difference between natural necessity and what is in fact an historical teleology. Just because history is not a natural science it cannot be treated by scientific criteria. The criticism of historical materialism is not that it is determinism but reductionism. It does not rob men of a belief in their own

124. *Ibid.*, p. 11.

destiny but makes them intolerant to fulfil it, whatever the cost.

It is no exaggeration to say that the core of Marxism is its interpretation of history. From it derives ultimately all its value and originality (including Marxian economics). It is also the source of its greatest failings in inspiring its adherents with the mystique of history: it becomes both a science and the oracle of universal wisdom, whereas we have argued it is neither. Historical development is not an invariable progress through social revolution from one mode of production to another, nor society a symmetry of basis and superstructure, nor men mere personifications of the historical process and their ideas simply its justification. On the contrary there is a complexity, an asymmetry, an imponderability about history that eludes the categories of historical materialism or for that matter any attempt to render it transparent.

Yet this does not nullify historical materialism or make the search for historical understanding vain. Marxism has come closer to achieving this understanding than any other out-look and confined within the limitations inherent in such an aim historical materialism can be fruitfully treated for what it is—a methodology and a point of departure in the study of society. It is here that its value lies and where the contribution of Marxism has been so pronounced.

In the first place it has made us think historically. To this, the awareness of historical change and development, rather than the sterile categories of dialectics, Marxism's much-vaunted sense of movement belongs. All social phenomena, including man's control of nature, are to be conceived as the outcome of a given mode of life, with its own specific conditions and causes. They are all brought within the dimension of historical space-time as the prerequisite of historical understanding. That such a conception is, albeit for the most part implicitly, coming increasingly to be accepted as necessary to historical method confirms the achievement of Marxism.

In the second place, this has gone together with liberation

from immutable categories. Where such inscrutable qualities as human nature served to explain most of men's practices, whether for good or evil, Marxism has translated them into actual historical terms. They have become timebound, moments in a continuous process, not sovereign and final. Thus for the first time attempts at genuine historical explanations have supervened: the tautologies—that man fights because he is warlike or that he worships because he is godlike—have been displaced by analysis, and the comparison of one epoch with another. Men and their institutions and values have been taken in the context of 'their reciprocal activities': the tasks in which they were engaged, the ways in which they organised themselves, their social relations and so on. They and their ideas are accordingly treated as rooted in a given milieu. This is where the concept of class has been so fruitful: for if men are the products of a particular way of life, they are so in virtue of the group to which they belong and whose activities, interests, and values they share. These stamp them indelibly—with rare exceptions—and only by viewing them thus do they become intelligible. So too with the relations between classes: we must recognise, in general terms at least, the existence of class rule and with it of class antagonisms in all societies so far. We do not need to adopt the classifications of Marxism to see how indispensable these concepts are. They constitute nothing less than a sociology based upon history. As such Marxism has provided us with the most fertile means for their fuller understanding.

Finally, of its very nature Marxism has become a mode of thought. It requires that we never take things as they appear; that we seek for connections; that we think in terms of time and space; that we regard things in their totality. Now this can easily become a cult, as I think it has with Marxism; it is only too easy to defeat the original purpose by falling victim to a new tyranny of concepts; and many Marxist discussions become little more than the bandying of categories.[125] Yet at the same time it generates an unmistakable mental alertness

125. See, for example, the discussion in *The Modern Quarterly*, Winter, 1949–50, pp. 81 ff.

and discipline that vastly enhance the grasp of essentials, as is apparent in the best Marxist work. Whether or not this is attainable without embracing the full range of Marxism it remains true that its technique of analysis constitutes an invaluable methodology, not easily dispensed with. Indeed it is this aspect, perhaps more than any other, that needs to be transmitted to the study of history and society generally; for it provides an insight which, properly directed, is the best antidote to the tyranny of concepts no less than to that of blind forces.

III

FREEDOM AND NECESSITY

◆────────

Hitherto we have considered the theoretical foundations of Marxism. In the following two chapters I wish to turn to those aspects with a more direct bearing upon practice: namely moral conduct and political action. It would be misleading to make any sharp distinction between them, save that the topics now to be discussed are concerned with what we may call the practical implications that arise out of the Marxist world view we have been examining.

The question of moral conduct has two distinct facets: firstly, the scope and limits of human action, that is to say, the problem of freedom and its relation to necessity; and secondly, as a consequence, the principles that govern men's dealings with one another. According to how the first is interpreted the second will be understood, for it is only when it has been decided what degree of freedom, if any, man possesses that it becomes possible to discuss how far he is responsible for his own actions and how their morality is to be judged. Clearly, if man has no independent area of free choice, the question of moral responsibility does not arise; and conversely, if he is a free agent, we are faced with establishing the ethical basis of his actions. Nowhere is this interdependence more apparent than in the case of Marxism. Its concern is so exclusively with the *conditions* in which men act that it gives no separate attention to the nature of their actions; or rather it subsumes the latter under the former, with the result that ethics, like ideology in general, are conceived as aspects of a given mode of production. Thus goodness and virtue, like truth and knowledge, are not concepts to be treated in their own right but in terms of the society whose way of life and social structure they reflect. In a backward society where men are far more subject to nature as 'an alien thing', men's power will be correspondingly more limited and their freedom of action circumscribed. Their moral standards will be likewise determined: in slave society, slavery will be preached as a law of nature, and under feudalism, subservience to a lord. Right and wrong, justice and injustice therefore merely articulate the prevailing practice and owe nothing to any external or eternal order of values.

It is in this sense that we can say that Marxism has no distinct theory of ethics, apart from that of society. It regards the problem of free will and determinism as a false one, since neither can be treated meaningfully as separate from a given social milieu. They are both essentially aspects of an historical situation, and only through accepting the necessity imposed by circumstances, and thereby acting in conformity with them, can men be free. As Plekhanov put it, 'In freedom there must be necessity'.[1]

This position was first formulated by Engels in *Anti-Dühring*[2] as follows:

'Freedom therefore consists in the control over ourselves and over external nature which is founded on knowledge of natural necessity; it is therefore necessarily a product of historical development. The first men who separated themselves from the animal kingdom were in all essentials as unfree as the animals themselves, but each step forward in civilisation was a step towards freedom. On the threshold of human history stands the discovery that mechanical motion can be transformed into heat. . . . The steam engine will never bring about such a mighty leap in human development, however important it may seem in our eyes as representing all those powerful productive forces dependent on it—*forces which alone make possible a state of society in which there are no longer class distinctions or anxiety over the means of subsistence for the individual, and in which for the first time there can be talk of real human freedom and of an existence in harmony with the established laws of Nature.*'[3]

1. G. V. Plekhanov, *In Defence of Materialism* (London, 1948), p. 128.
2. Pp. 128–9.   3. My italics. G. L.

It rests on the famous dictum of Hegel 'that freedom is the appreciation of necessity': ' "Necessity is *blind* only *in so far as it is not understood*". Freedom does not consist in the dream of independence of natural laws, but in the knowledge of these laws, and in the possibility this gives of systematically making them work towards definite ends. This holds good in relation both to the laws of external nature and to those which govern the bodily and mental existence of men themselves—two classes of laws which we can separate from each other at most only in thought but not in reality. Freedom of the will therefore means nothing but the capacity to make decisions with real knowledge of the subject. Therefore the *freer* a man's judgement is in relation to a definite question, with so much the greater *necessity* is the content of this judgement determined'.[4]

This passage contains the essence of the Marxist doctrine of freedom and necessity; despite numerous glosses upon it from the time of Plekhanov onwards, it has remained in essentials unmodified and unamplified. The reason lies in the definition itself; for if freedom consists 'in the control over ourselves and external nature' and 'is necessarily an historical product', we can only measure it by examining the specific circumstances in which it is to be found, that is, we go to history and society for its different forms and phases. But, and this is where it has to be distinguished from the similar treatment of knowledge or art, freedom involves practical actions. Therefore to diagnose freedom is to regard it in terms of a particular form of necessity, and according to how we define the latter so we shall conceive freedom. Our view of freedom depends, that is to say, upon our view of necessity and if the one is misconceived, so will the other be. Consequently if what we regard as necessary, and thereby as prescribing the scope and limits of freedom, is mistaken, we shall suffer the practical effects of such error. It is here that the Marxist conception is more than merely an idle speculation. Unlike, say, its view of ideology, it is no mere theory but of vital practical consequence, since ultimately the entire field of

4. Engels, *Anti-Dühring*, p. 128.

moral conduct is involved, as we shall see. For this reason we must examine it more closely.

Once again we owe to a paradox of Engels a whole canon of doctrine. In this case, starting from the proposition that freedom is the recognition of necessity he reached the position of equating the two, so that the greater the degree of freedom a man possessed the greater the necessity it contained: 'Therefore the *freer* a man's judgement is in relation to a definite question, with so much the greater necessity is the content determined.' What begins as a half-truth ends as fallacy; for it does nothing less than reduce freedom to necessity such that they become directly proportional to one another. This has been taken up by Marxism with the inevitable result that freedom as a meaningful concept goes out of the window and we are left with necessity. Thus Plekhanov, in *In Defence of Materialism*, speaks of passing 'from the realm of freedom into the realm of necessity' in virtue of the consequences of 'the conscious free acts of individual men [which are] unexpected for them and unforeseen by them'[5]; and conversely. This may or may not be true, but once freedom is interpreted in these terms, it is the shortest step to making the two concepts virtually interchangeable and this is what Christopher Caudwell does when he says, that 'they are aspects of each other'.[6]

The arguments against such an interpretation are both theoretical and practical. From a theoretical point of view the first thing to be noticed is that neither freedom nor necessity is adequately defined; or rather the definition is circular with each defined in terms of the other. What in fact do we understand by them? Let us pass over the literal definitions in which they are treated as antonyms; let us also grant that there is an element of truth in Engels's paradox mentioned above, so that even if they are not proportional to one another they bear some correlation. We will then find that each has two main connotations. Freedom can be

5. P. 129.
6. Christopher Caudwell, *Studies in a Dying Culture* (London, 1947), p. 196.

understood either negatively, as independence of necessity and constraint, or positively, as the power to do. Necessity for its part, can be interpreted either unconditionally as inexorable fate, or compulsion, or conditionally as causality, as that which will happen given certain circumstances. Now although Marxists do not explicitly specify their choice, from the context in which the terms are employed there can be little doubt that they regard freedom as a positive activity and necessity as the laws of causality, knowledge of which enables men to be free. More specifically their relationship is conceived in the words of Engels as, 'Knowledge of these [natural] laws and in the possibility this gives of making them work towards definite ends'.[7]

The weakness of this standpoint is, firstly, that it is inadequate just because it omits to observe these distinctions. Marxism thinks only in terms of a particular form of social freedom and thereby discounts its very real other aspects, as we shall have cause to mention: freedom is not only the power to do (socially); it also applies to the ability to be (personally). If I want to sleep, my freedom is no less the real for needing only to be left undisturbed; it requires no positive actions on my part that require me to gauge necessity. Similarly I can be free merely by being able to make a negative choice or not following a course of action; that is, in being unconstrained.

Secondly, in spite of assertions to the contrary the Marxist conception once again falls into the familiar dialectical trap of hypostatization. It tends to assume that freedom can stand in juxtaposition to necessity so that we can point to a state or action and say, 'That is free'. In fact, however, freedom is never more than conditional and relative; at best we have a greater or lesser degree of power to act as we choose, but always within certain defined limits. There are certain things we cannot do and certain constraints to which we are always subject. We are bounded by the laws of nature that prevent us, say, from living forever, as well as by the restraints inherent in living in any society. To pretend that by acknow-

7. *Loc. cit.*

ledging these we thereby transform them into attributes of freedom is unfounded; for even when we do so the necessity remains. That I cannot give vent to desires that may injure others is a social necessity and one from which I shall never be free no matter how I regard it. Such necessity is not merely causal; it is unconditional. Conversely, and here the crux of the Marxist case, to have the requisites for positive action is not the same as thereby to be free. No one would deny that a man is not free by the mere fact that he does not have to do something; for if he lacks the wherewithal for utilising the absence of such constraint he will then be subject to other needs that he cannot satisfy. Thus, as Marxists have never rightly ceased to emphasise, a worker, who is unemployed and is without the necessities of life, cannot be considered free just because he is not coerced to a particular course of action. Equally because men have sufficient control over nature to be able to live without deprivation they are not thereby free. We can make the 'laws of necessity work towards definite ends' without being free either socially or personally, as in the case of say cotton operatives during the industrial revolution or of class society generally. Power and knowledge are not the same as freedom; they may be its prerequisites, but we can know, say, how to control a furnace and yet be enslaved to doing so, through social coercion or economic pressure. Moreover, in the same way as freedom is relative so are our conceptions of it. What may appear as unrelieved toil to say a London office worker, in doing a five-day week, would probably seem like emancipation to a Congo copper miner; in fact it is neither absolute servitude nor absolute freedom. Do we then say that because it could be greater it is not freedom at all? That is, how are we to measure freedom save in relative terms? Accordingly the Marxist notion is one more example of treating as self-subsistent fact what is really an anthropomorphic judgement. Freedom is neither this nor that *in se*, but the result of a number of different relations—personal, social, economic, positive, negative, and so on. It cannot therefore be taken as an absolute.

From this it follows, in the third place, that where necessity is absolute there can be no freedom. To be able to act freely there must always be an alternative; otherwise, however knowingly we act, we are acting because we are compelled to do so, and therefore in reality we have no genuine choice. That is to say, freedom to act as we choose is more than to accede knowingly to what we have to do. It is to have the power to choose; and it is in the degree to which necessity is not absolute that freedom of action exists. Now the Marxist doctrine ignores this because its conception of freedom is restricted to the positive view, of power to do; it thereby confuses the ability to act with freedom to act, whereas, in fact, the two are distinct. Thus when Engels says that 'freedom of will is nothing but the capacity to make decisions with real knowledge of the subject', he is in effect excluding the subjective or personal element from an action and designating it as free simply because it can be performed. He thereby eliminates freedom by subsuming it under the necessity of action.

But freedom to do only what has to be done is not freedom; and there is a vast realm of experience where we are not free, however much we may recognise our subjection to necessity. That we must breathe to live, for example, is a law to which we must submit unconditionally on pain of death. To do so willingly and with full knowledge in no way diminishes the degree of necessity involved. In that sense we can never be free; at most our knowledge that we cannot do otherwise mitigates the sense of compulsion, but it confers no genuine faculty of choice. Much the same applies to most instinctual activities; and even where it does not, as in say harnessing water power, rather than praying to a rain god, we are still confronted with the problem of what we mean by freedom. While it may mean freedom in the control of nature it can, as we have said, entail subjection socially and personally for those engaged in such an operation.

Freedom, then, is a conditional state that can never be judged independently of what is to be attained. It depends essentially upon the intention of the subject. That is to say, the difference between a free and a necessary act is determined by the nature of the end in view. If we are constrained to act in a certain way or for a certain object such that the decision to do so lies outside our own choosing, then, whatever the means that enhance its attainment, they will not spell freedom even though other means could have been used. Thus if an army private is detailed to peel potatoes, a task that he has to accomplish on pain of punishment, he cannot be said to be doing so freely even though he may take only half an hour instead of the customary hour. A fish and chip merchant, on the other hand, because he freely wills to produce as many chips as he can in the shortest possible time is that much the more free. Now the Marxist notion confuses the two, for it assumes the end, whatever it is, as given, and only looks to the comparative efficacy with which it can be attained: hence on these grounds a man who peels potatoes in half the time of another is correspondingly more free by virtue of having gained greater mastery over his medium, regardless of the circumstances.

It would appear therefore that the Marxist definition of freedom rests on a fundamental misconception. Since freedom is impossible without knowledge the latter has been identified with power to attain an end, and this in turn has been taken as freedom; such a view is both incomplete and contrary for it concentrates upon the conditions needed to achieve an object instead of the nature of the object itself. Accordingly means have displaced the end.

Such a misapprehension is more than a mere matter of confusion, widespread though it is; it has also serious practical implications; indeed we can go so far as to say that the ready invocation of necessity by Marxism accounts in no small measure for its ruthlessness. It has bred an attitude of almost predestinarian submission to the ineluctable forces of history which, as its agent, the proletariat must foster. It has induced the belief in an invariable sequence from necessity to freedom, so that however daunting the tasks to be confronted, their overcoming is the 'precondition of freedom'. This has coloured Marxist theory and practice from the time of Lenin onwards.

It is in this context that I think one can speak of the tyranny of necessity in Marxism. It has its source in the very propositions we have been discussing. For once it is conceded that freedom lies only through accepting necessity two consequences follow. The first is to preach submission to necessity in the name of freedom; the second is to define necessity in accordance with expediency. That is to say, it leads only too easily to the principle that what is to be has to be and that its accomplishment is for the best of all possible worlds. It is at this point that the Marxist laws of historical development enter; for they enable us to prognosticate the necessary course of social action that history has prescribed. Therefore we have only to follow it to be on the road to freedom.

The weakness of this point of view is that there is no guarantee that what is held to be necessity is necessary and therefore the prerequisite of freedom. Herein lies the flaw in the freedom-necessity argument for human conduct. It seeks to make an objective criterion out of what can never be more than a particular set of emphases. It is we who evaluate what is necessary; hence necessity rests upon our evaluations of it and changes with them. When we are confronted with natural forces we are usually in no doubt as to what is necessity: when the sun goes down it will be dark; if I stand in the rain I shall get wet. In each case I have to accept these as necessary conclusions over whose operation I have no control, although I may be able to take appropriate action to avoid being either plunged into darkness or made wet. The case is quite otherwise in our social actions. Even if we accept the necessity of our antecedents, our natural endowments, and our historical situation, this does not mean that we have thereby to accept our personal condition as necessary and unalterable. If I am conscribed into the army and have to comply with military discipline, it is not through the operation of an immutable law of the universe 'that all adult men have to serve in the army' which I must accept; I may have no alternative but to submit to serving in the army; and in that sense I can be said to be subject to necessity. Even so, as necessity, it will differ from natural necessity: for I can contest the desirability of the end that it is supposed to serve, namely to strengthen the state; though I may see no means for the realisation of an alternative social order I can still regard the present one as invidious or unjust and so not worthy of defending. I cannot however say the same in the case of the action of sun or rain.

The difference is fundamental; for the only justification we have in bowing to necessity is that things could not be otherwise. In that case, as we have seen, we are not ensuring our freedom but merely recognising our lack of it. If, however, we can postulate an alternative or even merely reject without an alternative, we have left the realm of necessity, and the freedom of action that is available to us is in proportion to the absence of necessity.

Accordingly when we come to consider the implications of this outlook for practical life, we are in effect presented with a justification of tyranny; for it identifies what is considered desirable with what is necessary, and its acceptance with freedom, when in fact, as we have seen, neither implies the other. It means jettisoning any principles of moral conduct other than the pragmatic one of expediency (with what results can be seen from the changes and purges in the communist states); and it is this aspect that I now wish to examine.

As Engels says, 'It is difficult to deal with morality and law without coming up against the question of so-called free will, of human responsibility, of the relation between freedom and necessity'.[8] When, as we have seen, this question is resolved by making freedom lie in the recognition of necessity, the nature of human responsibility is correspondingly determined. It can consist only in the acceptance of that necessity, since not to do so would be to remain at the mercy of blind forces; in Hegel's words, 'Necessity is blind only in so far as it is not understood'. Clearly, then, there is no place for moral choice in such a procedure; at most we can all moral that which accedes to the demands of necessity; and this is the sense in which Marxism speaks of people and activities as progressive

8. Engels, *Anti-Dühring*, p. 127.

or reactionary. Thus the *Communist Manifesto* declares that 'The lower middle class, the small manufacturer, the artisan, the peasant, all these fight against the bourgeoisie to save from extinction their existence as fractions of the lower middle class. They are therefore not revolutionary, but conservative. Nay, more, they are reactionary, for they try to roll back the wheel of history'.[9] Such evaluation is in terms of what Lenin called 'recognition of objective law', whether in nature or in history. It therefore eliminates individual responsibility beyond demanding conformity with it. Accordingly the whole of the Marxist argument for socialism is not in moral but in teleological terms: 'Marx', says Lenin, 'deduces the inevitability of the transformation of capitalist society into socialist society wholly and exclusively from the economic law of motion of contemporary society.'[10] It is not a matter of capitalism being 'worse' than socialism, even though personal revulsion against the evils of the prevailing system has always been one of the driving forces in all revolutionary protest as we can see from the account of factory conditions in volume I of *Capital*; it is that the science of society and revolution cannot be founded upon personal sentiment, but must be rooted in 'objective law'. Hence the absence of the 'utopian' appeal to the dignity of man as one of the prime justifications for social change; hence, too, the absence of a 'utopian' blue-print for the new society. Just as capitalism is governed by objective laws with their appropriate forms, so the same will apply to socialism. The difference is that the latter, as constituting 'the immense majority in the interest of the immense majority', has 'the mission to destroy all previous securities for, and insurances of, private property'.[11] In doing so it ends the exploitation of man by man that marks 'the prehistoric stage of human society'. It is as a higher stage of social evolution, superseding the bourgeois relations of production that 'are the last antagonistic form of the social process of production', that socialism is a superior system. Its justification lies in its consonance with historical

9. P. 24.   10. *Selected Works*, Vol. XI, p. 33.
11. *Communist Manifesto*, p. 25.

necessity; that is the source of its moral fitness. The corollary is that morality consists in furthering the interests of socialism and therefore of the proletariat; they are to be served independently of any other considerations. In the words of the *Communist Manifesto*, 'The Communists fight for the attainment of the immediate aims, for the enforcement of the momentary interests of the working class; but in the movement of the present, they also represent and take care of the future of that movement. . . . In short, the Communists everywhere support every revolutionary movement against the existing social and political order of things.'[12]

The shortcomings of this interpretation would appear to be manifest. We can all admit that the Marxist emphasis upon the positive nature of freedom has been a salutary and necessary counterpoise to the negative view; that without the power to act there cannot be real freedom; and that to confine the latter to the mere absence of overt constraint has come all too frequently to mask the lack of any genuine faculty of choice, personal and social. Yet this in itself is not enough. We have to ask what end freedom is to serve and to what purpose? That is to say, freedom becomes an essentially ethical question and cannot merely be subsumed under the recognition of necessity. There comes a point where we are confronted with the need to state the principles of freedom and their justification. To do so entails arriving at its precise import. How are we to understand it? Do we conceive it as primarily personal or social, positive or negative? And according to our emphasis what is to be the relationship between these different aspects? Only if freedom is treated thus, can it be meaningfully considered. It therefore becomes a moral issue, the province of ethics at both the general and the individual levels. Marxism, in abdicating to whatever is decreed to be objective law, fails to recognise this: hence its inadequacy as a moral code and as a system of conduct.

So far as morality in general is concerned Marxism ignores the first requisite of all ethics, namely that of right doing. This is not a matter of metaphysics or logic, but of examining

12. *Ibid.*, pp. 47–8.

the grounds of our conduct and the intentions that actuate it. Now the weakness of so much ethical discussion is to attempt to reach such understanding by metaphysics or logic. That is, either to try to arrive at the nature of the good and right or to deduce the reasons why one course of action is good and another not. Neither seems to be viable. Goodness is not an entity but an abstraction; and like all abstractions it is derived from a diversity of individuals.

Whenever we say 'this is good', we are referring to a particular thing that for one reason or another evokes in us a feeling of pleasure or approval or respect. There is nothing inherently good in giving alms to a beggar or bad in a smack in the eye to an inoffensive stranger, other than the connotations we bring to these actions; and we do so because our experience and standards tell us that one is beneficial and the other is harmful. Similarly, when we talk about vegetables being good for us and too many sweets being bad we are describing their effects upon us; and when we say that one man is a good tennis player and another bad, we are judging them by the effects of their playing. Each of these cases constitutes a different kind of designation of good and bad: the first is what we may call a moral judgement; the second a statement of fact, that, given so many vegetables or too many sweets, the effect will be either beneficial or deleterious to the body; the third states the relationship between a man's capacity to play tennis and the requirements of the game. They are united by nothing save the approval or condemnation that we bring to them; and in this sense we cannot speak of goodness as a self-subsistent quality, or essence, but as a statement of approval.

For this reason there cannot be any logical grounds for positing good and bad. That is to say, there can be no a priori reason or proof for saying that to help a man is good and to attack him is bad, for good is not self-evident in the way in which rain is wet. Hence every statement that 'this is good' can be met by the counterstatement that 'it is bad'; and according to the definition given each is logically as tenable as the other. This is confirmed by the most cursory glance at history where human custom and behaviour vary from generation to generation and society to society. They belie any conception of good or right as absolutes; and ultimately the question why one man thinks that something is good and another that it is evil rests upon conviction: 'we believe that it is right to eat one's enemies' rather than 'it is right to do so', is the only tenable basis for an ethical judgement.

At the same time if good and evil are not simply a matter of absolutes, nor are they simply reflex actions. They rather express man's situation at any given time; they are both transitory, as historically conditioned, and common to all human needs. Thus, on the one hand, a cannibal will regard it as meritorious to eat his fellows, where in normal circumstances a twentieth-century European would regard it as among the blackest of crimes. There is clearly no unifying link between the two conceptions; they can only be explained in terms of social evolution and not in terms of human nature. On the other hand, men have in common certain fundamental needs that are a condition of their existence and so of their morality: love and security; protection from their enemies, whether natural or human; co-operation in the attainment of the essentials of life, the dependence upon which grows the more complex society becomes, and so on. These are the prerequisites of life, which in one form or another, according to historical circumstances, are the object of the overwhelming majority of mankind. In that sense, the fulfilment of these requirements is inherent in all morality; they are the stuff of which it is made.

We can say, then, that morality is both arbitrary, in that its forms and standards will depend upon a multitude of factors that are peculiar to each time and place, and universal in that it refers to certain inherent needs in men by means only of which they can exist as human beings. However self-interested the prevailing morality of a society may be, in expressing the interests of the dominant class, it must also contain those elements of genuine value to men as a whole. Their basic needs must in some degree be met, no matter how perfunctorily. Even the peasantry of medieval England received some protection from their lords and some recognition of their status as God's creatures, subject though they were. As with knowledge, so with morality, there has to be a more permanent validity in its products; in each case they tend to outlast the epoch from which they spring, whether Euclid's theorems or precepts like 'love thy neighbour'.

For that reason ethical values become a matter for conscious evaluation: it rests with us not merely to state the grounds for preferring good to evil but to specify what we understand by good and evil. Moreover, our choice can be founded upon practically demonstrable considerations. Thus it can be argued from experience that as a general rule happiness is better than misery, co-operation better than repression, love better than hate, because they benefit human beings; in logical terms alone there is no conclusive argument for the superiority of these states, for it could be equally asserted that men were undeserving of happiness and so should endure misery. Hence it is not enough to look to the laws of historical development for moral arbitrament as the Marxists do. Rather our conviction in a certain form of society must be founded upon our assessment of men. Only if we are prepared to acknowledge their needs, worth, and potentialities, can we reach an outlook founded upon ethical principles. Without such a moral code with its own priorities, political expediency will triumph every time, and freedom will be hostage to necessity.

At the level of individual conduct, Marxism in confining freedom to the recognition of a particular kind of necessity has excluded anything that can be called moral choice and with it personal morality. The effect has been to efface free will, or, as Engels called it, 'the question of so-called free will'. Since personal freedom cannot be conceived in its own right, conscience, intention, motive, volition, are all disregarded, or when acknowledged, as with conscience, derided as bourgeois.

That they cannot be thus dismissed hardly needs stressing. They are not only inherent in all conduct, but their presence belies the Marxist conception of freedom; for if freedom 'consists in the control over ourselves and over external nature which is founded on a knowledge of natural necessity', what becomes of the diversity of impulses and predilections, some merely whims, others the promptings of conscience, that go to make up our personal intentions and the actions to which they give rise? But a fraction of them is directed to the control of necessity as described by Engels, yet does that invalidate the rest? And conversely are we only to regard men as free when they are pursuing a socially necessary goal? To do so would be to discount the greater part of human conduct and values: for, and this is the central point, it is men who decide their own necessity and freedom by relating themselves to what they must and what they can do at any given time. The necessity and freedom that ensue are not solely of one kind, as Engels seemed to imply, but are determined by the totality of conditions that obtain at any given time. Consequently, there is never—or only very exceptionally—one necessity, to which all men must bow and with it one freedom, but a variety of situations that give rise to their own needs and opportunities. These vary not only from society to society, but from class to class and from individual to individual, over and above the ever-present realm of men's need to confront nature for self-preservation. Hence, as we stressed earlier, to talk of freedom and necessity as self-subsisting categories is untenable and can lead only to mistaking them and denying them where they are present. This is the fault in the Marxist notion; it fails to allow that many of our necessities and freedoms are without reference to an overriding social necessity. Thus one man needs eight hours of sleep, where another wants only four; one man craves company, where another demands solitude; one desires activity, another leisure; and so on. These are no less real for being personal, and their realisation no less an essential part of a man's freedom. Conversely a man can be master of a kingdom socially and yet be personally circumscribed by unending obligation.

This is not to deny that social necessity and freedom are not ultimately the foundation of all the human necessities and freedoms, but rather that they can be thus arbitrarily divided and their specific import ignored. Necessity and freedom are not separate entities that we can discern to the exclusion of anything else, as we suggested in the example of the absence of any hard and fast designation for the status of a London office worker. Even more, there is often no agreed way of understanding freedom. Nowhere is this so apparent as in the divergence between communist and non-communist interpretations. To take an instance cultivated by Marxists: a worker in a communist state is held by them to be free because the exploitation of man by man has been abolished, and so in working for the state he is working for his own freedom. Accordingly the obligations imposed upon him are in his own interests as the guarantee of this freedom. Yet if this prevents him from having the liberty of movement of, say, a Sheffield steel worker who is exploited for five days of the week, but who can spend the weekend in fishing, who is the more free? How are we to compare 'socialist construction' at the community's behest with fishing as a personal pastime? Clearly there is no means of comparison; or rather, to make one will depend upon how we understand freedom. However we do so, it is groundless to say that the former is freedom and the latter is not, as the Marxists do, in their exclusive insistence upon social freedom.

On the contrary since freedom and necessity are concerned with men's power to act or not, it is as they ultimately affect individual men that they arise. Whether we act freely or under constraint we do so through our own agency. Our actions are therefore the domain of individual volition or they are nothing: even if we are ordered to perform a task it rests with us in the last analysis to obey or to refuse (I exclude of course the use of torture or other circumstances where a man is not in command of his normal faculties). For this reason conscience is so important; there is an entire range of actions that are due neither to personal inclination nor the necessity of external compulsion, but which we perform from what, for want of a better term, can be called a sense of duty. The peculiarity of this feeling of obligation, or conscience, is that it frequently goes against our own desires and interests and yet it is too compelling to deny, with the result that we tend to feel the freer for having yielded to it.

This conflict between what we want and what we do is one of men's outstanding attributes. If it arises, as we suggested in the last chapter, from the constraints of society and thereby is inherent in any group, human or animal, it is none the less significant for that. For its pecularity lies in its very power to make man override sheer self-interest, even when as with, say, Socrates, or Cranmer, or Péri, the alternative is death.

No one would pretend that conscience has been to the fore-front in human conduct down the ages; indeed one of the frustrations of history is the tantalising glimpse of the discrepancy between how men could act and how they act; so that, at most, we are confined to a few outstanding occasions as evidence for man's better self. The history of morality belongs as much to cannibalism, the Roman circus, the crusades, and Nazism as to their martyrs. But this is not the same as to deny the existence of morality in all human societies and with it of the sense of obligation that is transmitted to their members. Most of us are brought up with defined attitudes towards theft, murder, adultery, God, and our neighbour, and these permanently colour our conduct (even if we rebel against them). We also have a conviction of what it is to be a man; and this sense of empathy with other human beings is one of the fundamental elements in a more highly developed system of ethics. That they vary from society to society is only confirmation of their indispensable need in every society as the condition of social cohesion.

In consequence freedom and necessity cannot be meaning-fully separated from moral conduct and conscience. They are inherent in every action that involves men in relation to one another. Even the most apparently casual deed such as buying goods in a shop entails a moral obligation to pay for them. This is not the same as saying that what is moral is necessarily right, or that in paying so much for something, I am not in fact being exploited; as Marxism has taught us, men give a moral habit to the most blatant injustices and are taught to believe that they are just, whether it be eating one's enemies or burning heretics. The point is rather that in being bound by a particular code of conduct, regardless of its intrinsic value, they are subject to a moral as well as a legal and coercive necessity.

Now the Marxist view entirely discounts this moral aspect. With its conception of freedom as men's power to act socially, it can find no place for the role of conscience and personal choice in 'the problem of so-called free will'. There could scarcely be more convincing testimony to its adherents' attitude than in the structure of the Communist Party itself, to whose aims of social change, as we shall discuss in the next chapter, nothing is more inimical than any form of personal autonomy. It is therefore not surprising that communists reject all such claims as bourgeois individualism.

In one sense they are right; personal morality is essentially the product of bourgeois society. Where they err is to see it merely as an aberration that can only retard the attainment of socialism. By adopting such an attitude Marxists do violence to their own interpretation of history no less than to history itself. They fail, in the first place, to take account of their own axiom that men in changing their circumstances change themselves, so that the standards by which they live are not mere external adjuncts detachable at will, but part of them. Men are what they are no less by what they believe than what they do; the two are indissoluble. A cannibal is a cannibal not merely in virtue of eating his fellow men but because of his attitude towards his fellow men; we regard a man as civilised not just because he drives a car or can read but because of his values. If the definition is arbitrary it is so from the arbitrariness of human history. The existence of a particular form of society is as independent of logical justification as eating and sleeping. We have to take them as given. At best we can look for their causes, and in the case of society attempt to change it for the better. What we cannot do is to turn away from the prevailing mode of life and the outlook that accompanies it, and to pretend that, since it is mistaken, it is of no account. This is just what the Marxists do with bourgeois morality. Since they regard its individualism as retrograde they dismiss it. In doing so they are attempting to dismiss an entire epoch in human development and, with it, failing to confront men as they have come to be as the result of bourgeois society.

Secondly, as a consequence, the Marxist view misconceives what it calls bourgeois morality. When we have made due allowance for the inconsistencies and cant that accompany the use of terms like freedom, conscience, the sovereignty of the individual, and so on, it remains undeniable that these values are integral to the capitalist ethic. Abused and betrayed they may be; but this is not in itself reason either to disregard them or to treat them as a mere snare and delusion. On the contrary, the desire for liberty in one form or another —whether as national independence or as political freedom —has been and is the most single potent force in history since the American Revolution, and it is a force that cannot be discounted. Its importance shows, what the Marxists appear unable or unwilling to grasp, that so-called bourgeois man with his bourgeois values is not an anomaly, a spectator on the margins of history,[13] but a living historical product standing for an entire phase of historical development. These values, whether we like them or not, have been transmitted to a great part of mankind so that men have come to regard the attainment of liberty as one of the foremost necessities.

Nor is this surprising; for the greater men's technological power, and the greater the knowledge that accompanies it, the less dependent they are upon the arbitrariness of nature and the inexorability of some kind of fate. This has been the inseparable accompaniment of advanced industrial society, which has seen the unprecedented growth of men's freedom not only materially but also mentally. What previously had been inviolable and unknowable, the preserve of a select minority and God, has become accessible to men generally. However weighted the scales are against the majority of the

13. This is the expression of A. C. MacIntyre in the *New Reasoner*, No. 7, Winter 1958–9, p. 92, in what seems to me a mistaken diagnosis of the moral problem of Stalinism, largely through his failure to recognise this very point.

people, capitalist society still represents the change from fixed hereditary status to one that is legally free, from belief through the mediation of the Church to knowledge based upon enquiry, from morality as a choice between conformity or heresy to recognition of individual conscience. It has transferred to the individual what previously rested with authority; and even if the majority must still submit, it has introduced the element of personal choice and with it of personal responsibility. In these circumstances personal morality assumes a new importance; where God disposed men can now propose. This individualist ethic has its epigraph in Luther's cry of defiance. 'Here I stand' is an appeal to man's power of choice; it is a recognition of individual responsibility in the face of which any other authority is of no avail. As such it has come to be the archetype of an entire ethos; it underlies countless acts of personal heroism as well as the attitudes of whole nations in preferring death to slavery. To attempt to override it is to fly in the face both of history and its necessity.[14]

Yet this, paradoxically, is the effect of the Marxist conception. In its invocation of social necessity it is reverting to an outlook far more akin to the medieval ethic; for it seeks to impose, albeit in the name of a higher morality, a new orthodoxy. If achieved, it could not but put the clock back; it would mean nothing less than the dismemberment of the faculty of individual responsibility that is the greatest achievement of bourgeois ethics. Such a consequence, for which there is only too much evidence in communist practice, makes the inadequacy of Marxist morality self-evident.

It is to this, then, that the Marxist sacrifice of morality to historical necessity leads. It discounts the validity of ethical values and in doing so discounts men themselves; for it fails to recognise that this morality has become integral to them. To separate them is to fail in the first requisites of historical

14. Including that of the Soviet Union, the unsurpassed heroism of whose peoples in resisting the Nazis was founded precisely upon the acceptance of death rather than slavery. It is added confirmation of the all-pervasiveness of the ideal of freedom, even if it has yet to be acknowledged by Marxism for individuals.

and human understanding. Accordingly when the Marxist says that freedom is the recognition of necessity he begs the entire question, of whose necessity? Man as an organism needing protection from nature? Man as an economic being who needs to understand its laws? Man as a social being who needs to co-operate with others? Man as an individual who demands dignity, freedom, and self-respect? Man as the maker of history that must go inexorably onwards? These are not the same men; some are not men at all; nor are they all found together. We can feed a man and yet tyrannize over him; we can accept him socially and yet deny him individually; we can respect him individually and neglect him socially; we can understand the laws of nature and ignore human nature; we can talk of man and yet forget men.

Let us by all means recognise the impasse of selfishness to which bourgeois freedom has brought us and the need to reintegrate the individual into society. Let us recognise the travesty of genuine freedom that often goes by the name of personal freedom. But to do this is not to abjure the individual as he has developed or to negate the importance of individual morality. Rather they must be our starting point.

This is where Marxist morality fails: it omits to think of man as a living historical being as he exists here and now. It assumes that it is enough to grasp the laws of historical development to compass man. But what in fact results is an abstraction, an abstraction over which Marxists appoint themselves arbiters. Man for them becomes a series of activities, the maker of history, the master of nature, the creator of socialism; and his morality a series of reflex actions, man the co-operator, man the social being, man liberated from all past constraints and oppressions. In the circumstances how could freedom be other than the acceptance of such an order and those who impede it be other than its enemies? The symmetry is so exact that it allows no place for the irregularity of men themselves, who may be all these things but are yet something which is none of these—specific beings in real circumstances. Here, ultimately, lies the difference between orthodox Marxism and some form of socialist humanism. For the former any measures can be justified—purges, secret executions, breaches of pledge, the suspension of law, liberty, and so on—in the attainment of the ideal; for the latter once such expedients are employed the ideal has become a frankenstein. It is the difference between refusing to start from men as they are, and accepting them as they are; between wanting to impose a pattern upon them in the name of history's pattern, and of making in their needs and desires the starting point; between a teleology in which the demands of an ultimate goal overrides the present, and a humanism that takes man as the measure of things. It is the difference, in short, between a morality based upon necessity and one based upon ethics, in the way we have suggested.

The significance of their difference is not academic; it bears upon the nature of society. The Marxist conception inevitably means dictatorship and repression because it sets the achievement of its end above all other considerations, even if it does so in the name of humanity. The humanist conception denies the validity of such an order of priority in that it denies that the present can or should be hostage for the future: men are as much men today as tomorrow, equal in their needs and in their value; living under capitalism does not make them second-class human beings as compared with members of a future socialist society. They cannot therefore be dragooned into following a particular course just because humanity will benefit in the long run. It will be objected here that Marxism is also concerned with men in the present and that the distinction between ends and means is an irrelevance. No doubt, but in subjecting them to the arbitrament of history, whatever the extenuating circumstances, its will must be done. It is not unlike the Catholic doctrine of predestination: God wills all men to be saved yet some are nevertheless damned. The reasons in each case may be impeccable, but the result is to put man before men.

For this reason it is not unjust to speak of historical necessity as the *deus ex machina* of Marxism; despite all the protestations that it is made up of real living men, it is yet endowed with its own momentum that will wait on no man; the goal is .

so clear that no impediment, even if it is the inclinations of men themselves, can be allowed to stand in the way. In that sense we may well say that the tyranny of Marxism lies less in any specific political mechanism than the tyranny of concepts that engender it. We are dealing less with a science than with a mission.

In contrast the humanist position must rest upon a belief in what it is to be human not in man as a mere unit in the historical process. When we say that these should include life, liberty, and the pursuit of happiness, we are not thereby degenerating into flabby idealism; we are stating a fact as surely as when we say that he needs food and air and sleep. 'Love is wise, hate is foolish' is a dictum of self-interest as well as altruism; it rests on no hypothesis but on the facts of human existence. Oppress a man and he will hate; and to cause him to hate is to inflict suffering and to generate more hate. We all share certain needs; we all desire certain satisfactions, and these can only be assured if each man recognises that 'the condition of the free development of all is the free development of each'. Hitherto such a condition has never been realised, though a few have been aware of its truth for centuries. Today it has become practicable, indeed indispensable, to human survival. It rests upon only one assumption, respect for each person's humanity. If it is accepted it follows that society must be organised in man's interests. Any system, or policies, that violates them is to be condemned. That is to say, there is all the difference between the Marxist view that in the end judges a situation not on its intrinsic merits—how much suffering will be caused or *vice versa*—but on its long-term implications, and an outlook that refuses to sell the present for the future.

No outlook can ever overcome the central dilemma inherent in all human existence—of the need to choose between evils—but only that which is firmly wedded to an ethical principle, based upon respect for men rather than subservience to history, can limit the area of injustice. For that reason, above all, Marxist morality both in its theory and its practice must stand condemned.

THE DICTATORSHIP OF THE PROLETARIAT AND SOCIALISM

1

Marxism, its exponents claim, is above all a guide to (political) action. It must therefore stand or fall by its practice; and largely because this has followed an almost undeviating pattern of repression, deceit, and narrow privilege, evocative of the worst features of class rule wherever communism has come to power, Marxism as political doctrine can no longer be accepted.

Nowhere does this apply more than to the dictatorship of the proletariat which is the model for the seizure and exercise of power by the Communist Party. According to Lenin it is the hallmark of Marxism: 'Those who recognise *only* the class struggle are not yet Marxists. . . . A Marxist is one who *extends* the acceptance of the class struggle to the acceptance of the *dictatorship of the proletariat*. This is where the profound difference lies between a Marxist and an ordinary petty (and even big) bourgeois. This is the touchstone on which the *real* understanding and acceptance of Marxism should be tested.'[1] Although the concept was only made explicit after the experience of the Paris Commune of 1871 and did not receive its full delineation until Lenin's classic of *The State and Revolution*, it goes right back to Marx's early thinking. Even in the *Economic and Philosophic Manuscripts of 1844*, Marx writes of 'The positive transcendence of all estrangement—that is to say, the return of man from religion, family, state,

1. V. I. Lenin, *The State and Revolution, Selected Works*, Vol. VII (London, 1946), p. 33.

etc., to his *human*, i.e. *social* mode of existence'.[2] Three years later in *The German Ideology* the state is described as originating 'out of this very contradiction between the interest of the individual and that of the community . . . [which] takes an independent form as the *State*, divorced from the real interests of individual and community. . . . Just because individuals seek *only* their particular interest, i.e. that not coinciding with their communal interest (for the "general good" is the illusory form of communal life), the latter will be imposed on them as an interest "alien" to them, and "independent" of them . . .'[3].

The state therefore is the preserve of the ruling class, enshrining its economic and social hegemony that 'has its practical-idealist expression in each case in the form of the state; and therefore every revolutionary struggle is directed against a class, which till then has been in power'[4]. Already the conclusion was drawn that 'in order, therefore, to assert themselves as individuals they [the proletarians] must overthrow the state'.[5]

With the *Communist Manifesto* the formulation becomes more precise. 'The executive of the modern State is but a committee for managing the common affairs of the whole bourgeoisie'[6]; and since 'political power, properly so called, is merely the organised power of one class for oppressing another',[7] 'the first step in the revolution by the working class is to raise the proletariat to the position of the ruling class, to win the battle for democracy'[8]. In these statements we have the twin essentials of the Marxist doctrine of political action. The first is that the state is 'the organised power of one class for oppressing another', that is to say, its function is to impose authority where there is no longer a natural community of interests. As Engels was to put it later, 'The state is by no means a power imposed on society from without; just as little is it "the reality of the moral idea", "the image and the

2. *Economic and Philosophic Manuscripts of 1844*, p. 103.
3. *The German Ideology*, p. 45. 4. *Ibid.*, p. 85.
5. *Ibid.*, p. 95. 6. *Ibid.*, p. 16. 7. *Ibid.*, p. 35.
8. *Ibid.*, p. 34.

reality of reason", as Hegel maintains. Rather it is a product of society at a definite stage of development; it is the admission that this society has involved itself in insoluble self-contradiction and is cleft into irreconcilable antagonisms which it is powerless to exorcise. But in order that these antagonisms, classes with conflicting economic interests, shall not consume themselves and society in fruitless struggle, a power, apparently standing above society, has become necessary to moderate the conflict and keep it within the bounds of "order"; and this power, arisen out of society, but placing itself above it and increasingly alienating itself from it, is the state.'[9] Moreover, 'As the state arose not only from the need to keep class antagonisms in check, but also arose in the thick of the fight between the classes, it is normally the state of the most powerful, economically ruling class, which by its means becomes also politically the ruling class, and so acquires new means of holding down and exploiting the oppressed class. The ancient state was, above all, the state of the slave owners for holding down the slaves, just as the feudal state was the organ of the nobility for holding down the peasant serfs and bondsmen, and the modern representative state is the instrument for exploiting wage-labour by capital. Exceptional periods, however, occur when the warring classes are so nearly equal in forces that the state power, as apparent mediator, acquires for the moment a certain independence in relation to both'.[10] Engels's last qualification apart, we have here the Marxist view of the state as a product and an instrument of class rule.

The second essential is the need for the working class to constitute itself into the ruling class. In this way it 'makes despotic inroads on the rights of property, and on the conditions of bourgeois production'[11] and 'as such sweeps away by force the old conditions of production' and hence 'the conditions for the existence of class antagonisms and of classes generally'.[12] Engels, in *Anti-Dühring*, outlined the

9. Engels, *Origin of the Family, Private Property and the State*, pp. 193-4.
10. *Ibid.*, p. 196.   11. *Communist Manifesto*, p. 34.
12. *Ibid.*, p. 35.

main stages in this process: 'This solution can only consist in the recognition in practice of the social nature of the modern productive forces, in bringing, therefore, the mode of production, appropriation and exchange into accord with the social character of the means of production. And this can only be brought about by society, openly and without deviation, taking possession of the productive forces which have outgrown all control other than that of society itself. . . . By more and more transforming the great majority of the population into proletarians, the capitalist mode of production brings into being the force which, under penalty of its own destruction, is compelled to carry out this revolution. By more and more driving towards the conversion of the vast socialised means of production into state property, it itself points the way for the carrying through of this revolution. *The proletariat seizes the state power, and transforms the means of production in the first instance into state property*. But in doing this, it puts an end to itself as the proletariat, it puts an end to all class differences and class antagonisms, it puts an end also to the state as state. Former society, moving in class antagonisms, had need of the state, that is, an organisation of the exploiting class at each period for the maintenance of its external conditions of production; that is, therefore, for the forcible holding down of the exploited class in the conditions of oppression (slavery, villeinage or serfdom, wage labour) determined by the existing mode of production.'[13]

Accordingly, the proletariat seizes power and constitutes itself the ruling class for the purpose of putting an end to all classes and with them of the need for the state at all. As Engels describes it in a celebrated passage:

'When ultimately it becomes really representative of society as a whole, it makes itself superfluous. As soon as there is no longer any class of society to be held in subjection; as soon as, along with class domination and the struggle for individual existence based on the former anarchy of production, the collisions and excesses arising from these have also been abolished, there is nothing more to be repressed which would

13. F. Engels, *Anti-Dühring*, pp. 307–8.

make a special repressive force, a state, necessary. The first act in which the state really comes forward as the representative of society as a whole—the taking possession of the means of production in the name of society—is at the same time its last independent act as a state. The interference of state power in social relations becomes superfluous in one sphere after another, and then ceases in itself. The government of persons is replaced by the administration of things and the direction of the processes of production. The state is not "abolished", *it withers away*.'[14]

So much for the general principles; in this form they did not posit any specific mechanisms or phases by which the goal of a classless society was to be reached. These did not emerge until after the Paris Commune of 1871, when for the first time the experiences of what Engels described as the 'dictatorship of the proletariat' were at hand. It was in 1875 that Marx in his *Critique of the Gotha Programme*, first publicly[15] spoke of the 'dictatorship of the proletariat'. 'What we have to deal with here', he said, 'is a communist society, not as it has *developed* on its own foundations, but, on the contrary, as it *emerges* from capitalist society; which is thus in every respect, economically, morally and intellectually, still stamped with the birthmarks of the old society from whose womb it emerges'.[16] Accordingly, 'Between capitalist and communist society lies the period of the revolutionary transformation of the one into the other. There corresponds to this also a political transition period in which the state can be nothing

14. *Ibid.*, pp. 308–9.

15. Although as early as March 1852 he had written in a letter: 'And now as to myself, no credit is due to me for discovering the existence of classes in modern society, nor yet the struggle between them . . . What I did that was new was to prove: (1) that the *existence* of *classes* is only bound up with *particular, historic phases in the development of production*; (2) that the class struggle necessarily leads to the *dictatorship of the proletariat*; (3) that this dictatorship itself only constitutes the transition to the *abolition of all classes* and to a *classless society*' (Letter to Weydemeyer, *Selected Correspondence*, p. 57). In the *Critique of the Gotha Programme* he reiterated the need for such an order of development.

16. Karl Marx, *Critique of the Gotha Programme*, *Selected Works*, Vol. II, p. 21.

but the *revolutionary dictatorship of the proletariat*.[17] This is a necessary stage in the final withering away of the state, which Engels had discussed in *Anti-Dühring*, and later described in a letter of 1883 thus:

'Since 1845 Marx and I have held the view that *one* of the ultimate results of the future proletarian revolution will be the gradual dissolution and final disappearance of the political organisation known by the name of the *state*. The main object of this organisation has always been to secure, by armed force, the economic oppression of the labouring majority by the minority which alone possesses wealth. With the disappearance of an exclusively wealth-possessing minority, there also disappears the necessity for the power of armed oppression, or state power. At the same time, however, it was always our view that in order to attain this and other far more important aims of the future social revolution, the working class must first take possession of the organised political power of the state and by its aid crush the resistance of the capitalist class and organise society anew'.[18]

It did more than crystallise the state form that was to mark the transition to socialism; it 'implied', as Lenin said, 'the recognition of the state right up to the time when victorious socialism has grown into complete communism'; and it was on this assumption that Lenin founded the entire theory and practice of proletarian revolution. These may be formulated in six logical moments.

First, 'the state is a special organisation of force; it is the organisation of violence for the suppression of some class'.[20]

Second, 'what class must the proletariat suppress? Naturally only the exploiting class, i.e. the bourgeoisie. The toilers need a state only to overthrow the resistance of the exploiters, and only the proletariat can direct this suppression, carry it out; for the proletariat is the only class that is

17. *Ibid.*, p. 30.
18. Marx and Engels, 'Letter to Van Patten', *Selected Correspondence*, pp. 416–17.
19. Cf. *State and Revolution*, *Selected Works*, Vol. VII, pp. 82 ff.
20. *Ibid.*, 24.

consistently revolutionary, the only class that can unite all the toilers and the exploited in the struggle against the bourgeoisie, in completely displacing it'.[21]

Third, 'the doctrine of the class struggle, as applied by Marx to the question of the state and of the socialist revolution, leads inevitably to the *political rule* of the proletariat, of its dictatorship, i.e. of power shared with none and relying directly upon the armed forces of the masses. The overthrow of the bourgeoisie can be achieved only by the proletariat becoming transformed into the ruling class, capable of crushing the inevitable and desperate resistance of the bourgeoisie, and of organising *all* the toiling and exploited masses for the new economic order.'[22]

Fourth, 'the proletariat needs state power, the centralised organisation of force, the organisation of violence for the purpose of crushing the resistance of the exploiters and for the purpose of *leading* the great mass of the population—the peasantry, the petit bourgeoisie, the semi-proletarians—in the work of organising the socialist economy'.[23]

Fifth, 'by educating the workers' party, Marxism educates the vanguard of the proletariat which is capable of assuming power and of *leading* the *whole people* to socialism, of directing and organising the new order, of being the teacher, guide and leader of all the toiling and exploited in the task of building up their social life without the bourgeoisie and against the bourgeoisie'.[24]

Sixth, 'but if the proletariat needs a state as a *special* form of organisation of violence *against* the bourgeoisie, the following deduction arises automatically: is it conceivable that such an organisation can be created without first abolishing, destroying the state machine created by the bourgeoisie for *itself*? The *Communist Manifesto* leads straight to this deduction and it is of this deduction that Marx speaks when summing up the experience of the Revolution of 1848-51'[25, 26].

21. *Ibid.*   22. *Ibid.*, p. 26.   23. *Ibid.*
24. *Ibid.*   25. *Ibid.*, pp. 26-7.
26. See the passage by Marx in *The Eighteenth Brumaire of Louis Bonaparte* referred to by Lenin: 'Finally, in its struggle against the revolu-

These propositions together constitute the essentials of the Leninist case for the dictatorship of the proletariat under the hegemony of a Communist Party organised on the paramilitary lines of the Bolsheviks. It envisages the transition to communism, no less than the seizure of power, as a period of continuous struggle against the dispossed elements. While it endures 'suppression is *still* necessary; but it is the suppression of the exploiting minority by the exploited majority. A special apparatus, a special machine for suppression, the "state", is *still* necessary, but this is now a transitory state: it is no longer a state in the proper sense; for the suppression of the minority of exploiters by the majority of the wage-slaves of *yesterday* is comparatively so easy, simple and natural a task that it will entail far less bloodshed than the suppression of the risings of slaves, serfs or wage-labourers, and it will cost mankind far less'.[27] Then gradually 'when the resistance of the capitalists has been completely broken, when the capitalists have disappeared, when there are no classes . . . *only then* does "the state . . . cease to exist" '[28]; and with it comes full freedom. This is the second and higher stage of communism in which the 'birthmarks of the old society', still present in the first phase of the dictatorship of the proletariat—injustice and inequality—have been obliterated. It can only be reached in the manner outlined.

Before discussing the dictatorship of the proletariat let us note in passing that the doctrine of the state on which it is founded is too narrow and over-simplified.[29] As in the case of ideology, it must serve a wider purpose over and above solely asserting class interests. While it may be an instrument of class rule, and often of oppression, it also acts as an arbiter,

---

tion, the parliamentary republic found itself compelled to strengthen, along with the repressive measures, the resources and centralisation of government power. All revolutions perfected this machine instead of smashing it' (*Selected Works*, Vol. I, p. 301).

27. *State and Revolution, Selected Works*, Vol. VII, p. 82.

28. *Ibid.*, p. 81.

29. For a fuller treatment of this theme, see *History and Social Theory*, chap. 9.

as Engels recognised when he said that it was to ensure that the different classes 'shall not consume themselves . . . in fruitless struggle'.[30] To this end it has to maintain some measure of protection to even the most down-trodden, and in modern society very much more. It is significant that this aspect was ignored by Lenin and the entire emphasis, as we have seen, laid upon the coercive, oppressive nature of the state.

This said, the first and most obvious reply to Lenin's analysis is that it has not worked out and, what is of even greater importance, shows no sign of doing so. On these grounds alone we can reject the Leninist doctrine of the dictatorship of the proletariat. We have but to mention some of Lenin's now utopian prognoses to realise the divergences between theory and practice. It indeed makes ironical reading today to be told 'of a *more* democratic, but still a state machine in the shape of the armed masses of workers who become transformed into a universal people's militia'[31], of '*all* taking part in the administration of the state'[32], of the control of society 'not by a state of bureaucrats, but by a state of *armed workers*'.[33] Yet for this reason it is important to try to locate the causes for the discrepancy.

It lies, I suggest, in a complex of reasons. Central to it is the failure to allow for the need to distinguish between the seizure of power and the creation of a new society. Lenin's writings abound in military and para-military imagery, such as we have mentioned above: struggle, destruction, victory, army, vanguard, armed workers are the elements that go to compose the dictatorship of the proletariat. If this is inevitable in the accomplishment of revolution, to envisage the entire first phase of communism in these terms is to damn the venture at the outset. There is all the difference between para-military dispositions for the seizure of power and for the creative work that has to follow: to posit the same order for both is to fail to establish the conditions of trust, stability, and

30. See p. 221.
31. *State and Revolution, Selected Works,* Vol. VII, p. 92.
32. *Ibid.*   33. *Ibid.*, p. 89.

free expression, in which alone people can exercise their initiative and talents. If the whole of society is conceived as an armed camp, with an enemy ever-present within to be destroyed, how can anything but an atmosphere of suspicion and repression result? To use Marxist terminology, the qualitative difference between destroying and building has been ignored; nor can they be reconciled in any dialectical syllogism. If society is to be on a para-military basis, then obedience and authority will rule the day as they do in any army; and the ideology will give expression to that state. Men will grow up as they have in the Soviet Union thinking and speaking in terms of errors, deviations, enemies, machinations, plots, and so on. The last thing in the world to be engendered will be an atmosphere of brotherly love that one might have thought the only worthwhile foundation of socialism. This is just what communism has failed to achieve; instead it has transformed the building of socialism into a joyless and coercive activity.

As a consequence the entire theory and practice of its rule have suffered the effects. The first, and the most general, has been an inflexible and mechanical conception of dictatorship. From the premise that every state is for the oppression of one class by another, the proletarian state was also to be a dictatorship, but with two differences: whereas, in the first place, previous states were an almost insensible expression of the prevailing class relations, the proletarian state was constituted for the express purpose of oppressing its exploiters; and in the second place, it represented the interests of the vast majority where formerly the state belonged to the minority.

Now these distinctions are fundamental and should have led to fundamental differences between the proletarian state and all other states, differences of quite another order from those which have in fact emerged. If the state is regarded as a transition to a society in which it will wither away, it should from the beginning, or as soon as possible, attempt to introduce the change from 'the government of persons to the administration of things'; it should be far less bureaucratic and far more genuinely uncoercive than any corresponding bourgeois state; even if, as at first, repression was unavoidable, it need not have been exalted into a law. Yet this is what Stalin did in his doctrine of the intensification of the class struggle under socialism; and it is not without significance that its rejection by Kruschev was in the forefront of his attack upon Stalinism. The result has been that personal freedom, the unrestricted expression of opinion, the free interchange of ideas, all of which should be inherent in a socialist society, have been taken as signs of bourgeois weakness. Throughout the communist countries, with the possible exception of present-day Poland,[34] conformity has reigned. Over and above *raison d'état*, matters of opinion, art, and thought have been judged by whether they accord with the current dictates of authority. This has been the filter through which everything must pass so that at best we have paternalism—'the state knows best and the state says that T. S. Eliot is not good for you'—and at the worst thought control as at the time of Zhdanov's Olympian pronouncements on music, literature, and art, in 1947 and 1948. Similarly what, in theory, should have been a political dictatorship over the minority of enemies of the new state has become a clamp upon the free movement and expression of the majority.

Consequently when we compare the communist countries with the most developed capitalist democracies we see a much greater degree of personal freedom among the latter; instead of the communist peoples being able to give expression to their new-won power they are regulated in a way reminiscent of the most class-divided societies. It is the proletarian states that have created a new orthodoxy and with it new heresies; and this reversion to a pattern more in keeping with feudalism than with socialism is their most distasteful feature. That mistakes, even calamities, were bound to occur on the way few would deny; but the devious attitude towards all difficulties that has developed is another matter. Not only can friend and foe, good and bad, black and white change overnight; perhaps more alarming is the unquestioned acceptance

34. This is no longer true, a further commentary upon the logic of Leninism.

of such metamorphoses by the rank and file, even in the most flagrant cases. It is nice point, for example, had Molotov and his associates triumphed over Kruschev and his followers in 1957, whether there would not have been the same arguments—and the same assent to them—to the opposite effect? This endless manoeuvring for conformity leads one to ask why it should be necessary for a society in which, according to Lenin, 'the suppression of the minority of exploiters by the wage-slaves of *yesterday* is comparatively so easy, so simple a task'? Do the proletariat in fact have more active direction over their lives under communism than under capitalism?

This question brings us to the central issue of the role of the Communist Party. Its relation to the working class was clearly formulated in the *Communist Manifesto* as that of vanguard of the working class: 'They have no interests separate and apart from those of the proletariat as a whole.... The Communists, therefore, are, on the one hand, in their practice, the most advanced and resolute section of the working class parties of every country, that section which pushes forward all others; on the other hand, theoretically, they have over the great mass of the proletariat the advantage of clearly understanding the line of march, the conditions, and the ultimate general results of the proletarian movement. The immediate aim of the Communists is the same as that of all the other proletarian parties: the formation of the proletariat into a class, overthrow of the bourgeois supremacy, conquest of political power by the proletariat.'[35]

With Lenin, mainly through the struggles of the editorial board of *Iskra* from 1900 to 1904, in *What Is To Be Done*, written in 1902, and *One Step Forward, Two Steps Back*, written in 1904, the party became a disciplined, tightly knit body at once distinct from the working class and its advanced 'detachment' in virtue of its organisation. It was not to be a 'mere agglomeration' of members but 'to be built upon the principles of democratic elections, of *democratic centralism*'.[36]

35. *Communist Manifesto*, pp. 26–7.
36. *History of the Communist Party of the Soviet Union* (Moscow, 1945), pp. 47–9.

'Formerly', wrote Lenin, 'our party was not a formally organised whole, but only the sum of separate groups, and therefore, no other relations except those of ideological influence were possible between these groups. *Now* we have become an organised party, and this implies the establishment of authority, the transformation of ideas into the power of authority, the *subordination of lower party bodies to higher party bodies*.[37] It was in this form, with the subordination of the lower party bodies to the higher party bodies, the acceptance of all majority decisions as binding, and attempts to have them rescinded punishable as 'factionalism', that the Communist parties exist everywhere. They are parties of a 'new type', chracterised by their monolithic structure that vests supreme authority in the highest organs. That it has made them renowned for discipline and cohesion is undeniable; but equally undeniably it has bred the authoritarianism, dogmatism, and duplicity, that characterise every Communist Party in its dealings with its own members and with the outside world. Authority, like charity, begins at home; and the communist leadership in its responsibility for the well-being of the working class has also to guide its own members, as anyone who has been a member of the party knows.

Now it is to their position as the vanguard of the working class that the communists owe their *raison d'être*. Since they are able to see farther and more clearly 'the line of march' than the main body of their brethren, they must lead them. They do so not in any way as a separate entity, with its own interests, but solely as part of the working class. Accordingly it is as the representatives of the latter that they conduct the seizure of power and then its exercise under the dictatorship of the proletariat. Only thus is the working class finally emancipated and society made truly classless. Hence the indispensability of the Communist parties in all socialist revolution.

This doctrine seems to me to be plausible neither in theory

37. *Ibid.*, p. 49. My italics, G. L.

nor in practice. Far from the Communist parties, of the Leninist model, being indispensable to the proletarian revolution and the dictatorship of the proletariat, their very presence has been the 'germ of iniquity' in those which have taken place. This is not to deny that within the context of Tsarist Russia Lenin was not *tactically* correct in insisting upon a select organised fighting body as the only effective means of combating illegality and the secret police. But then the same applies to any wartime operation; Britain introduced commandos in the last war, yet we do not, for that reason, say that all the army, let alone the whole of society, should be organised on a commando footing. The effect of Lenin's action was to institutionalise dictatorship and thereby render a body blow to socialism. The sanctification of unity and authority above all things has meant the triumph of the party and the party man, so that it is perhaps not accidental that men like Stalin, Rakosi, and Ulbricht have become the archetypal communist leaders. Nor have the workings of democratic centralism been confined within individual parties; it has led to a veritable hierarchy as between the different parties and the Kremlin. It is equally apparent in intellectual matters where Marxist theory was until the schism between Russia and China the preserve first of one and then of both. Is it mere coincidence that until then only Stalin and later Mao Tse-Tung were considered to have developed Marxism since the death of Lenin? Is it intellectual power alone that marked Stalin off from, say, Plekhanov and Lukács or Western communist thinkers? In these circumstances it is hardly surprising that official Marxism has not been notable for its original thinking.

But it is above all in its relation to society, and the working class in particular, that the Leninist conception of the party has proved so mistaken. Instead of the dictatorship of the working class we have that of the party, which has power of life and death over its own members and those of society. This has come about from a number of reasons. The most important is the identification of the party with the working class so that their interests cannot but be the same; when the

Party prescribes a course of action it is *ipso facto* that of the working class as well.

The fallacy lies not simply in the dictatorial nature of the party—to which we shall advert later—which in effect makes it an autonomous body; but in the very condition of the working class. Marxists never tire of enumerating the reasons in support of the working class as the instrument of socialism and the abolition of all classes; and its importance in any such change is undeniable. What they have never asked is whether this necessarily qualifies them for the leadership of this movement. If the working class is at the very point of exploitation and so of the discrepancy between the social character of production and the private nature of appropriation, it is by that token also its greatest victim. Its very emphasis upon the group, upon mutual co-operation is also the measure of its lack of opportunity, and of responsibility. Even today, whatever the prospects for individual working-class children, for the majority it is a scamped education in overcrowded schools and a childhood in obsolescent houses. It is the culture of the 'have nots', less in the strictly material sense—so far at least as this country is concerned—than in the attitude that is bred from being at the base of society: a lack of identification with society at large, a disavowal, indeed fear, of responsibility, a distrust of authority, whether it be the organs of the state or the boss, a lack of a social, as opposed to a personal conscience ('you don't do what you're not paid for'), an acceptance of limitations in culture, dress, and habits. All these are strongly marked working-class traits. They go with a lack of education, of divorce from the cultural heritage (which in Britain is essentially a minority one), of the absence of intellectual training and mental interests, and of lack of opportunity for the cultivation of personal habits and individual pursuits. Together these constitute an outlook that in itself is anything but constructive and visionary; on the contrary, it tends to be gullible in its uncritical acceptance of prevailing prejudices, such as jingoism (to be found in the widespread attitude to people of other races, which is only too familiar to anyone who has canvassed a working-class district), nationalism (the need to be stronger than the other side), fatalism (there will always be war), and so on.

Now these are severe handicaps, and they hardly conduce to a sense of or capacity for constructive leadership in the creation of a new society. Nor are they compensated by the ability to be revolutionary about pay or conditions. Yet it is on this tenuous basis that Marxism allots the leadership to the working class, or rather to the Communist Party in the name of the working class. And it is precisely at this point that the sleight of hand is committed; for by reason of its position in capitalist society, the mass of the working class is constitutionally unfitted to lead. Its whole inclination, for the reasons given above, is to follow, which is in effect what has happened in all communist revolutions.

To say this is not to make aspersions upon the working class; still less to deny the indispensability of its organised strength in capitalist and socialist society. It is rather to recognise that it is not a deity, and that to idealise it in the manner of the Marxists is to do it, and genuine socialism, the worst possible service. In the first place, to claim that socialism can only come about through the dictatorship of the proletariat is to give it the right to hegemony over all other sections of society. It is to introduce the principle that society can only be changed by coercion and repression; and it is on this principle that the communists found their right to rule. In the second place, however, this is in fact nothing but the justification for the dictatorship of the Communist Party alone; for in ruling in the name of the working class the Communist Party is in fact ruling by itself. Its entire position is founded upon the inability of the working class to rule; indeed its need for guidance and leadership makes it dependent as never before once the revolution has come about: it has to renounce the ways of capitalism and to take upon itself the responsibilities it previously eschewed. This can only be done by the constant exhortation, encouragement, and intimidation that are so common in Eastern Europe today. That it has to be done is the measure of the working class's inability to do so itself. This may be a justification for the Communist Party but it is certainly not for socialism, as preached by it.

What we are presented with, then, in the dictatorship of the proletariat is the dictatorship of the Communist Party. The relationship between the two is analogous to that between a puppet and its master, and, however genuine the love of the latter for the former, the master he remains. It derives from the failure to reckon with the working class as it is, and not as its 'historical mission' calls it to be. They are not indeed the same; and Marx and Lenin both failed to apply the logic of their analysis 'dialectically', that is, they failed to see the negative as well as the positive aspect of the working class as the product of capitalism. If it is its main victim materially, so it will be ideologically; if it is confined in its activities, so it is in its outlook; if it has to make do with the dregs of the economic products, so too with its intellectual and cultural products; if its body is undernourished (today only comparatively in Western Europe), so its mind; if it breathes the air of industrialism, it also breathes that of chauvinism and nationalism; if it lives at the base of society, it also confines itself to the base. The list could be continued indefinitely and leads to the inescapable conclusion that if the working class is to lead, it has to be led to do so; it is not a natural leader, and it is in pretending that it is that the communists both delude themselves and the working class.

It is this that is largely responsible for the communist dictatorship; for it has put the latter into the position of supreme arbiters. By claiming to act in the name of the majority of the exploited, communists have insensibly arrogated to themselves the right to lay down a complete pattern of life. I emphasise the word insensibly, for such a course was the inevitable outcome of the whole notion of the dictatorship of the proletariat; if the working class is to rule and the Communist Party is the vanguard of the working class, then in effect it is the Communist Party that rules; and in ruling with the intent of changing the whole of society it takes control of all conduct, from the use of cosmetics to foreign policy. Lenin obviously anticipated otherwise in his frequent references to the armed workers; and the cause of his miscalculation lay in his superficial view of the working class. Nor was it merely an aberration, but sprang from a basic misconception. This was to think in essentially abstract, idealised terms. I am aware that applied to Lenin, the epitome of realists, this sounds paradoxical in the extreme; but in making the assertion I am concerned less with any personal quirks on his part than with an inherent characteristic of Marxism, to which we have frequently alluded—the tendency to think of concepts, classes, and movements, to the exclusion of things and people. The whole course of proletarian dictatorship appears to me to be an illustration of this failing.

Let us examine it more closely. When broken down Lenin's analysis consisted in the juxtaposition of a series of concepts, freedom, dictatorship, class, the state, and so on, from which he was able to evolve a relationship between them: dictatorship was equated with the state, the socialist state with democracy and the withering away of the state with classless communist society. The thread that united them all was the leadership of the Communist Party, and *ipso facto* the more pronounced this leadership the better, and the more complete the dictatorship of the proletariat the nearer to socialism. Freedom and class domination would take care of themselves, or rather would be taken care of in this very process.

What it failed to take account of was, as we have said, the discrepancy between the working class and the Communist Party, so that the hegemony of the latter did not necessarily mean the supremacy of the former. Instead Communist Party leadership has become increasingly a law unto itself. From the first it was a minority and in the achievement of political power it has remained a minority; the directing minority. As such, on good Marxist principles, its experience is inevitably different from that of the majority of the population, and so also is its outlook. It regards society from a position of privilege and authority; and, like all privileged minorities, however much it thinks in terms of the people's good, it does not have to share its experiences. Hence the remoteness between the hierarchy and the mass that can be discerned in Soviet novels like Vera Panova's *The Factory* (the interest of which is that it takes the disparity for granted). Lenin assumed an umbilical community of interests between the two and therein lay his mistake. As a consequence, the dictatorship that he planned on the basis of democratic centralism has not so far evolved, or looked like evolving, to the stage where a withering away of the state becomes possible. On the contrary, it has led to three outstanding evils to which Lenin gave no consideration, simply because he made no allowance for an asymmetry between his different categories.

The first has been the failure of democracy and freedom to develop. Here we have a clear example of Lenin's abstract, indeed perfectionist, conception. In spite of his castigation of Kautsky for failing to ask the question of 'democracy for whom?'[38] Lenin's own notion of freedom is scarcely more realistic. 'While the state exists,' he says, 'There is no freedom. When freedom exists there will be no state'.[39] What is this if not a premise of absoluteness, of all or nothing? Either we have freedom or we do not. It is to disregard the first principle of Marxism: that men and society must not be judged by abstract criteria but by the stage of historical development to which they have attained. Bourgeois freedom may be less, far less, than the ideal but it is real nevertheless to those who possess it. It is no mere trapping; and once known it is not easily relinquished, just as once extinguished it is not easily rekindled. For Lenin freedom was automatically subsumed under the rule of the toilers as incidental to their possession of power. It would come with the ending of the state. It had no other function and hence no provision to guarantee it was made. Accordingly we must still await its advent. With democracy, likewise, Lenin's was a counsel of perfection because he failed to appreciate its positive value:

38. See *The Proletarian Revolution and the Renegade Kautsky, Selected Works*, Vol. VII, p. 130.

39. *State and Revolution, Selected Works*, Vol. VII, p. 87.

'Bourgeois democracy, although a great historical advance in comparison with medievalism, nevertheless remains, and under capitalism cannot but remain, restricted, truncated, false and hypocritical, a paradise for the rich and a snare and deception for the exploited, for the poor'.[40]

No doubt, but it is still better to preserve those of its practices that have made for greater tolerance and equality rather than to 'smash the state machine' and all its laws and institutions. To destroy just because of past associations is a wanton exercise that goes against human interests and practice. We are all dependent upon the heritage of the past, and it is far better to select those elements that are regarded as enhancing life than to consign them all to oblivion on account of their past uses. It may well have been apposite in the case of Tsarist Russia, but if you destroy *habeas corpus*, representative government, and the institutions associated with them, what will be the result? In what way will the ground be cleared for fuller democracy? It is far more likely to lead to the converse.[41]

Both these cases lead to the same conclusion: that neither freedom nor democracy is an automatic accompaniment of the dictatorship of the proletariat, in theory or in practice. Theoretically, the argument for their emergence rests on the assumption that the dictatorship of the proletariat entails ever-increasing freedom; if that cannot be established then the argument falls to the ground, as I think has been shown to be the case. Practically, the short answer is that in every communist dictatorship up to the present the personal, political, and juridical freedoms are almost as non-existent as economic freedom. The ending of exploitation has yet to see the burgeoning of freedom.

The second feature of the dictatorship of the proletariat has been the abuse of power by those in authority. According

40. *The Proletarian Revolution and the Renegade, Kautsky, ibid.*, p. 130.
41. The British Communist Party recognises this in its plan, *The British Road to Socialism*, where it speaks of 'transforming' Britain's democratic institutions: it would thereby seem tacitly to have departed from the Marxist-Leninist doctrine of 'smashing' the state machine.

to Marxism the aphorism, 'Power corrupts and absolute power corrupts absolutely', is merely an example of the bourgeois mystique of human nature. We have already discussed the place of power in human conduct, and here it remains to examine why communism has not proved the exception to the rule. The reason, I suggest, lies in the very role of the communist party: as a minority exercising absolute power it has been uncurbed by any countervailing authority. In the final count it need be, and is, guided only by the effects of its policies, as in the frequent, and often understandable, adjustments in economic and other matters. Now such supreme authority is bound, even on ordinary Marxist grounds, to find expression in the attitude of those who exercise it. If a man like Stalin is lauded to the skies and treated as a demi-God his own estimate of himself will tend to change correspondingly unless he is a very exceptional man; and we have it on the evidence of Kruschev himself that he became a tyrant. Similarly if a whole group comes to regard itself as the repository of all wisdom, if its role is constantly to hector, exhort, and moralise on every aspect of life, it will come sooner or later to act and think of itself as an élite— which is the case with all communist parties in or out of power. It is in this sense that they, like all other autocracies, can be said to be corrupt in acting as they consider best without constraint; and the more absolute their power to assert themselves the greater the degree of corruption. Hence it is no accident that all communist parties in power have been guilty of the abuse of power, and that arbitrary authority becomes inextricably confused with the enforcement of principle. 'Social consciousness reflects social being'; the atrocities of Stalin, Rakosi, or their fellows show that communists are not exempt from this condition; if they exercise unconstrained power they are as likely to fall prey to its abuse as their victims are to fall prey to them. Once again Lenin's simple touchstone of class solidarity has shown itself inadequate.

Finally, arising directly from this is the fallacy that to abolish class is to dispense with caste or, put another way, that once the toiling masses have taken control of the state, and the exploitation of man by man is ended, there should be a corresponding ending to class distinction. This is not the same as saying that there are no inequalities, for as we have seen both Marx and Lenin stressed that the first phase of communism would be characterised by 'differences, and unjust differences, in wealth . . . but the exploitation of man by man will have become impossible, because it will be impossible to seize the *means* of *production*, the factories, machines, land etc., as private property'.[42] At the very least, then, the differences that remained should have arisen from those enjoying differences in wealth, but not from the disparity between the vanguard and the workers. This was emphatically stressed by Marx, Engels, and Lenin, all of whom regarded as central to the entire experience of the Paris Commune the self-denial of its leaders; it was part of the very process of purging the old state as Engels shows when he wrote the following passage, quoted with approval by Lenin:[43]

'Against this transformation of the state and the organs of the state from servants of society into masters of society—an inevitable transformation in all previous states—the Commune made use of two infallible expedients. In the first place it filled all posts—administrative, judicial and educational—by election on the basis of universal suffrage of all concerned subject to the right of recall at any time by the same electors. And, in the second place, all officials, high or low, were paid only the wages received by other workers. The highest salary paid by the Commune to anyone was 6,000 francs. In this way, an effective barrier to place-hunting and careerism was set up, even apart from the binding mandates to delegates to representative bodies which were also added besides'.[44]

Lenin's comment on this passage, in the light of subsequent Soviet history, is instructive: 'Engels here approaches the interesting boundary at which consistent democracy is *trans-*

42. *State and Revolution*, p. 85.
43. *Ibid.*, p. 71.
44. Karl Marx, *Civil War in France, Selected Works*, Vol. I, p. 439.

formed into socialism and at which it *demands* socialism. For, in order to abolish the state, the functions of the Civil Service must be converted into the simple operations of control and accounting that can be performed by the vast majority of the population, and, ultimately, *by every individual'*.[45]

Even if it is argued that Lenin conceived this as the ultimate aim, it is hard to see that even a start towards it has been made. On the contrary over the past generation we have witnessed the growth of a new élite in the Soviet Union, which can only be termed a caste: a group whose privileges are derived from the exercise of power and positions of authority, by virtue of which they and their children are marked off from the rest of society. The days of 6,000 francs as the maximum wage or even of Lenin's simple mode of life have long been superseded by fast cars, villas, private schools, vast differentials, provision of children to important posts, that together constitute the whole paraphernalia of privilege whether under capitalism or under socialism. They share the same source as the rest of communist hegemony, and are indeed but the trappings of power, the figure of authority in full dress.

Taken together these different aspects present us with the very divisions that Lenin envisaged the dictatorship would eliminate. Instead of greater freedom, fuller democracy 'a thousand times better than that of capitalism', the ending of inequality, the withering away of the state, the rule of the vast majority, we have dictatorship, and whether or not it is viewed as in the interests of the mass of the people, dictatorship it remains. It has arisen from the false premise that any one (minority) group is able to judge best the needs of the majority and that in order to achieve its interests it must resort to all expedients of repression. In the event, it is the majority that is repressed and the minority that has repressed it.

This is the source of the false dawn of communism. From the outset the communists isolated themselves from the rest of society, among it but not of it, by arrogating to themselves a sovereignty that could only be maintained by coercion. In

45. My italics, G. L.

the name of the people they have brought everything within their purview; socialist values have been transmuted into party values with the consequent impoverishment of spiritual and intellectual life; the great work of art, the arresting idea, can neither be born nor survive in such an atmosphere, and that they have not is the measure of communism's failure to engender a genuine socialist culture. What we see is not a new respect for man as an individual but the triumph of a political orthodoxy to which all men must bow or face the consequences (*cf.* Pasternak); not the liberation of the vast majority of mankind but the replacement of one élite by another. That it is often selfless, largely uncorrupt, and dedicated still does not change its authoritarian and frequently repressive character. Government for the people is still not government of the people, and all the enlightenment in the world cannot make it so. To Lenin the distinction was meaningless; to us, over fifty years on, it spells the failure of a system.

2

The moral of this failure is not the abandonment of socialism or socialist theory, but of Leninism. In its stead we must recognise that there can be no universal pattern in the achievement of socialism. The experience of Russia or China has as much bearing for Britain as the Indian Ocean upon its climate: centuries of representative institutions, however imperfect, and a degree of individual freedom must be the starting point for improvement, not the first target for attack. On the other hand, it is equally fruitless to expect feudal states to follow the path of parliamentary democracy and to condemn them as dictatorships for not doing so. These are truisms; and so must be the theoretical conclusion, namely, that Leninism—with its insistence upon a para-military Communist Party for the seizure of power and forcible reorganisation of society—is of its nature incapable of establishing the conditions for a truly classless society. It is guilty of the very narrowness of vision for which it arraigns all previous class society; it is content to establish its rule by the power of the minority (albeit acting for the majority). As a result it has bred repression and all the accompaniments of abuse of power—caste privilege, conformity, and suspicion. Like breeds like, even in the cause of socialism, and there is no more reason to expect that coercion will suddenly be changed into brotherly love than capitalism into socialism. Man as Marx said, is 'the ensemble of social relations': if these are authoritarian, he will bear its stamp whether as a bully or one of the bullied.

Instead of exalting dictatorship therefore as essential to socialism let us recognise that its exercise is an impediment; that so long as it prevails there can be no real break with the past; and that only when the conditions for majority rule and open decisions openly arrived at have been reached can the first foundations of socialism be laid. It means dispensing with the very apparatus that Leninism wishes to erect, for if socialism is not to be founded upon trust it is nothing.

But, it will be argued, what of the state and the expropriated class? How can these be ignored in the transition? The answer is that if socialism is the rule of the majority, then the state will be democratic and the expropriated class forced to submit. It is precisely because Lenin while talking in terms of majority rule in fact thought in terms of minority rule that he conceived the dictatorship of the proletariat as a repressive force; and so long as the assumption is of political sleight of hand, of the seizure of power, of its exercise in the name of the working class, so long will it be dictatorial in nature. It is a minority that must scheme and manoeuvre, plot and counterplot, to establish and maintain itself in power, not the majority; it is a minority that becomes a caste by virtue of its exceptional position; it is a minority that is corrupted by power simply because it has the majority over which to rule. Reverse the order to that of genuine majority rule and all changes: the seizure of power, its exercise, and the tempo of development are no longer the prerogative of an autocracy, nor their vicissitudes a matter of political expediency, to be judged solely by the criterion of the immediate *political* objective, but become the concern of society as a whole. The same applies to intellectual life: certain ideas and art forms are not good or bad because the party so decrees, but must be judged by their effects. It is in these conditions where the norms of society arise out of the co-operation of its members that a genuine socialist culture can alone flourish. Communist experience has shown only too clearly that socialism is not simply achieved by the juxtaposition of class relationships, important as this is. The first condition is the access of the majority to genuine participation and this means a new and higher respect for men as individuals and not their treatment as units; for only thus can they rise above the anonymity to which hitherto all class society *and proletarian dictatorship* has consigned them. Socialism therefore can only begin where dictatorship and minority rule end.

From this it follows, secondly, that power can only be attained when the majority desire change. Lenin recognised this when he said that, 'The fundamental law of revolution, confirmed by all revolutions and particularly by all three Russian revolutions in the twentieth century, is as follows: it is not sufficient for revolution that the exploited and oppressed masses understand the impossibility of living in the old way and demand changes; for revolution it is necessary that the exploiters should not be able to live and rule in the old way. Only when the *"lower classes" do not want* the old and when the *"upper classes" cannot continue, in the old way*, then only can revolution conquer.'[46] But whereas for him this was to be the signal for the advent of the dictatorship of the proletariat, for a genuine socialist movement it must be achieved through majority assent, and subsequent participation. The forms that it may take will vary, but unless it is carried through as a majority movement and enshrined in fully representative institutions we shall be back at the incubus of the dictatorship of the proletariat. There is no overwhelming reason to believe that if there is a genuinely democratic movement involving the support and participa-

46. Lenin, *'Left Wing' Communism, an Infantile Disorder, Selected Works*, Vol. X (London, 1946), p. 127.

tion of the people that it will fail unless organised as a dictatorship; even assuming that there were initial attempts to overthrow the new order it can be defended by what Lenin called 'the armed militia' of the people without the need of a self-appointed, monolithic party set permanently above it.

The Marxist contention that the minority must be oppressed under the direction of an omniscient and omnipotent vanguard falls to the ground unless it can be shown first that oppression of the expropriated class is necessarily prolonged over a whole epoch as Marx and Engels assumed, and second that even if it were so prolonged that dictatorship is the only or most effective method of enforcing it. So far as the first is concerned there is nothing either in theory or in communist practice to support it; theoretically, the greater the support of the people for change the greater the odds against prolonged resistance; but only circumstances can make known the nature of the resistance and its effectiveness. It cannot be gauged from communist practice, because, from the admittedly appalling handicap that faced the Russian Revolution, the Communist parties have always acted on the assumption that resistance will invariably be of that order and that they must act in advance to crush it. The effect is to be seen in the continuous pressure, sometimes coercive, sometimes hortatory, upon the whole of society, and the periodic opposition to which it gives rise, alike from the peasantry and the working class, as in the East Berlin risings of 1953, and the Hungarian and Polish rebellions of 1956. This helps us to answer the second condition, for by the same token repression has always led to resistance where other methods of change and reorganisation might not have done so. There is all the difference between stamping upon the recalcitrant minority, who refuse to accept anything but the old order and do all that they can to overturn the new, and drawing upon the participation of those who are unco-operative. At the very least, it is elementary self-interest, to act on the assumption that such people are misguided rather than evil, and that conviction not coercion is the only satisfactory attitude to be adopted towards them. To act otherwise, as the communists have done, on the grounds that the 'dis-possessed elements' must be treated as the class enemy, leads straight to undiscriminating ruthlessness in the name of the revolution. Socialism should be as much a matter of reformation as reorganisation and not a mere exercise in dictatorial authority upon which the communists have largely relied. As we have frequently emphasised, if the new society genuinely represents the vast majority the use of force should be minimal: it is an approach that has yet to be tried. Until it is, there are no grounds, theoretical, practical or ethical, for positing the indispensability of dictatorship. Nor are the arguments drawn from the past any better founded. Even granted that all previous states have been for the repression of one class by another, that is no reason why the qualitatively new socialist state should emulate them: the reading of history should not consist merely in the extrapolation of a trend; and in the case of socialism, its entire *raison d'être* lies in its decisive breach with the past. Only if it is founded upon genuine co-operation and respect for minorities can it overcome the repression and privileges that have marked all previous societies.

This brings us to the final question, 'how should power be wielded in society if not by the dictatorship of the proletariat?' There are three aspects to be considered. Firstly, if it is to be genuinely representative of the majority of the population, it must be multiform: that is to say, in contra-distinction to the monolithic conception of a one-party, one-line, one-leadership state of the communists it must draw its support from all sections. The fallacy of the doctrine of the dictatorship of the proletariat, as we have seen, is to conclude that because the proletariat is the bedrock of capitalist society it alone is fitted to *lead* to socialism. That in fact this does not happen in the countries of the dictatorship of the proletariat but that the leadership often consists largely of intellectuals is evidence of the emptiness of the ideal. For the truth, as we have remarked, is that in the transformation of values that the change from an acquisitive to a co-operative society entails, the workers are more in need of counsel than

246

ever before; it is now not simply a case of fighting for their rights but of discarding many of the habits, one should almost say reflexes, engendered by capitalism and of being prepared to enter into the full heritage of society, accepting the responsibility that full participation involves. This is where the intellectual and professional minorities have a unique role, for in virtue of their greater freedom of movement, training, opportunity for thought, acceptance of responsibility, humane callings, and comparative detachment from the exigencies of deadening routine, they have an indispensable part to play in the fashioning of a new society. Their importance here is not an academic one but of fact and can be seen by the comparative preponderance of non working-class intellectuals, in the formation of the communist movement alone, from Marx, Engels, Lenin, and Stalin to Mao Tse-Tung, Togliatti, and Palme-Dutt. Apart from their overt political role, however, it rests largely with the cultured minority to transmit the vision of a better society to those who have lived at the base of present society. This is not a question of teaching all to appreciate the works of Beethoven, Rembrandt, and Shakespeare but of communicating a new world of spiritual and intellectual experience, so that, as in Britain, culture is no longer regarded as the preserve of the minority together with responsibility. Just as 'it's not worth the responsibility' must cease to be the badge of a class, so must 'it's not for the likes of us': instead each should merely express a state of personal preference.

Accordingly, the intellectual and professional, far from having to abase themselves before the superior worth and wisdom of the working class in the shape of an omniscient Communist Party, and to conceive of their activities as subordinated to and governed by political considerations, must recognise their own importance. Their very privileged position provides them with the knowledge and perspective denied to the majority; their function in transmitting, applying, and adding to the wisdom of mankind, as doctors, teachers, writers, and thinkers, gives them a contact with values from which their own value springs. In exercising their vocation therefore they speak not for themselves but for the experience and knowledge of all men and for that reason their duty is not to jettison their principles and truths before superior numbers but to assert them.

In the same way there is no reason why there should not be minority political or cultural groupings; not all men need belong to the same party or be of the same principle. While there is all the difference between the irreconcilable interests of a tory and a socialist party, socialists should be able to emphasise different aspects of socialism; and in doing so ensure that no single group becomes all-powerful. Nothing is more specious than the communist assertion that parties *ipso facto* represent different classes: it depends upon the circumstances. It is quite as conceivable to have groups for different sections as it is to have different trade unions; we do not regard the latter as being of fundamentally different interests or of the T.U.C. as anything but the sum of its parts. So with society. There is a place for every viewpoint that embodies some genuine facet of society; and although none may be accepted in its entirety, together they should cover the gamut of human experience. It is precisely in the wealth and diversity of experience that monolithic communist society is so singularly deficient; it may be sound politics and economy to have only one party or five brands of hats but human happiness and colour suffer for it.

Secondly, if society is to be genuinely multiform, there must be institutional safeguards against the possession and exercise of excessive power by any one group. It may be true as Marx scornfully said that bourgeois democracy consists in 'deciding once in three or six years which member of the ruling class was to misrepresent the people in parliament';[47] but better even this than no such right at all. The first principle of socialism, however, must be the guarantee of individual and popular rights to expression; and whatever form this takes it must begin from the very premise that Marxism decries, namely that 'power corrupts and absolute power corrupts absolutely'. That is to say, in contradistinction to

47. *Civil War in France, Selected Works*, Vol. I, p. 472.

Leninism that considers power simply as the lever of proletarian dictatorship and pays no regard to the effects it is likely to have upon those who wield it, socialism must make the distribution of power its central theme. Communist experience has shown that it cannot be allowed to be taken care of simply as part of the process of governing. The guiding principle must be to avoid its concentration in any one monolithic body and the greatest safeguard against its abuse lies in the type of multiform society mentioned. There seems no reason at all why a planned society should not from the outset be designed to reduce to a minimum bureaucracy by allowing the fullest possible participation of its members in the running of its industries and government. Even if it involved, as would be bound at first to happen, numerous mistakes and shortcomings, is this not to be preferred to a faster tempo of change by means of dictatorship? Who is to say that ultimately the Hungarians or the Poles[48] have benefited more by gaining ten years of industrialism plus dictatorship than if they had been allowed to move at their own pace? Above all who has the right to arrogate to himself, in the name of history, the sacrifice of one generation's liberty and its pursuit of happiness to the next? If it were a matter of free choice, the case would naturally be different.

This leads to our final conclusion that true socialism must be based upon humanism; its foundation, as we suggested before, must be the worth of man as an individual and not just as a species. It must therefore take as its starting point man's needs, spiritual no less than economic, and not the dictates of history. Now such an outlook need not be any the less scientific for being based upon deliberately chosen ethical principles: on the contrary only if these are kept to the forefront, can the direction of society be in terms of men's needs and not as a mere exercise in planning. By this yardstick, the greed, the waste, the class privilege and exploitation of capitalist society cannot but be rejected for one of planned

48 In the case of the Soviet Union such speed was perhaps necessary of survival; the trouble has been to exalt it into a universal law of socialist development.

co-operation and social justice, for only that way lies hope. At the same time we need not be slaves to the historical process to recognise that now for the first time the conditions for the ending of class rule and exploitation have arisen, and that to do so is the one rational path for mankind upon which its survival depends. All the 'scientific' considerations that orthodox Marxism regards as its preserve are equally accessible to the socialist humanist; the difference is that he refuses to make them his sole *raison d'être*; or rather, he is a socialist not because of ineluctable historical laws, but because he has a vision of life. He is not concerned simply to keep his eye on the chronometer of history, in order to gauge his route and rate, but to know whether men are happier, more fulfilled, and better for their new experience; if they are, the experiment is successful; if not, then it has somehow failed and must be re-examined. Ultimately this is the difference between the two conceptions: for the Marxist, hardship, sacrifice, hunger, and misery are all worth it in the interests of history; for the socialist humanist, history is nothing apart from the men who make it and it must be judged according to them, not *vice versa*. The choice is plain and it is for us to see that the right one is made.

INDEX